THE KRAY FILES

THE KRAY FILES

The True Story of
Britain's Most Notorious Brothers

COLIN FRY

MAINSTREAM
PUBLISHING

EDINBURGH AND LONDON

First published in 1998 by
MAINSTREAM PUBLISHING COMPANY
(EDINBURGH) LTD
7 Albany Street
Edinburgh EH1 3UG

Reprinted in 1998
This edition 1999

ISBN 1 84018 185 0

A catalogue record for this book is available from the British Library

Typeset in Garamond
Printed and bound in Finland by WSOY

To the sergeant 'orders is orders'.

CONTENTS

ACKNOWLEDGEMENTS

Being given the chance to write a book is something that doesn't happen very often to too many people. I have been fortunate in that respect, since this is my second offering – and it is all thanks to Bill Campbell at Mainstream Publishing in Edinburgh.

My wife Eva has, as usual, kept me supplied with coffee and sustenance during the small hours and my children Alexander and Christian have always been on hand to mould the plot into shape and to stop me from being too conservative in my thoughts.

I would like to thank my twin brother, Rod, for reading through my chapter on twins. I know it was a pain, but his efforts were much appreciated. Likewise my mother has always encouraged me with my work.

Friends have been supportive of my new profession as well. Lalit Bagai in Denmark and Charles Rosenblatt in Florida, USA, have always given me the best pragmatic advice based on their long years in business. Thanks to you both.

Newspapers have always been an invaluable source of information – although not exactly reliable for investigative endeavours – and the Internet is proving to be a tremendous source of all kinds of useful knowledge; but who do I thank here? These two sources in particular, coupled with my own intimate knowledge of the Krays, have helped me greatly in the early stages of my investigations. Sifting through the inaccurate and sometimes misleading stories becomes simply a habit, but then this is the stuff of legends and make-believe plays its part in creating the imagery of the celebrity.

But we must not forget the academics who gave this book a new interpretation on the Krays. Professor Chris Jenks at

Goldsmiths College (Head of the Sociology Department) in London has co-written a paper with Justin J. Lorentzen entitled 'The Kray Fascination' and I have regularly referred to this work within my own text. Also Tim Trimble, who lectures in psychology at King Alfred's College, Winchester, was invaluable in the psychological analysis of the background material. Without their guiding framework, this investigative part of *The Kray Files* would have been almost impossible. Other academics include Dr Dick Hobbs at Durham University, with whom I share a book title *Doing the Business*, and Audrey Sandbank who is a family psychiatrist with the Twins and Multiple Births Association (TAMBA). Audrey has just completed editing a new book on twins entitled *Twin psychology – from conception to grave* which will be published by Routledge sometime in 1998. Thanks for the help; it was outstanding and led me in all directions, enabling me to build up the 'big picture' that I was aiming at.

Thank you all for helping me in my quest to write an objective and in-depth analysis of the Krays.

INTRODUCTION

When deciding on the format of this book, three distinct categories arose immediately: past, present and future.

The past is now history and well documented from many varying sources, the only problem being the grouping of such information into intelligible and readable chapters. Additionally, however, I decided to investigate the background that had so affected the Krays – the East End of London, with its sociology, history and significance within the country's capital. In this respect I was extremely fortunate in that a conversation with Alison McDonald at the Institute of Psychiatry in London led me to Professor Chris Jenks at Goldsmiths College, who had recently lectured on the sociology of the East End and in particular the Krays. A brief telephone conversation with the learned professor soon showed that he was exactly the right man, in the right place, at the right time. Indeed, he sent me a recent academic paper entitled 'The Kray Fascination', that he had written with a colleague, Justin J. Lorentzen. This paper helped to open my mind about the East End of London and I make no apologies for often quoting from his original manuscript (see Volume 14, Number 3, August 1997, Theory Culture & Society, publ. SAGE Publications, London).

But these chapters are about more than just the sociological aspects surrounding the Krays, so it was absolutely vital to my investigative work that I found a reputable source within the field of psychology to help create the background analysis so necessary for my investigation. This ultimately led me to Tim Trimble at King Alfred's College, Winchester, and his detailed accounts of psychological behaviour helped me in focusing my attentions on the right areas of study.

Also, Audrey Sandbank at TAMBA, the twin organisation – with whom I had been in contact some years ago when I was considering writing a book on twins – supplied me with much intriguing information and material. This, coupled with the fact that I am, myself, an identical twin, enabled me to gain considerable insight into what the 'twins', Ron and Reg, were like.

My only loose end was getting hold of Scotland Yard and gaining access to their own Kray files. Even though I was initially told that the files would be made available to me, they pulled the 75-year rule and have put them away for safe-keeping in a dusty drawer somewhere at Scotland Yard. It became obvious that there were officials in high places who didn't want me to see these files and to access their data. So, without their help, I created my own extensive files and these form the basis for this book.

My history of the Krays was now complete; indeed the entire outline of the book was taking shape at a rapid and all-encompassing pace. The problem would be what to leave out rather than what to include.

Drawing on my inside knowledge of the Krays I decided on the following structure for my book and I have endeavoured to give a brief account of the reasoning behind why I consider these topics as being the most important and relevant to any work on the enigma known simply as 'The Krays'.

Initially the Krays were known only as able boxers and petty crooks. It was the out-and-out ferocity of their violence, man to man, gang to gang, that made the Krays what they are today. They didn't lose fights – unlike during their boxing days – for Ron and Reg Kray it was a win–win situation. It was this incredible ability that first brought them to the attention of Scotland Yard. Hence the title for chapter one: 'Once Upon a Time There Were . . . The Gang Wars'.

All three Kray brothers were always anti-police, ever since the days of hiding their deserter father from the inquiring eyes of local constables, keen on apprehending 'old man Charlie' for desertion from the British Army. The environment of the East End of London did the rest. The Krays never asked for favours from the police nor did they give any. Their worlds were worlds apart and even now in the 1990s they remain the same, stuck in their own particular time warp with only hatred as their guide; it would appear that the Krays will be forever trying to outsmart Scotland Yard, hence the title for chapter two – 'Trying to Repay the Old Bill'.

When researching the Krays many names arise unexpectedly only to disappear swiftly without trace. Are these people victims of the ruthless methods of organised crime and especially those practices as adopted by the Krays? Or did they get out while the going was good? Indeed, some did manage to escape to South Africa and other Commonwealth countries; but not so George Cornell, shot and killed by Ron Kray in The Blind Beggar public house; not so Jack 'The Hat' McVitie, stabbed to death by Reg Kray; not so the 'Mad Axeman', Frank Mitchell, killed by Kray lieutenant, Freddie Foreman. The list continues, hence chapter three – 'Another One Bites the Dust'.

What made the Krays different, and one of the main reasons for their continual cult status, is their craving for publicity. It was Ron Kray in particular who directly sought the general public's attention, by being photographed with George Raft, Lord Boothby, Henry Cooper, Barbara Windsor and other celebrities. This was all part of his strategy, his own brand of image building. The Krays have become icons of a sort, and celebrities by association. They are, or so it would appear, now part of the establishment, that same establishment that they always feared. Hence the title for chapter four – 'Stars in their Eyes'.

When it came to working closely with the US Mafia no one came nearer to being a part of 'Murder Incorporated' than the Krays. Their involvement was extensive – they protected their clubs in London; they laundered their illicit dirty money; they even protected their close pals. When visiting celebrities from the USA needed 'minding' it was the Krays who got the phone call and the Mob even asked them to protect young Frank Sinatra Junior when he was on a tour of the UK. As a special favour the whole Kray family were invited to see Frank Senior perform when he was on tour in London and to attend the reception party afterwards. Chapter five is therefore entitled – 'Mob Rules'.

Who was the good twin and who was the bad one, or were they both just as bad as each other? A complete psychological profile has never been attempted on the Krays – not, that is, before now. With the assistance of the academics and a number of well-informed and creditable sources, this chapter attempts the impossible. It is not to apportion blame or to excuse anyone for their actions, but to gain insight into the Kray phenomenon and to assist in the understanding of their actions, both now and then. Hence the title for chapter six – 'Twins'. This sets out the basis for a complete understanding and appreciation of the Krays but it is only by looking at events after their appre-hension in 1968 and imprisonment the following year that the big picture can be established.

We have now come to the present and this is where my own in-depth knowledge of Kray business activities comes into focus. Remember, at one time I shared an office with Charlie Kray which made me privy to many of his business ventures, or as I like to call them, business adventures. I also made many visits to see Ron and Reg Kray, discussing various business deals with them on each occasion. Let me say here and now, however, that I am not, nor have I ever been, a part of any Kray firm.

This extensive inside knowledge has formed the basis for this section, which starts with an extension of the chapter entitled 'Stars in their Eyes'. As previously, each chapter is preceded by a brief description of its contents.

How has this Kray iconisation come about? Why are all three Kray brothers 'household names' – something that Ron Kray in particular achieved after the notorious 'Boothby Affair' (and in this context I use the word 'affair' advisedly)? Are the media really to blame or are there deeper and more sinister aspects to be considered? Is the celebrity status awarded to crooks and criminals like the Krays and Ronnie Biggs the same as that of those amongst the higher echelons of society, such as Diana, Princess of Wales? Is it 'Myth or Mythology' – my title for chapter seven?

My next chapter is right out of the old days of the Kray empire, but it happened in 1986 and it involved my own personal contribution. Supposedly a genuine music venture in which I had invested much time and money, it was really the creation of a Mafia front company for laundering drug dollars into clean British pounds. This is just one example of the Krays' continuing Mafia connection, and of their power. This chapter is entitled 'Music Mafia Please'.

Many of the 'nice little earners' often favoured by the Krays pitted brother against brother. They were all always on the look-out for easy money, honest or dirty. And Reg and Charlie, after the death of Ron Kray on 17 March 1995, are still at it – after all these years. Some things don't change, do they? Ron and Reg were always serious in their schemes, although they were not clever businessmen by any means. At one time in the mid-'80s they wanted to take over London again and were using a couple of cheap hoods to front the deal. But the whole thing misfired when the petty criminals chosen decided to aim for the major league by killing off Ron and Reg and taking over the business for themselves. Charlie Kray, on the other hand, looks more like a 'Del-boy' derivative by the end of this chapter – entitled 'Still Wheelin' and Dealin''. But they did manage to net £255,000 for the sale of the film rights for their story, called *The Krays*.

Chapter ten goes behind the scenes at Broadmoor. Ron Kray always hated the idea of being locked away with no date for his release. But that is just what he got, and he died in Broadmoor in the spring of 1995. His only form of escape was to get married, write books, get married again, write more books – and to make friends and, sometimes, enemies. Peter Sutcliffe, the Yorkshire Ripper, was a sworn enemy – they hated each other (something that I witnessed for myself). He often told me of his dreams – sailing around the world, seeing old friends. This is the story of those lost years, years of insanity. Reg Kray has toured the UK over the past 30 years, going from one jail to the next, heading for parole (due in 1998). I went to see him in Nottingham Gaol where he was steadily getting drunk on vodka and orange juice, smuggled in to him by friends. These friends had a young baby with them, so the vodka was in the baby bottle, but Reg didn't appear to mind. This is his story; one of brutality, of charitable involvement and finally of marriage. Chapter ten is entitled 'Lifers'.

Charlie Kray will now always be known as a drug dealer. This is ultimately the story of a deal that went catastrophically wrong, ending with a 12-year sentence for cocaine importation and dealing. Was it a last ditch-effort to make a fortune and retire, or was it just a 'nice little earner' that went wrong? I have attempted to clear the picture and to explain the events, but in the end it was a deal too far for Charlie Kray. Hence the title for chapter eleven – 'Will Charles Kray, Drug Dealer, Please Stand'.

When discussing the Kray fascination it is difficult to get away from the ladies. Indeed, not many would want to get away from the delightful and sexy ladies in the lives of all three Kray brothers. Reg has had many such 'fans' while in prison, leading ultimately to marriage inside the walls, but his first wife committed suicide. Ron was married twice within the walls of Broadmoor, although he had other intimate associations while in the institution (men only). And Charlie Kray had an affair with Barbara Windsor. So what is the fascination of the Krays? Why do they appeal to women the way they obviously do? Are there really any answers to this intriguing riddle? Chapter twelve is called 'The Women in their Lives'.

So what is the future for the Krays? Some would say that it's all over for the Krays, some that it's only just begun. So what is the truth? Since no one yet has been able to predict the future in an accurate and intelligible way anything I have to say is pure guesswork.

Chapter thirteen makes an effort at predicting the future for the Krays. Ron Kray is now dead, so there is no future for him apart from his undeniable place in history. Charlie Kray, at the age of 70, has just started a 12-year prison sentence so what future is there for him? Are Charlie Kray's champagne days really over? And Reg Kray, at 60-something, has just got married again, this time to a well-educated school-teacher. So what can she teach him that he doesn't already know? What then of the Kray dynasty? Is it the end or the beginning, the beginning of a new life? The only man who can answer that is Reg Kray, and what is his future likely to hold? He has been doing time for 30 years now. But surely his celebrity status, which has prospered while inside, will make him a wealthy man. He will certainly be able to make more money from legitimate business dealings than from a life of crime. But is this right? Should Reg Kray be able to make easy money in this way? After all, he is a killer. Chapter thirteen is called – 'The Kray Legacy'.

Happy reading!

1. ONCE UPON A TIME THERE WERE . . . THE GANG WARS

If you have ever wondered what it was like in the bygone, war-torn days of London, then I suggest you take a magical mystery tour past Tower Bridge and head east along the Whitechapel Road, through that area haunted by Jack the Ripper, and then out along the Mile End Road to the East End of London.

It is like a time warp, a virtual reality *Goodnight Sweetheart* experience, for any other dweller of suburban London or for any inter-galactic tourist trying to find a worm-hole leading home. It is a strange new (out of the old) world waiting for discovery by anyone who dares enter its dwindling domain and for those thirsting for the ultimate time-travel experience.

This is an area of tradition, a place where family ties and old-fashioned values still come first. But what are these values, the social aspects of daily life still cherished and worshipped by Eastenders, young and old alike?

It is time to put on your thinking cap and to get your head into gear as we go back in time to the early days of the East End after the Second World War; a time of those great aristocrats of crime, Billy Hill and Jack Spot, and to the scene of criminal innovation (often imported from the USA) that rose from the ashes of the *blitzkreig*. This is a time of lawlessness like in the early days of the Wild West of America, an age of personal freedom and cultural change, and a mish-mash of new thinking and political ideology that eventually led to an event that was to change the way of life for almost everyone in the country – and beyond.

This was the time of the gang wars!

The following is an attempt at relating information in a reasonable, articulate and sensible manner in order to give the reader an appropriate sense of what the East End of London is really all about. In the name of communication, however, academic terminology has been 'dumbed down' into a more easily recognisable vernacular, although this comes mainly in the latter part of the discussion. In each and every case where I have used academic research papers or previously published academic books, I have sought advice and acceptance from the original author and I am very appreciative of this collaboration. Original text referred to in this book is attributed, enabling the reader to access the original research material.

So come with me back in time to an era of innocence and guile; to a time of progress and stagnation; to a wonderland of imaginative ideas and devious dealings.

We start by looking at the emergence of these gangs as a post-war phenomenon. Later on in the debate, the history of the area is seen through the eyes of the sociologists. Readers can find further information in an academic paper, entitled 'The Kray Fascination', written by Professor Chris Jenks and Justin J. Lorentzen, of Goldsmiths College, London. In this Professor Jenks and his colleague look into the background of the East End of London and of the Eastenders themselves.

Another sociologist, Dr Dick Hobbs of Durham University, in his book *Doing the Business*, tells of how the working-class background of the East End helped to maintain and strengthen the position of the Krays within its social structure. (This title is one we share – I also published a book called *Doing the Business*, Smith Gryphon, London, 1993 – dealing with the Krays.)

So, just why and how did the Krays, like so many other gangs, emerge from the ashes of the Second World War? And how did the Krays come to dominate the '50s and '60s, which saw an explosion of criminal underworld activity and a developing and sensitive society full of opportunities for those who were willing and able to impose themselves through violence, fear of retribution and intimidation?

The pre-war community of the East End of London was a very closely knit collection of multiple ethnic groupings. Almost all immigrant groups were there – Jewish, Italian, Maltese, Irish, Bangladeshi and Romany. All were represented among the ancient fabric of the East End in its mainly working-class domains.

'London, like many large conurbations, expanded initially in relation to function and density but divided latterly in terms of largely social and cultural factors,' say Professor Chris Jenks and Justin J. Lorentzen of Goldsmiths College. The East End, we are told, was a disease-ridden den of iniquity, where deprivation and poverty were the order of the day and criminal and political dissidence the norm. Or so it was up until the end of the 1939–45 war, when most of the area lay in ruins. There was no option other than to build it up all over again.

Before the war, crime was a known phenomenon but people left their doors unlocked since there was little or no fear of being robbed. Neighbour supported neighbour and when there were problems, everyone wanted to help; they were supportive to the extreme.

But the war changed all of that. Violence crept in, weaving its bloody trail through the winding streets of both East and West London. There was a blossoming of protection rackets, drinking and gambling clubs and prostitution. The war was a great time for the villains. They ran the black markets and used the Blitz as cover for their ram-raiding and theft from the West End stores where they would dress up as ARP wardens or police or ambulance crews to deceive their way into the West End. 'For the West End to know the East at all was to apprehend the threat and intimidation, the exotic and even the bizarre,' says Chris Jenks, reflecting on this urban 'great divide'.

Everything was rationed, but people had incurable desires which led to almost everyone buying something through connections or off the back of a truck. Get it at all costs was the name of the game. And people didn't mind how they got it. They turned a blind eye to theft and to crime in general. Everyone managed their own lives the best they could. This was the start of the egoistic era of the '50s and '60s. Acquisition became the order of the day. Eggs, meat, clothing, fuel coupons – they were all highly marketable products in the hands of the crooks. The material world was born.

The criminal has always looked after himself first and everyone else last. And so it was with the war. They defied the call-up, using any means at their disposal to get out of joining the forces. Hitler was seen as a guiding light – he killed and maimed, and succeeded. So the gangsters of the East End began turning the screws. They became more violent, more sadistic, more aggressive.

One such small-time gangster, by the name of Frankie Fraser, actually caused such a rumpus at his medical that he was certified insane and sent to an asylum. The crooks and criminals would go to any lengths to get out of the call-up. No trick was barred. Indeed, if you didn't escape the clutches of the military, you were not a member of the club. All the best villains got out of military service in one way or another, so it was these people, the tricksters and the petty villains, who came to rule the East End of London during the Second World War.

Even the West End was full of deserters. Soho attracted them in their droves. There was money to be made and suckers to rob. Business was good and the villains and rogues of the East came West in search of an easy target.

The cultural inheritance of the East End of London 'does not conform to either proletarian or bourgeois cultural stereotypes' says Dick Hobbs, referring to the attitude of the East End villain. This covers both the materialistic and the ideological, since the Krays, for example, came from both Jewish and Romany stock, but 'showed a response to poverty and hardship which was at once protective, itinerant and entrepreneurial'. Being a rogue in Bethnal Green was not just accepted, it was welcomed.

The fires of the Blitz shielded the villains who coolly went about their business. They were all kept busy with their robberies and easy-money dealings and there were few police officers around to hinder them; they were all kept busy with the bombs. There was a certain freedom for the villains and they exploited it as much as they could. The war was a watershed in the history of crime.

The villain, previously only tolerated by the Eastenders, became a true friend who could get the good things of life. He became an acceptable part of everyday life. The rogues didn't exist any more, only the villains survived.

By the early '50s, the world of the East End had changed. London was in the grip of violent criminals, men who would stop at nothing to get what they wanted. Billy Hill and Jack Spot, real name Comer, had run the underworld successfully for more than ten years, from their base in the West End of London. Hill was a thief with a passion for organisation, whereas Spot was the minder who arranged the heavy stuff. They were the very best and everyone knew it – from the Krays to the Richardsons and throughout the entire city of London, both East and West. These men were the uncrowned kings of crime.

By 1955 things were changing and the team of Hill and Spot had a falling-out. They disbanded the old guard and formed new allies. Jack Spot turned to the Krays. Spot took Ron and Reg Kray to Epsom races in April of 1955 and introduced them to real money. Organised crime has always seen supplying protection to bookmakers as an easy racket. If the bookmakers didn't pay then they would be roughed up. So they ended up paying people like the Krays for protection. Violence was now the tool of the gangster and knives and guns became the tools of the trade.

Jack Spot was not a young man and had recently been badly cut around the face by the evil 'Mad Frankie' Fraser, who had joined Billy Hill's forces. So getting the Krays on his side was a bit of a coup. The twins were keen to learn and took time off from the Regal Billiard Hall to size up the opposition. They were fast becoming good businessmen themselves and were quick to spot an opportunity. They could smell the money.

Billy Hill was not a man of violence. He would sooner make a deal and share the profits rather than risk war. It just wasn't good for business. But he could see that the whole underworld scene was hotting up. Violence was now the key.

Gang met gang in minor skirmishes, only using knives or fists. They would arrange for a meet on one of London's many bomb sites, where rubble still littered the streets and back alleys. But these were not important events; they only showed which gangs were the dominant ones. The big business was making money, not war.

Robberies were executed with bloody efficiency. The stakes were high and crimes of violence commonplace. The crooks wanted the good life, no matter what. Callous people committed the most violent of crimes. These people knew that once caught, they would face harsh treatment in prison. The cat o' nine tails was still around and the birch was available for serious offenders; sentences were long. In this dark world of the criminal brutality bred brutality and there was no one better than Ron and Reg Kray when it came to out-and-out violence.

It was the time of the gun and it was also time for Spot and Hill to beat a hasty retreat. In the summer of 1956 Billy Hill retired to his villa in the South of Spain, and Jack Spot took over a furniture business in the West End. They got out while the going was good and before the killings started. It is a pity that the Richardsons and the Krays couldn't have done the same.

For the bosses of the underworld it was a very busy time. They began stock-piling weapons of all kinds in readiness for the war that was sure to come. In the end, however, it was only a war of words – not of deeds. Each of the prominent gangs was ultimately responsible for its own downfall, and the bosses never met each other in the expected gangland brawl. Just who was the biggest and the best was never decided. The clash of the Titans never took place.

The Nash Gang

In the early part of 1960, one of the Nash brothers was involved in a car accident. The other driver was Selwyn Cooney, who ran a spieler in Whitechapel in an area frequented by known villains; it was also the site of the last Jack the Ripper murder. Unfortunately for Cooney, the other guy came off worse. And when the other guy is a Nash then you can expect trouble.

At around midnight on 8 February, Jimmy Nash, the leader of the gang and one of the most respected villains in London, arrived at the back door of the club with two other men. Inside were Cooney and his moll, Fay Sadler; they weren't expecting trouble, but that is just what they got.

Jimmy Nash was a powerful man and, at 28 years old, was thought by many to be destined to remain a top underworld figure for many years to come. He and his six brothers had a string of gambling clubs and were involved in theft and other corrupt activities, and he was a very popular figure throughout the London underworld. There was no need for Jimmy Nash to be there, but he took it personally and retribution was on his mind.

When Nash stepped into the spieler brandishing a gun, Billy Ambrose stepped in between Nash and Cooney. Ambrose was only a customer, so he really should have known better. Nash shot him. Then Nash turned to Cooney and shot him at point blank range. Cooney died instantly with a bullet in the brain.

When the police arrived at the club, they found carnage. It was Jack the Ripper all over again. There were three witnesses including Fay Sadler, and they were all willing to talk.

The trial, however, had to be staged twice due to threats and attempted intimidation of the jury. But in the end Jimmy Nash was sent to prison for five years for killing Cooney. At the time many people thought he would be hanged.

The Nash family gave up most of their business enterprises in Islington, North London. They slowly and quietly disappeared. The last I heard of them was that they were all living peacefully on the Costa del Sol, but that is another story.

The Richardson Gang

The most powerful of all the gangs, and the richest by far, was that belonging to Charlie and Eddie Richardson. Charlie Richardson was a shrewd businessman and after the war he had entered the field of surplus stocks and scrap metal, but he also ran a wholesale chemists' business, which shows the versatility of the man. The Richardsons, from Lambeth in South London, spent many years building up a respectable business empire, but there was an evil side to their nature and they had a side-line in debt collecting, blackmail and extortion. It was over-indulgence in violence that was eventually to be their downfall.

Charlie Richardson had contacts everywhere. He even had corrupt policemen on his payroll, from Scotland Yard itself. A phone call from Charlie and cases were dropped. Even when it came to government contracts he had friends in high places. Corruption was the name of the game. It was the '50s and the '60s, a time of good living and everyone wanted more of the same. An office in Park Lane was a natural consequence of his success, and the gold mine in South Africa was a constant reminder to other gangs, like the Krays, that here were real adventurers; they would go anywhere and do anything for the dosh.

As a part of the debt-collecting set-up, Charlie Richardson hired Mad Frankie Fraser, a real thug who was hungry for trouble. Fraser was feared by all. He was the best at his game and had even sliced up Jack Spot, the old gangland leader. Fraser was afraid of no man and in 1962 he went to work for the Richardson gang.

The hiring of Fraser was a big mistake, since it forced everyone and everything up a gear. The pace got hotter, the events more violent and serious and there was always trouble in the air. Exactly why Charlie Richardson hired Mad Frankie Fraser is also a bit of a mystery, since he had good working relationships throughout London and had secured recognisable boundaries for his business operations. The threat, however, was to come from another madman, Ronnie Kray, but in a way this was set up by Fraser himself.

With his Scotland Yard pals behind him, keeping the gang out of trouble, Charlie Richardson set about a period of expansion. The 'long firm' frauds continued, but he wanted more income from them. Debts of £25,000 became normal at this time, so profits were naturally good. The idea of a 'long firm' is to build up debts, only to fold the company overnight and get away with the money. The Richardsons were good at it.

The Krays were also involved in 'long firm' frauds. Leslie Payne, their business manager, had set up a whole string of them throughout the East End. Again, money was good, so the Krays continued to build up their empire on the back of dishonest, devious dealings.

However, the Richardsons had ideas of grandeur; they wanted to be the underworld bosses and the Krays had no place in their business strategy. A meeting was called, with the Richardsons and the Krays putting their own particular point of view and trying to establish some kind of territorial domain for each gang. The Richardsons didn't see how the Krays could fit into their plans and the meeting broke up with everyone expecting out-and-out war. 'Clear off, we don't need you,' was Charlie Richardson's closing remark to Ron and Reg Kray.

The Krays went home and brought out the arsenal. Once again, it was not needed, much to Ron's disappointment.

Billy Haywood was a thief and together with his pal Billy Gardner he ran a spieler in Lewisham. It gave them a good living and gangsters were not allowed. Thieves were, however, allowed into the place and many came to talk and chat and to plan deals. Thieves kept to themselves, they didn't like the gangsters who wanted to take everything away from them.

Eddie Richardson, together with Mad Frankie Fraser, visited the club and asked for protection money. Haywood and Gardner weren't interested. Eddie Richardson and the much-feared Fraser left empty-handed.

Fraser had a reputation to live up to, or to live down, if you like it better that way. So he phoned Haywood to invite him and Gardner to a meeting at Mr Smiths, a gambling club in Catford. Haywood had already been warned, so he and Gardner and a group of pals turned up at the club, heavily armed. Fraser, with Eddie Richardson and a dozen or so members of the gang were already there. They too were heavily armed. Guns galore!

The shooting had to start sooner or later, but it happened sooner than anyone had imagined. Eddie Richardson said only a few words and that was it. Shots were fired everywhere. All the gang members dived for cover and there was blood and guts all over the floor of the club.

Dickie Hart, a member of the Kray gang who was by chance with the Lewisham gang that night, fired at will. He wasn't very accurate, but he did manage to hit one of the Richardson gang. Fraser saw the incident and managed to shoot and kill Hart, but not before Hart had managed to shoot Fraser in the leg.

When the police arrived all they had to do was to go around and pick up the bodies. There was no resistance and even Fraser went peacefully. The battle scene at the back of the club where the police took away the bodies resembled a blood bath. The police found weapons everywhere. There were guns, iron bars, knives – anything and everything that could be used to kill or maim.

Incredibly, only one man was killed – Dickie Hart. Mad Frankie Fraser stood trial for the killing of Hart, but he was found not guilty.

But Eddie Richardson and Fraser were convicted of causing grievous bodily harm and given five-year sentences.

For Haywood and Gardner the game was not finished. Over the next few years everyone who had taken their side in the battle was killed. Only Haywood and Gardner themselves were left unscathed. Whether or not this was retribution on the part of Charlie Richardson has never been proved, but the thought remains ever present in the minds of Billy Haywood and Billy Gardner.

Charlie Richardson kept the business going with new recruits and he continued to collect money on behalf of his clients. One of his debtors was a man called Jimmy Taggart who actually told the police of his treatment. Knowing that the Richardsons had spies everywhere, he was afraid to sign a statement. But he did agree to give a statement, if he could sign it only when Charlie Richardson was safely behind bars.

Taggart's statement was staggering. It revealed everything

about the Richardson gang's use of electric shock, pliers to pull out fingernails and to cut off fingers, drugs and such. It was serious torture according to anyone's standards and it all took place at a yard in Rotherhithe, just south of the River Thames. There was even medical evidence to back up the statement, since Taggart had treatment after the torture at a flat in North London.

Charlie Richardson was pulled in and Jimmy Taggart signed his statement. It was all over bar the shouting for Charlie Richardson. Only five months after his brother's arrest he received 25 years in jail for his part in the crimes, for violence and demanding money with menaces. It was only now that the police realised that there was a connection between the 'long firm' frauds and the beatings at Rotherhithe. That connection was Charlie Richardson.

But this wasn't the only reason why Scotland Yard were after Charlie Richardson. Other evidence was coming into the Yard from other sources, far away in South Africa, of Richardson's dealings there and of how he was involved in murder.

A man by the name of Thomas Waldeck had been murdered by two men, Harry Prince and Johnny Bradbury. Bradbury was an old pal of Charlie Richardson's and had escaped to South Africa in 1964. Harry Prince was the hired assassin, but he needed help from Bradbury to locate his man. The man in question was Waldeck, a man who had committed a most heinous crime – he had borrowed money from Charlie Richardson and hadn't paid it back.

Prince vanished and left Bradbury to stand alone in court. Bradbury was eventually sentenced to life in 1966 and spent 11 years in jail, but he told everything to Scotland Yard, who sent police officers to South Africa to question him. The game was over for the Richardsons. Even Eddie Richardson and Frankie Fraser were again tried and given 15 years each for their involvement. Charlie Richardson's 25-year sentence reflected his involvement in the South African affair. It was just another London gang who had apparently committed suicide and Fraser was the man with the shooter.

Sir Frederick Lawton, who tried the Richardsons and Fraser, called it 'the torture case' since he had never heard of anything so horrible as the evidence presented in court. Charlie Richardson kept complaining to the bitter end. 'I only want my money,' he would remark continually, as if he had done nothing wrong. But he and the others were this time found guilty, and his pals at the Yard couldn't help him.

The police method of investigation was to mark a significant change in tactics which had repercussions in later cases, even against the Krays. The fact that these criminals were locked up while police investigations could take place was a change in normal procedure and gave witnesses the chance of telling the truth, without the fear of reprisals. No bail was allowed for the Richardsons and their gang, so the police could collect the evidence they needed without retribution or threats of violence. This meant that the Krays were left alone to take over the West End of London, with a little help from their pals in the US Mafia.

The Kray Gang

By the start of the 1950s the twins had built up a sturdy reputation as boxers. All three Kray brothers boxed at the Royal Albert Hall on the same evening, something that has not been surpassed to this very day. The date was 11 December 1951 and the Kray brothers would never fight in a boxing ring again. Both Charlie and Ronnie lost that night; only Reggie won his match, but then he was a schoolboy boxing champion and a real prospect in the game. But the twins had already decided on another game: the game of crime.

The start of the empire was The Regal, an old dilapidated billiard hall. They bought new tables and Ron supplied the smoky atmosphere, just like in the American movies. They were only 21 when they bought The Regal and they had to borrow the money from elder brother Charlie. But it was a start and from then on their rise up the underworld ladder was relentless. Local crooks would come and trade goods or hide weapons; this was when Ron Kray started taking an interest in knives and guns.

Helping Jack Spot at Epsom was the next step on the ladder. But what really made everyone sit up and take notice was when a Maltese gang tried to get protection money from them. The Maltese were usually into prostitution and not known as fearless mobsters, but the events that night set the record straight about the Krays.

When the leader of the Maltese gang asked for protection money Ron stared him in the face. It went terribly quiet in The Regal. This kind of situation was unrehearsed so no one knew what would happen – except Ron and Reg Kray.

'Protection from what?' asked Ron as he drew a cutlass. Reg Kray pulled out a knife and the twins lashed into the Maltese gang. They fled in terror with the twins only building up a light sweat.

'They've not got a lot of bottle, these continentals, especially when the knives come out,' Reg was heard to remark about the battle. It showed everyone in the place that these two youngsters were here to stay. They would defend what was theirs with their lives; and anyone else's who got in their way.

There were other fights, such as that with the dockers who again wanted protection money from the Krays. Now anyone would have thought that they would have learned from the Maltese gang. But no.

The dockers, all from Poplar, invited the twins to meet them in a pub on the Mile End Road. The twins were busy that evening at The Regal, but everyone knew that they had been called out by the dockers. Again, they all waited to see and hear what would happen. At the end of the evening, late in the autumn of 1954, Ron and Reg Kray put down their teacups, put on their jackets, and walked slowly but deliberately out of The Regal.

It was only a short walk down to the Mile End Road and the dockers were waiting for them in the private bar, drinking light ale. They looked up when the twins entered the bar and began to grin at the two youngsters. Now that was not a good idea.

'Here you are, sonny,' said one of the dockers. 'You are just about old enough for a shandy.' That was it. This was downright disrespectful. Ron Kray, once again fearless in battle, laid into the dockers with his bare fists. Reg joined in and before long they had beaten the big men to pulp. Reg had to pull Ron off one of the dockers; Ron couldn't stop hitting him and could easily have killed him with constant punches.

It was all over as quickly as it had started. Ron and Reg Kray smartened themselves up and walked out into the brisk night air. The job was done, the record set straight. On the way back to The Regal they discussed plans for getting into the protection racket themselves.

Protection was the Krays' biggest business. They had all kinds of traders and trades people on their lists. If they wanted cars, then they would just go and get one. If they wanted food, then they would send someone over to collect. And if they wanted booze, then they would go out and drink all night and let the establishment pay for it. They paid for nothing and everyone paid them for it.

Clubs, too, became big business, especially after the 1961 Gaming Act and by the time the twins were eventually taken into custody they had shares in over 30 clubs, dotted all over the country. The Double R was the next club they bought after The Regal. Then came a few others leading to The Kentucky. But pride of place was Esmeralda's Barn, located just off Wilton Place, right in the middle of the West End. It was one of the best casinos in London and the guests were all from *Who's Who*. The Krays had climbed right to the top of the heap, but they soon found out that it was quicker tumbling down than climbing up.

The twins were bonded by both rivalry and devotion and they had quickly built up a reputation. It was in the mid-'50s that they started building their gang, the 'Firm'.

Headquarters was at 178 Vallance Road, where they and their mother had lived since the twins returned home from the country, where they stayed through the war. Old man Charlie joined them when he could, since he was still officially a deserter. This simple two up and two down was their fortress and they called the place Fort Vallance.

The Firm was a loose conglomeration of, in the main,

small-time gangsters. Ron, who called himself the Colonel, was the boss together with his brother Reg. But in any disagreement it was generally Ron who came out best. Charlie Kray was only involved when and as needed. He played no role in the protection rackets, but was deeply involved in the organisation of the clubs. He was good at his job; that is, when Ron allowed him to do it. For this was the real problem within the gang. Whereas Jimmy Nash and Charlie Richardson were the natural bosses of their respective gangs, the twins could never decide among themselves who really was the boss. It was always a joint decision, even if one of them disagreed. And Charlie was never asked for an opinion.

Members of the gang used the Kray name to sell themselves and to make some money. Tony and Chris Lambrianou are typical of these types of gang members. They would travel the country playing for high stakes with the names of Reg and Ron Kray. The deal was not complicated: if they made some money from one of their crooked deals, then the twins would receive a share. It was that simple. The twins never asked what they were doing; just how much was coming to them from the profits of the Lambrianou rackets. Most of these deals were connected to protection, but they were not limited to anything in particular. Tony and Chris Lambrianou could do whatever they pleased, as long as the twins were paid.

Other members of the Firm, for example Big Albert Donaghue, collected the protection money and shared out the pensions. They had two different kinds of lists: the big names for big pay-outs and the so-called 'nipping' list for smaller income. They would collect from the big names on the first list in ready cash, but collection from the smaller operators could be in goods, such as crates of booze or cartons of cigarettes. If Ron or Reg wanted a car then they would just stroll into the dealer and drive away with the latest American import. No one would stop them or ask for payment.

As for the clubs owned by the Krays, it was usually someone trusted who ran the establishment. They didn't trust many outside of the family, so there were many relations by the name of Kray employed in the business. But generally brother

Charlie was not on the board. Only in the case of the Double R did he figure as a boss. But when Ron Kray got out of jail Charlie was told to take a back seat, as usual.

Ron and Reg Kray did not favour their elder brother Charlie being involved in their business dealings. Maybe they thought that Charlie was too clever, or maybe they simply did not trust him. But the fact remains that Charlie Kray was never a partner, not even in their outrageous adventure in Africa.

Now not many people know where Enugu in Nigeria is. But to Ron and Reg Kray it was their chance to get into Africa, just like their main enemy (apart from Nipper Read) Charlie Richardson. They had been envious of the Richardsons. Any deal in Africa was something big. And Ron Kray wanted something big!

The deal was set up in the early part of 1964 by Leslie Payne who had a chance meeting with Ernest Shinwell, the son of Lord Manny Shinwell, the prominent Labour politician. The plan was for a major development in Nigeria comprising houses, shops, hotels, amenities of all kinds. The place was Enugu, right on the edge of the jungle, and Leslie Payne flew down to Enugu with Ernest Shinwell to check out the possibilities. Payne reported back that the Krays could expect to make £120,000 from the deal, so GAS (Great African Safari) was born.

Ron Kray visited the site a number of times and so did Reg. But they never went there together, since one had to stay in London to look after business. They decided that their brother Charlie should be sent along with any visitor to Nigeria, just to see that things were progressing well and that the Krays could be sure of the back-handers that Payne had reckoned on. Over the following months Charlie Kray was a regular visitor to Lagos and beyond, together with Payne, Freddie Gore the accountant, Shinwell, the construction company Tariff representatives and so on.

Unfortunately for the Krays, Leslie Payne thought that he had become the new great white hunter and started to get difficult with the contractors. It was these very same contractors who had paid the Krays good hard pound notes for getting their contracts. They didn't like being ordered around. One of them was a brother of the Chief of Police in Enugu and when he heard about the goings-on at the construction site, he swiftly put everyone in jail. All, that is, except for Charlie Kray. Charlie had no official position with GAS and was only there as an observer. So it was up to Charlie to get everyone out of jail and home to London.

The twins, back in the East End of London, didn't like Charlie's urgent plea for money. But they sent the Firm out at short notice to collect protection money. Soon it was on its way to Africa and the Great African Safari was over. The Krays ended up paying every penny back to the Nigerian contractors.

The only good point about the deal was that Ron Kray had participated in a guided tour of Parliament and had taken lunch in the Lords with Lord Shinwell and got the chance of meeting and clubbing with Lord Robert Boothby. This, in a way, was worth every penny to Ron Kray.

The Krays were all about reputation, but they had to live up to those reputations. When a gang member was cut up or shot by a rival gang, then as with the other gangs, retribution was expected. When Eric Mason, a member of the Firm, was kidnapped by Mad Frankie Fraser, who was working with the Richardsons, it was their duty to take care of business.

Eric Mason had had a run-in with the Scottish fugitive Jimmy Boyle, who was being wined and dined by Fraser at The Astor Club, just off Berkeley Square in the West End of London. Mason ended up being coshed by Fraser and dragged away in a car. His treatment at the hands of the Richardson gang was pure torture. They even tried to cut off his hands.

This meant to Ron and Reg outright war, but the shoot-out at Mr Smiths Club involving Eddie Richardson and Mad Frankie Fraser stopped the action. The Krays and the Richardsons never had their duel and Ron Kray's confrontation with Fraser didn't materialise. Ron had never liked Fraser, who had only a short time earlier taken over some slot machines in the West End, which was Kray territory and everyone knew it. And Fraser's pal and fellow Richardson gang member George Cornell had taken over a pornography business, also located in the West End. Ron Kray was all dressed up, but with nowhere to go.

The only outcome of the Kray/Richardson feud was the killing of George Cornell by Ron Kray covered in chapter three, which tells the story of the many killings during the reign of the Krays.

As gangs go, the Firm was no real success, apart from supplying the Krays with protection money. They did far better with the clubs and casinos like Esmeralda's Barn and their Mafia deals, such as sharing profits from The Colony Club, which was operated by George Raft.

The 'long firm' frauds also worked well, but when the twins decided to get rid of Leslie Payne, they lost their only business partner who could handle the intricacies of such deals. When Leslie Payne decided to get out, it forced the twins to try to get rid of him. The man chosen for the job was Jack 'The Hat' McVitie. But when he decided to keep the money and not kill Payne, it was his turn to be killed at the hands of Reg Kray. This too is covered in chapter three.

Scotland Yard just didn't know how to handle the Krays. When Cornell was shot and killed in The Blind Beggar rumours quickly found their way to the Yard where Assistant Commissioner Brodie was waiting for a break. He had already appointed Chief Superintendent Tommy Butler to the case, Butler having been successful with the Great Train Robbery case in 1963.

But Brodie thought Butler needed help and enlisted the services of Leonard 'Nipper' Read, who had previously worked with Butler on the 1963 robbery. Read had, however, some years earlier, caused a bit of a bother in police circles when his photograph appeared in the national press – pictured drinking in the company of none other than the Krays themselves. Nipper Read was cleared of improper behaviour and taken off the Kray case, but not before he was promoted. How often has this scenario repeated itself? So Leonard Nipper Read was no stranger to the Krays.

Read was once again moved on and an uneasy stalemate developed between the police and the Krays. This was broken only when Nipper Read was reassigned to the Kray case. It appeared that Scotland Yard just couldn't make up their minds about the Krays and about the involvement of Read, who eventually proved to be their greatest asset.

In the autumn of 1967 Read was back in the picture as a Detective Superintendent, assigned to the Murder Squad at Scotland Yard. The new Commissioner of the Metropolitan Police, Sir John Waldron, was concerned about the publicity surrounding the Richardson case and by the constant and embarrassing ways the Krays flaunted themselves in public, so he immediately put Read in charge of getting the Krays, once and for good.

It was Nipper Read who started contacting old pals of the Krays looking for evidence. But all he managed to get was a 200-page statement from Leslie Payne, Ron's ex-business manager (and the man who was targeted for killing by Jack 'The Hat' McVitie). This statement was not completely reliable due to Payne's own involvement, but it gave Read some good ideas on who to talk to and how to proceed. He had also learned from the Richardson case where the rats deserted the sinking ship only after the Richardsons were safely behind bars. So when he took his great gamble in May of 1968, he was fully prepared.

As with the Richardson enquiry, the police breakthrough came by accident when a moment of madness changed history. Ron Kray could not stop himself from killing George Cornell and that was to be his downfall. Ronnie's constantly provoking his own twin brother was also the final nail in Reggie's coffin, and this too was brought on by his chronic paranoid schizophrenic tendencies.

So Nipper Read won the battle of the gangs when he obtained authority from the Home Office to offer immunity from prosecution to key witnesses, who eagerly testified against their former associates, just as in the Richardson affair. The proof came in in abundance, but the police could only convict on the basis of the two killings, and not for any other crime such as the 'long firm' frauds or the Mafia deals. But this was good enough for Nipper Read and his team at Tintagel House. It was Read who got all the credit, but it was the team who did all the work.

The gangs of the '50s and '60s, in the main, all committed suicide. They thought they could get away with murder, but they couldn't. It wasn't Scotland Yard that caught them, however – they did it themselves with just a killing too far.

Before the killings, the Krays appeared to fit into a niche nicely positioned with the police on the one side and the East End community on the other. As Dr Dick Hobbs states in his book *Doing the Business*, the local police had little to fear from the Krays. He goes on to say: 'Their business enterprises served to reinforce a taken-for-granted sense of order built upon a solid foundation of independence, autonomy and tough masculinity.'

It is undeniably true that the East End of London had not been top priority for housing, employment and entrepreneurial considerations, which had led to the development of a type of class solidarity, but it is difficult to see the Krays as part of a social structure. This is, however, the case because the Krays saw themselves as the protectors of their own manor, manipulating some kind of control in their own inimitable way. 'When Reggie and me looked after things in the East End there was never any of this mugging of old ladies or child killing. If anybody had started pulling strokes like that they would have been stopped,' said Ron Kray to *The Sun* in 1984. So were the Krays your friendly society of local vigilantes? I don't think so, but this does show their position within the East End, since many people still today say similar things about the Krays. It may not have been true then, but it is now. It is all a matter of perception and selective memory.

'As integral parts of the indigenous social order the Kray twins were unproblematic to the local police force. In their world children, women and old people were respected and kept in their place,' says Dick Hobbs. He continues: 'The sense of decorum enforced at their establishments likewise rendered the police peripheral, their role being reduced to that of token representatives of the state.'

Other prominent sociologists and commentators have pointed out that as the old working-class communities of the East End have been replaced or dislocated by recent social and economic changes, then relations with the police have benefited. But the East End is still a collection of isolated communities, with diverse ethnic backgrounds; the influx of newcomers to London as a whole did not change things, since these 'outsiders' settled in other parts of London well away from the East End and the deprivation associated with this part of the capital. So the East End is still working-class, it still has a social order similar to that which existed prior to the Second World War and it still shows tolerance towards all ethnic groups. It appears to have a soul of its own.

Chris Jenks has defined the East End as 'a territory without a map, slowly it evolved into a precise cartography but the territory disappeared. Now it stands in a twilight world between urban place and museum space'.

'The Krays and Richardsons did not challenge social reality but reinforced it by conforming to behaviour traditional in entrenched urban working-class districts,' says Dr Hobbs. The police knew this at the time, although they may not have put it as eloquently as Dick Hobbs and they may not have been able to understand it, but they accepted it for what it was and they let the Krays go about their business, as long as they didn't do anything too rash or awkward, where the police were forced to take action. But that is exactly what happened. Homosexuality and mental illness were the two major factors that caused Ron Kray to go beyond the accepted parameters and this naturally enough forced a police commitment to find, arrest and convict the guilty.

When the killings occurred, the feeling changed in the East End. The Krays had overstepped the mark and were becoming an embarrassment both to the police and to the various communities of the East End. They weren't the sporting heroes that they were supposed to be. The police were forced into action by the grotesque events and the status quo was shattered.

The killings were all down to Ron Kray and his illness – some would call it madness. He could not stay within the boundaries and tolerances set by the social order of things. He just had to overstep the mark to prove a point. All he proved was that he was indeed crazy!

It was Ron's mental illness that provoked the killings of both Cornell and McVitie, but his twin brother Reg had to be sentenced to 30 years in prison just to prove a point. Dick Hobbs puts it well when he says: 'The local CIDs of both South and East London had coexisted with the Krays and the Richardsons for many years, as had their predecessors with the likes of Jack Spot and Billy Hill. Occasional arrests had always been necessary for some minor misdemeanour but both the Krays and the Richardsons made it impossible for the police to turn a blind eye in the case of murder.' It had always suited the police to accept the gangs, as they do to a certain degree in the USA, but killings were unjustifiable and unacceptable. The public outcry is such that an enquiry must be instigated and an outcome secured which brings the perpetrators to justice. Justice must not only be done, but be seen to be done.

2. TRYING TO REPAY THE OLD BILL

The Kray twins, Ron and Reg, were only five years old when their father, old man Charlie Kray, deserted from the British Army. At the start of the Second World War, in 1939, he had been conscripted into the armed forces, but he was more intent on serving himself than his country; even his family came off second best.

So the early days for the twins involved keeping their father out of the clutches of the local constabulary and away from the fighting line. Charlie Kray senior had been an able fighter, like all the Krays before him. Their pedigree went back to the bare-knuckle fighting days; they were proud and let everyone know it. But he wasn't interested in his country, only in his own well-being. And that meant staying a free man and not stuck in some army barracks in the back of beyond; or even worse, facing German troops in Europe. All he wanted to do was to travel the south of the country in search of anything from clothes to gold and silver. He worked throughout the south, even travelling as far afield as South Wales. He was often away, and he liked it like that.

On one occasion the twins hid their father under the dining-table when the house was searched by the police. When one elderly policeman glanced at the table Ron said nonchalantly, 'You don't expect to find him there, do you?' They continued to search the house, but not under the table. This was characteristic of Ron and Reg alike. Another time they hid him in a cupboard, again to great effect. The twins soon learned how to handle themselves and the police; and they were still only at infant school.

This led to a hatred of authority of any kind. They made up their own rules and they punished anyone who dared break these rules. This ideology was to stay with them all their lives. It influenced their way of being, their actions and their thoughts; indeed, it even culminated in them killing people. Killing, to the Krays, was the ultimate punishment for not playing the game according to their rules.

The only one who could influence Ron and Reg Kray was their mother Violet. They idolised her and always took her side in an argument against their father, no matter who was right and who was wrong. They would protect their father, all right, but not at the cost of causing their mother any harm. She wanted them to take care of their father and so they did. This was not because of any affection they may have had for him. It was simply because of a promise to their mother.

Old man Charlie had been away, in hiding from the police, at a very important time in the lives of the Kray twins. Their mother Violet and Aunt Rose, who lived nearby, took on parental responsibilities and they cherished and nurtured the twins into adolescence. For six long years Charlie Kray senior was on the run and generally not at home at Vallance Road. This mother–son relationship dominated their lives.

From day one, almost, the police had been their sworn enemy. Why should the twins talk to them? Why should they trust them? Why should they believe them? It was one of the principal tenets of their code. 'We'll take care of ourselves and we'll put no trust in the law' was order of the day, and each and every day Ron and Reg Kray lived up to that code. Ron was to die by it; Reg still has to live by it.

Being wary of the Old Bill was a way of life in the East End. As stated earlier, everyone knew a rogue or two, even an out-and-out villain, who could get hard-to-come-by goods at a fraction of the price. This was a normal occurrence in this socially deprived area of London where the working classes did not have the spending power of their West End counterparts. So buying something out of the back door or from the boot of a car was an almost everyday event. This had always been the case in the East End and became even more so after the Second World War, when the twins were growing up in Bethnal Green.

It was a time of opportunities for the Kray twins, who quickly developed their independence in the blitzed ruins. Their father was more often than not away in the country trying to make a living and keeping well away from the law. From the very early days Violet would call them 'special'. She also considered herself to be special, since no one else in the neighbourhood had twins. People would stop her in the street and gaze in amazement and friends would come around to the house to ask if they could take the twins for a ride in the pram. This was glamour in the eyes of Violet Kray, it made her feel different, just like her two lovely sons.

When the twins were only three years old they were ill with diphtheria. They were separated and kept at different hospitals. Violet saw them both every day, but it took some three months for Reg to come home to Vallance Road. Ron was still ill and doctors were not giving him much of a chance of surviving. 'I know my boys best,' said Violet Kray, diagnosing symbiosis, as she took her little Ronnie home. 'He misses his brother.' She was right, the one was missing the other – after all, a mother knows best. Soon they were both out playing in the street, happy and contented, but their brother Charlie had witnessed the care and attention given to the twins by his mother. He was now in second place, with the twins firmly positioned on top of the heap.

Exactly how this made their elder brother Charlie feel is not well recorded, but I bet he hated it. The twins had only just been born and straight away their mother treated them like royalty, pandering to their every wish. After all, it was Charlie who had to go out to work and to help his mother with the chores around the house. Six years older than the twins, Charles David Kray had many responsibilities in the house in Hoxton and he continued with his duties at 178 Vallance Road, Bethnal Green, when the family moved there shortly before the outbreak of the war.

So, in a way, Charlie Kray took over the responsibilities that the father would normally have pursued. He taught them to box and he advised them to turn professional and make a living from boxing. He encouraged them to fight, even fighting on the same bill with them at the Royal Albert Hall. He did everything an elder brother should. But he could not entirely replace the father that the twins so desperately needed.

Without any true guidance from their father, the twins made up their own rules and their mother encouraged them – after all, they were special. But one rule that they didn't have to make up was the one that said don't trust the Old Bill. This was just a way of life in the East End, so the twins didn't need any telling. The lower social classes of the East End always looked after themselves, that's just the way it was. Some might say that it still is.

Whether or not their father Charlie would have made any difference to their lives at this time is debatable, but there are good psychological grounds for saying that families without a prominent father figure have more problems with their male offspring than so-called normal two-parent families. This does not mean that single parents always have problems with their children, but it does mean that the chances for trouble are increased. That unfortunately is just a way of life and it can be verified statistically.

So, to summarise, the twins had no father figure. They lived in an environment that frowned on going to the police for help. They were constantly hiding their father from the police and they were continually running foul of the law because they lived by their own rules and not by the law of the land. This was a recipe for disaster.

The twins were always keen to fight. If they couldn't find someone to have a fight with then they would fight themselves. They were not cheerful children, not by any means. In fact they were serious most of the time, with one continually trying to outsmart the other. They had their own way of sharing things, but it often came to a fight to determine who would get his way. In general it was Ron who came out on top. He would urge his brother on only to knock him down. Even at this early age Ron Kray knew how to control his twin brother Reg. And remember, Ron was the younger of the twins.

When their parents argued Ron and Reg wanted to join in and always took their mother's side in any row. They didn't know their father very well, even after the war, since he was still a wanted deserter. So with all the years of buying and selling all over the south of England and Wales before the war and trying to escape the police after the war, old man Charlie Kray really didn't know his sons.

When the twins were eight years old, school began again in the East End of London but the twins didn't take to the education system very well. They were always fighting on the old bomb sites with one gang or another and soon had their own bunch of followers. The Krays always led from the front, they never followed. Of the two it was Reg who did better at school, but Ron got his own back as soon as school was over. They soon became known as the 'terrible twins'.

By the time they were nine the twins knew how to handle the law. Their street, Vallance Road, was called 'deserters corner' and the Lees (Violet was a Lee) were everywhere. There was Aunt Rose, Aunt May, Grandfather Lee, Grandmother Lee and many more all dotted along and around Vallance Road, and the twins used to go from one house to another through the open doors or through the backyards. When the police came to call the twins would tell them that their parents were divorced and that their father didn't live there any more. Aunt May's husband was also on the run, as were many friends of the family. Grassing to the Old Bill was a real no-no.

When their father did make it back home for a weekend, he often took them over to see old fighter friends across the river, pals who made a living as pickpockets and small-time crooks. He filled their ears with tales of conflict and of violence, completely different to the bedtime stories they had from mother Violet and Aunt Rose. The twins lived in a paradoxical world; one full of love on the one hand and full of hate on the other.

Every year there was a fair over at Victoria Park. The twins would go with Grandfather Lee, with their dad Charlie scowling in the background, since he was still a wanted man. They loved the fights, with blood and sweat pouring off the fighters. The most interesting part of the boxing was when one or more of the local lads got into the ring to fight one of the main boxers, hired to fight all comers. The twins watched and waited. Soon it was their turn.

'Who'll be the next?' asked the ringmaster, as one poor soul was carried from the ring. 'There's a fiver in it.' He looked around the marquee; no one was taking him up on the challenge.

'I'll do it,' said Ron Kray, only eleven years old but ready for the big time. The ringmaster looked at him and started to laugh. He couldn't see who he could fight, since he was so much lighter than the 'professionals'. The crowd began to laugh and it all got too much for Brother Reg.

'I'll fight him,' said Reg, getting into the ring. The crowd were ready and the twins didn't let anyone down. They bruised each other, gave each other bloodied eyes and noses and generally tore one another to pieces. Eventually the ringmaster had to call a halt and pronounced it a draw. Ron would have kept on fighting, but the crowd had had its money's worth, so he reluctantly decided to call it a day.

Their father had seen it all and was pleased with his boys, since they were living up to the fighting Kray and Lee names. Their family history was full of prize-fighters, drunkards and small-time rogues. Charlie was happy to see that the twins had inherited something, something that he could be proud of. Violet, however, was fuming when she heard about the fight and she made Ronnie and Reggie promise not to fight each other ever again. They promised their mother and from then on they would always fight on the same side, mostly against authority and especially against the police. They now had a common enemy, the Old Bill.

But their first real piece of trouble came when they were 12 years old. There had been skirmishes with the law before, but what happened now was to be repeated many times through-out their lives. They were put on probation when found guilty of firing an air gun in a public place – even at this age they were both interested in guns. But the probation meant nothing to them and they carried on as usual with their gang fights, which became more and more intense. They would both use glass or knives or chains – they would use anything as a weapon. And they would never stop when they had their opponents down. This was just the way it was. Get them down and keep them down was the order of the day.

At 16 they bruised and bloodied a young lad from another gang, using chains and bars. But there were witnesses who saw the wicked deed and the police were involved. At the Magistrates' Court they were remanded in custody, accused of grievous bodily harm, and sent to the Old Bailey for trial. However, the witnesses were soon scared off with promises of beatings and other sordid threats, so the police were unable to convict them. Even the lad they had beaten was encouraged not to give evidence; it just wasn't done in the East End of London, breaking as it did one of their oldest codes. 'You don't grass,' he was told, so he didn't. The Krays got away with it.

Only a short while later they were in trouble again. The twins were hanging around Bethnal Green Road on a busy Saturday afternoon chatting to some pals, when a young policeman, PC Baynton, approached and told them to move on. He didn't just tell them, he decided to shove one of them, hitting him in the stomach. And that someone was young Ronnie Kray. Just why he acted in that way when they were only out for a stroll is pure speculation. But Ronnie took offence at being shoved, especially in front of his friends, and punched the officer in the face. That was it. He was carted down the station, leaving Reg wondering what had happened.

Charlie Kray rushed down to the police station as soon as he heard about the incident and what he saw didn't please him at all. Ronnie's face was in a real mess, bruised and bloodied all over. 'What the hell's going on?' Charlie screamed at the officers near the cell, as he went in to look at little brother Ronnie. They were still sniggering and taunting Ronnie, but Charlie soon put an end to that by telling them that he would get a lawyer if they didn't stop. They did. Charlie then told them that he was taking Ronnie to see a doctor and the two of them walked out of the police station; no one tried to stop them.

Reg wasn't a happy young man. He felt that he had let his brother down so he searched all afternoon for PC Baynton. When he found him he punched him in the face, just like his brother Ron. He then casually went home and waited for the law to catch up with him. When they eventually came for him, Charlie told the police not to do what they had done to Ronnie, or the Kray family would sue for damages. So Reg went quietly. That evening he sat in the same cell that Ron had occupied earlier in the day but no one came near him.

The only thing that saved them at the trial was the good Reverend Father Hetherington, who said that it was all out of character for the twins, who had helped him in the past on numerous occasions. Despite the magistrate praising PC Baynton for his courage in such a cowardly attack, he put them on parole and the twins once again walked free. This was to become a bit of a habit throughout their lives, although they didn't beat the courts every time. They did what they wanted to do and in the main they got away with it. The more they got away with it the more they wanted to do and so it escalated until the killings of Cornell and McVitie. The seeds were now sown.

In February of 1952 the postman delivered two important letters to 178 Vallance Road in Bethnal Green. They were addressed to Ron and Reg Kray and the twins looked at them for a while before opening them. When they did open the letters they looked at each other and said nothing – there wasn't really much to say. Violet reached over to see what it was all about and then she gasped. Her little boys had just received their call-up papers; they were wanted in the army.

In the early part of March Ron and Reg Kray put on their best identical suits and took the bus to the Tower of London, where they were to be enlisted into the Royal Fusiliers. They had little difficulty finding the place, since it was the same regiment that their father had deserted from all those years earlier. He had often told them the story of his great escape.

A corporal took control and they were soon outfitted with their uniforms and various bits and pieces. After a light meal they and a bunch of other raw recruits were ready to be shown the ropes. The corporal spelt it all out, by the numbers. The twins weren't used to being told what to do and certainly not how to do it. The barracks were bare and tasteless, typical army grey. They didn't like it.

The twins listened patiently for a while, but the corporal was beginning to get on their nerves. Without saying a word and without motioning to each other in any way, they slowly walked towards the door.

'And where do you think you two are going?' asked the corporal, not used to anyone walking out on him. After all, these men were now in the British Army.

The twins stopped and turned round. They looked at each other, but said nothing.

'Well, where are you off to?' he asked again, not believing his eyes. He looked first at one and then at the other. Was it Ron or Reg, or Reg and Ron? He couldn't tell the difference.

'We don't like it here,' said Ron Kray. He could have said 'fuck the army' but he chose his words carefully. 'We're off home to our mum,' he added as they both turned again to face the door.

At that moment the corporal grabbed at the twins. He obviously didn't like anyone walking out on him, especially two at a time, but he overreacted and the answer from the twins came swiftly.

Suddenly the corporal was on the floor, knocked out cold. Just who had hit him was anyone's guess and there were plenty of witnesses in the barracks. But the twins had won the argument, so they went home to mum for tea, just as they said they would.

Later, the following morning they were picked up by the police at Vallance Road and taken back to the Tower. They caused no bother and went quietly. Once there they were delivered to the Military Police who threw them into the guardroom so they could spend the rest of the day in deep meditation. But the Krays were prepared. They knew what they were doing, all right. They may have been only 18 years old but they were smart and streetwise, not to be messed with.

The following day they were brought before the Commanding Officer, along with the other prisoners. The CO had a real problem to solve that day. His normal reaction would be to sling any man who had committed such an act out of the army, but he didn't know which one had punched the corporal. He couldn't court-martial the wrong man. The other new recruits in the barracks couldn't say which one had knocked the corporal down, they looked identical, so the CO was in a quandary.

'So which one of you attacked the corporal?' asked the CO. 'Was it you?' he asked, looking first at Reg and then at Ron.

'It wasn't me, sir,' said Reg, standing nose to nose with his CO.

'It wasn't me, sir,' said Ron, as the CO moved over to stare him in the eyes. Now staring into Ron Kray's eyes was a big mistake, since Ron could see through 'most any man'.

'It must have been one of you, so who did it?' screamed the CO. He was getting a little fed up with the charade. But he was beginning to feel defeated; the enemy were using tactics beyond his capacity.

'Do what, sir?' said Ron Kray, still keeping his cool. He knew he had gone far enough.

The CO had only one option left open. That choice was to send both men to the guardhouse for seven days, with only a blanket for company and bread and water to survive on.

This incident came to mark a turning point in the career of the twins. They had always been top dogs in Bethnal Green, but this was the British Army; if they could beat them then what couldn't they achieve? After all, they were only 18 years old.

Along with them in the guardroom was another lad from the East End, by the name of Dickie Morgan. Morgan had spent time in borstal and knew the system well; he also knew how to use it. The twins talked with Dickie Morgan about what they would do outside, where they would go, what they would get up to in the way of villainy. The strange and dismal setting of the guardhouse made cell-mates of them all. A bond developed that brought them closer together.

After seven days in the guardhouse Ron and Reg Kray, with Dickie Morgan in tow, were on the run again. They left the barracks and headed towards the docks where Morgan had friends among the petty crooks and villains of the area. They were introduced to booze, cigarettes and wild times and this was a bit of an eye-opener for the twins. They had never experienced anything like this before, but they were learning fast. And Dickie Morgan was a good teacher.

One day they took a trip to Southend in a pal's car, just for the fun of it. While there they found time to send the CO at the Tower barracks a postcard – it simply said: 'Having a great time from your pals Ron and Reg Kray and Dickie Morgan'.

The next months were spent in and out of the guardhouse at the Tower of London. They would be captured, then escape. Then captured, then escape. This routine was the order of the day right up until November, when they decided that it was time for a change.

They were enjoying their time of freedom sure enough, but they were also getting a little bored. They knew that they couldn't exist like this for ever, indeed they didn't want to live like this, so something had to give. One day when the twins were in a café on the Mile End Road, they approached a policeman who had arrested them earlier in the summer, PC Fisher, and gave themselves up. This was indeed a strange thing to do, since they knew what would happen to them. And to turn themselves in to a policeman – it was both the first and the last time.

This resulted in a one-month prison sentence in Wormwood Scrubs, the first time the twins were imprisoned in a real jail. The peculiar thing about their time in the army was that the authorities saw fit to keep the twins together, even sending them to the same prison. It was as though they thought Reg was a calming influence on Ron, but in the end it was Ron who had full control over his twin brother and this meant chaos wherever they went.

After prison there were more escapes and further re-captures, until finally in the spring of 1953, the army gave up on the Kray twins. They were sent down to Canterbury, along with their old pal Dickie Morgan, and summarily court-martialled on 11 June. Their sentence was to be a nine-month stretch at the military prison at Shepton Mallet, Somerset.

Once there, they continued to play their mind games with authority. They were completely uncontrollable and even Charlie was asked to come down to talk to them to see if he could calm them down. But it didn't help. Their mother Violet came to see them too but that didn't help either. They had decided that their rules were more important than any army regulations and they would beat them at all costs.

But the twins learned a lot from the army about the control and the manipulation of people, and they would put all of this to good use later in life. They met all the best (or worst) young offenders in the country, all gathered in one place where they could all learn from each other. The army also taught them about organisation, something that they would put to good use when they established their gang, known as the Firm, and Ron even took on the mantle of the 'Colonel'. This was not because he respected the army or any authority, but because in his mind he had beaten them at their own game. He deserved the title and he would use it.

By the early part of the new year, 1954, the twins were free men, dishonourably discharged from the army. They didn't care about the disgrace, since they were again back in Bethnal Green and in their eyes, kings of their manor. In their own way, the army had made real men of the Kray twins.

The twins now had time on their hands and time to turn those hands to small-time crime. They robbed trucks and delivery vehicles in the East End, even doing a little trading in stolen goods. But the life didn't suit them and they were on the look-out for something special. Of an evening they would hang around street corners with their pals and sometimes they would go and play billiards at The Regal, in Eric Street, just off the Mile End Road. The manager noticed an increase in violence when the twins became regulars there – the fights increased and the police were becoming regular visitors too. The manager bought an Alsatian dog to help guard the premises but someone threw fireworks at the animal and it went mad. By the summer of 1954 the manager had seen and heard enough and he wanted out.

It was no surprise to friends of the Krays when Ron and Reg were pronounced the new managers of the billiard hall. They had made a deal with the retiring manager and paid him off with £5 a week. The owners were satisfied and the twins took the place over. It was probably a wise decision since they would probably have taken it over anyway. The only problem for the twins was lack of ready cash to fund the purchase of new tables, sorely needed at The Regal. Their salvation came in the form of their brother Charlie, who lent them the money for the tables and some paint so they could clean the place up really well. They all worked hard and the place was an instant success. And the trouble stopped as abruptly as it had started.

With the billiard hall a success the twins had no need of getting involved in petty crime. In fact they had all they could handle at The Regal, since they would hide weapons for their pals, trade stolen goods and keep items hidden for customers who did not have a safe hiding place. Business was good and the money came rolling in. And the Colonel was firmly in control.

The police kept away from the hall, letting the Krays take care of business in the normal East End way. There were the normal gang fights, such as with the Maltese gangs, and there was trouble with other gangs trying to hustle in on the Mile End Road, but the twins took care of this and settled down as masters of their own universe. For over two years the Krays continued to run the business and stay out of trouble. The police didn't bother with them and the Krays didn't bother with the police. It was a long time for the twins not to be involved in conflict with the law, but they were running their own business with their own rules and no one said that they couldn't do it. So it worked well and even Charlie enjoyed himself at The Regal, without the fear of violence; well, almost without the fear of violence.

But it had to change and the reason had to be Ron Kray. The twins had already started their protection rackets and they were making more money than ever. But Ron was still building up a personal arsenal at home at Vallance Road, where they still lived with their mum and dad. One day there was some minor trouble at a car dealership that paid protection money to the twins. A dissatisfied buyer wanted his money back and threatened to get some help from south of the river. When Ron heard about it he rushed to the scene and shot the customer, wounding him in the leg. It was silly really, since the customer had returned to the car dealer to apologise. So Ron's shooting fit was a complete waste of time. Reg rushed over to the place, calmed people down and got the man treated. No police were involved, but the rumours began to spread.

But shortly afterwards, on 5 November 1956, Ron Kray was convicted of causing grievous bodily harm and sentenced to three years' imprisonment. He caused the police no bother and went quietly. This gave Reg three years to work on the business and to prepare for his brother's return. He grabbed his chance.

By the spring of 1957 Reg Kray, together with his elder brother Charlie, had opened The Double R Club, just off Bow Road and, typically for the Krays, very near Bow Street Police Station. It was a great success as a club, which was something new to the East End. Reg sorted out the internal arrangements and the boxing ring upstairs, while Charlie took care of drinks and amusement. It was a good mixture and the club was extremely successful. It was one of those times in Charlie Kray's life when he would say, 'It's going so well, something's got to happen.' By the spring of 1959 Ron Kray was back on the scene and everything changed – for the worse. They had two great years, with Reg going frequently to the West End and becoming a bit of a playboy, while Charlie kept the club going with slick panache. Now it all lay in ruins because Ron swept back into their lives.

With Ron back, the police were back too. They had been keeping an eye on the club ever since Ron Kray had made his escape from Long Grove Asylum, near Epsom (this is covered in chapter five). They visited the club on a regular basis, looking for thieves and goods, but Reg protected his twin brother and wouldn't let Charlie have a say in the business any more. While Ron had been in prison it had been okay to share with Charlie, but now with Ron back in his life, he only wanted to share with his twin brother.

But it wasn't to be Ron who caused the downfall of the Double R Club; it was Reg and his moral code, the one that said 'Don't grass.' It wasn't anything really to do with Reg Kray, but the police didn't see it like that. Ronnie Marwood, an acquaintance of Reg Kray's, was wanted by the police for killing a policeman. It was a very serious offence, as it still is, but Reg just couldn't betray his code; he couldn't tell the police what they wanted to know. He knew where he was hiding and everyone knew he knew. But still he couldn't 'grass' on a fellow Eastender. The police couldn't do anything about it, but when the club's licence came up for renewal they opposed and the renewal was refused. Reg Kray couldn't betray a killer by telling the police of his whereabouts, so the club had to close. It was something else that made Reg Kray hate the police and authority in general. His brothers agreed.

It had been great while it lasted – at least for Reg and brother Charlie. Ron spoiled all that with his aggression and his madness. But it was that moral code, held strongly by both twins, that ruined the business and threw their progress into reverse.

Soon Reg would be behind bars, convicted of extortion. He just happened to be there when the incident occurred, but due to his track record he was guilty in the eyes of the police. It was definitely extortion, although Reg has always denied being involved. Others were pulling the strings and he got caught up in the mess. A man by the name of Shay, who ran a car dealership, asked for a discount on a briefcase he had purchased. It wasn't the fact that he asked for a reduction in the price that upset the owner of the shop, it was the use of phrases such as 'or I'll cut you to pieces' that he objected to. The police called on him just in time to arrest Shay together with Reg Kray, who was just along for the ride. It was totally out of character for Shay, so Reg got the blame and an 18-month prison sentence; 1960 was beginning to be another bad year for the Krays.

This scenario was to play itself out on many occasions during the late '50s and throughout the '60s, like a game of chess between the Krays and the Metropolitan Police. The Krays had many reasons for hating the police and the police tried in numerous cases to convict the Krays, but with limited success. It was a cat-and-mouse game, but who was the cat and who were the mice?

With Reg back out and surprisingly enough Ron still at large in the East End, the Krays took over Esmeralda's Barn in Wilton Place in the West End. The Krays had moved up a gear and were entering the big time in a big way. And the police didn't bother them. They were men of property and therefore to be respected, though still to be kept an eye on. As long as the twins didn't overstep the mark and do something really stupid then the police would leave them alone. 'They didn't want the aggro,' Ron told me once in Broadmoor. But he couldn't let things lie, he had to press everything and everyone to the limit.

The skirmishes with the law continued, including being arrested on suspicion of burglary, and even loitering with intent to commit a felony. Ron made the most of these incidents to get much-wanted publicity and to make it look as though he was being persecuted by the police. His newspaper adverts were very convincing and the twins were acquitted of all crimes – they even managed to get costs. It was simply a case of 'us' and 'them' to Ron Kray, although Reg didn't try to take it so personally. He had learned his lesson from the Marwood case and wasn't prepared to go to jail for anyone ever again. But Ron felt that his propaganda had worked, he was invincible. Charlie just looked on in amazement, trying to stay out of the way of Ron and getting on with his own concerns at Esmeralda's Barn, where he had many responsibilities, including the amusement laid on for gamblers and drinkers.

More clubs opened and more interest in their concerns was taken by the police. There were more knifing attacks by Ron Kray on so-called friends, for various long-forgotten reasons. Ron became increasingly unpredictable and depressed and Reg and Charlie could do nothing about it. Ron had taken pills even before he went into Longrove Asylum, but the mixture of booze and tablets didn't always have the desired effect. As the Krays struggled to hold things together, the police looked on, waiting for their chance. It was all just a matter of time.

They were investigating the Krays when the Lord Boothby case arose, spread all across the national newspapers (see chapter three). A denial by Scotland Yard, stating that they had not been keeping tabs on the Krays, meant that the twins were free to continue their business, almost unimpeded by the police. In fact it was a lucky break for the Krays, but not for the police. They had to scrub the slate clean and start all over again. Because of the denial, no evidence gathered in this period could be used in a court of law.

But when the Krays were arrested for asking for protection money from Hew McCowan, at The Hideaway Club in Soho in January of 1965, Nipper Read thought that he had won at last. It was their old pal 'Mad Teddy' Smith who called at the club on their behalf, asking for money. When he didn't get any he started smashing up the place. McCowan, seeing what was going on and fearing the Krays' involvement, immediately phoned Scotland Yard and Nipper Read arrested the twins.

Although they tried very hard, the twins were refused bail. Their next move was to hire a good legal team and Reg, always keen to learn from past mistakes, took on the lawyer who had beaten him in the Shay case. They also hired private detectives to dig up any dirt on the unfortunate McCowan and soon found him to be a homosexual. They used this in court to ridicule McCowan and to make his testimony unreliable in the minds of the jury. That the Firm may already have intimidated and/or bribed the jury has never been proved. In either case, the Krays were found not guilty and walked free. The very same evening they bought the club from a despondent Hew McCowan. The Krays had won again.

Nipper Read's photos the next day in the national press did, however, cause a bit of an uproar. He was invited to the party held at The Hideaway to celebrate the twins' victory, but newspaper photographers were also there. Although this time it ended in an embarrassing police enquiry, Scotland Yard were now sure that the Krays were getting too big for their boots. The police knew that one day soon the twins would put their foot in it.

When the Krays rescued Frank Mitchell, known as 'The Mad Axeman', from Dartmoor in 1966 the police thought once again that they could get a conviction.

They couldn't find the body, but they arrested Ron and Reg Kray, together with their old pal Freddie Foreman. It took some time for the police to get a case strong enough to defend and this involved getting witness statements. However, when Albert Donaghue gave a statement to the police they thought their case was secure. So they went to the Old Bailey with testimonies from both Donaghue and Mitchell's girlfriend, known as Lisa. But the jury didn't accept the testimony of a known villain and found that Lisa's evidence was not reliable, so once again the Krays beat the law of the land and walked free.

Nipper Read was furious and immediately put the Krays at the top of his 'most wanted' list. It wasn't long before his own investigations into the Cornell shooting in 1966 took an unexpected turn when information concerning the killing found its way onto his desk. He couldn't prove it yet, but he was at last beginning to get the big picture, by putting all the pieces of the jigsaw into place. Read was a man who worked by the book and did his homework in a routine and logical way, so when he suddenly arrested the twins on 9 May 1968, it was totally out of character. But Scotland Yard had had enough of the Krays. They had overstepped the mark and they had to take action to secure a decision in their favour. This time the Krays would not be getting away from the Old Bill.

Even when the police were closing in on the Krays, they managed to maintain their activities right to the end. But they knew they were in danger, they had gone too far down that slippery slope to total villainy. This was symbolised by the purchase from Harrods of two pet pythons, which they called appropriately Gerrard and Nipper, after the two most prominent Scotland Yard chiefs after their hides. The twins learned how to control these snakes (unlike their complete lack of control in the case of Nipper Read). But Ron and Reg wanted to feel the power of being in control of the situation, and hence the charade with the pets. I am sure it made them feel better, but it did them no good at all.

One last attempt was made at fooling the Old Bill when they tried to get the Firm to take the rap for the Cornell and McVitie killings. 'We'll look after you,' they were all told. 'We'll even take care of your families and there'll be something for you when you get out.' But the loose assortment of crooks and criminals that made up the Firm were not so easily fooled by the twins any more. They knew that they would only look after number one – the Krays were always more important than anyone else, or at least that was the way the twins saw it. But by denying the murders the twins guaranteed that their own brother Charlie would get a long sentence for his involvement in the killings, even though he was nowhere to be seen on either occasion. So Charlie got a seven- to ten-year stretch because the twins pleaded not guilty. Being a brother he too felt that he couldn't grass to the law. So he had to serve seven years in prison for upholding his moral code.

The statements by the majority of the Firm made sure that Scotland Yard would get victory over the Krays, but even here not everyone joined in. Tony Lambrianou, who was present at the McVitie killing, lived by the same East End code that meant that you did not 'grass' to the police. For being quiet and honouring that code he received 15 years in jail, a harsh sentence for behaving with dignity.

The situation has changed now, even in the East End of London. It is no longer a sign of morality or respect to say nothing in a difficult situation when approached by the police to give evidence. It is now called stupidity. And the current East End gangs are not stupid. They may be nasty, corrupt, deceitful, dishonest and dirty criminals, but stupid they are not. They have the money to buy the brains, just as the Krays had the cash and know-how to lure Leslie Payne and Freddie Gore. It all started to fall apart when the twins decided they didn't need the business acumen of these two men, so the downfall of the Krays was all their own doing. The Old Bill didn't get them, they did it all themselves.

3. ANOTHER ONE BITES THE DUST

The Kray twins will always be remembered as killers, out-and-out villains afraid of no one and quick to exact revenge through that ultimate of acts – murder.

But according to Judge Melford Stevenson, at their trial back in 1968 and 1969, they were only accused and convicted of killing one man each: George Cornell in the case of Ron Kray, and Jack 'The Hat' McVitie in the case of his brother, Reg. So why were both men given sentences of 30 years with no chance for remission?

This has been a contentious issue and it continues to be a source of debate and media attention even now.

The question is really whether or not they killed, or caused to have killed, more than just these two men. Were there other bodies to be found; other Kray victims? Could they be found propping up flyovers, supporting new city skyscrapers, featuring in pigswill, or merely buried in unmarked graves? The stories are numerous.

'I ran the pig farm,' one man told me. 'We got rid of him [Jack 'The Hat' McVitie] at sea,' said another. 'We dumped him [Frank Mitchell, 'The Mad Axeman'] off the Kent coast,' said yet another.

But how much of this is true and how much mere speculation? Were these people telling the truth? Did they actually do these things? Or are they just hangers-on, trying to inflate their own meagre and miserable egos on the strength of the Kray legend?

The Kray twins and their brother Charlie lived longer than many of their contemporaries. Even their Mafia pals were silenced, one by one. So here are a few of the more well-known stories of Kray associates (and others). Some lived to tell the tale, others were never seen again. Is this, then, the real reason for the long life sentences of 30 years?

Make up your own minds.

The Killing of George Cornell

The first, and most important, killing of all was that of George Cornell, shot and killed by Ron Kray at The Blind Beggar public house, in Whitechapel, on 9 March 1966. The importance of this killing is that it had such immense repercussions throughout gangland and broke all the rules previously regarded as standard practice.

George Cornell was the only Richardson gang member to escape from the Mr Smiths fiasco of the previous evening and why he had to go and have a drink on Kray territory is anyone's guess. He was a loner and not an established part of the gang; he was a mean man who had a reputation of being a tough customer to deal with and Charlie Richardson was not one of his favourite people.

The East End grapevine is a mysterious phenomenon and it has ways of reaching those parts previously not reached by other grapevines, so news soon got to Ron Kray that Cornell was alive and well and drinking in The Blind Beggar. This was out-and-out provocation. The fact that Cornell had apparently called Ron 'a big fat poof' at a recent gangland meeting only made matters worse for George Cornell. Maybe he knew his days were numbered?

Whether Cornell actually did utter those fateful words is pure conjecture, but rumours were enough to sour the reputation of Ron Kray. He didn't care if it was true or not – it was time for justice as he saw it.

Ron rushed to Vallance Road to collect his 9mm Mauser handgun. He took his driver John 'Scotch Jack' Dickson and his minder Ian Barrie with him for the ride. He also supplied guns for them.

Soon they were heading in the direction of The Blind Beggar. Ron Kray's moment had come. Dickson was told to remain with the car, while Ron and Ian Barrie loaded themselves with weapons. Slowly but surely Barrie opened the door to the pub and the two men went inside. It was almost deserted, with only a handful of drinkers downing their mid-week pints. Cornell and a man by the name of Albie Woods were standing near a partition at the end of the bar, quietly having a few beers. There was no rush or alarm on the part of George Cornell. Ian Barrie fired a few shots into the air just for the sake of it. It was a warning of what was to come, but Cornell wasn't much bothered by it all.

Ron Kray approached the bar and stood face to face with Cornell. Cornell sneered back at him. 'Well, look who's here,' he said as he raised his glass. It was last thing he ever did. At that moment Ron Kray pulled out his 9mm Mauser and shot Cornell in the head. As he did so, the barmaid was putting on a new record. It was by the Walker Brothers and entitled 'The sun ain't gonna shine any more'. It was rather poignant but the playing of this particular song happened completely by accident. What had happened to poor George Cornell, however, was no accident. It was cool, deliberate murder!

Albie Woods had already slid off his bar stool and was crouching on the floor, trying to bury himself somewhere in the darkness. When the shots rang out the bloody body of George Cornell came gradually down to join him. Once again he came face to face with his old pal. But this time he was almost unrecognisable. Woods tried to help him but it was too late, so he phoned Cornell's wife to tell her what had happened to her husband. He couldn't console her.

John Dickson drove Ian Barrie and Ron Kray back to the Mile End Road and to home territory. He still wasn't aware of any killing.

In fact George Cornell, even with a bullet in his face, wasn't yet dead. It was only later that night in hospital that he actually died. Ron got to hear about it and he laughed out loud. And when the Colonel laughs everybody laughs. Now the whole Firm knew that he had his 'button' (American slang for a killing). There was no turning back.

It was some time later that the news got out, but the few witnesses there that evening were all told to be quiet, so the police couldn't collect even one statement. It was only after

Scotland Yard's Nipper Read took his gamble by imprisoning the Krays that people began to talk. It was a repeat of the Charlie Richardson affair and the police were learning fast.

In 1993 I had a memorable chat with Ron Kray about the Cornell killing. The trip to Broadmoor had been the usual hour's drive and I was looking forward to seeing Ron and to hearing stories about the old days. After locking away my briefcase at one of the reception security boxes, I made my way together with a guard through the maze of locked doors that make up the most secure hospital in the country. Before long I was in the meeting area, where tables and chairs were strewn around the room and smiling staff were sitting in corners, waiting to help any visitor or inmate requiring assistance.

The buildings were grey and uninviting and the meeting-place was in need of a coat of paint. But the atmosphere was congenial enough and I could see Ron seated at his usual table, being waited on by a white-coated figure who brought him his favourite non-alcoholic lager and lit his cigarette for him.

The normal pleasantries over, we immediately got down to business. And business that day was the story of the killing of George Cornell. Ron was very much matter-of-fact in his telling of events. He showed no sign of remorse or regret. In fact it looked like he was enjoying it thoroughly.

'Just how did you feel that day, Ron?' I asked him thoughtfully. He looked right through me as he said with a glint in his eye, 'Bloody marvellous!'

The gun featured in the Cornell killing is now the prized possession of Scotland Yard's Black Museum. Some years ago the police dragged the River Lea in London's East End and found the small 9mm Mauser automatic, rusty and looking its age. Like its victim it can't tell the story of the killing or why it took place. Even John Ross, the curator of the museum, doesn't know the whole truth about the incident. And now, like Ron, it will forever hold its secrets.

The Death of the 'Mad Axeman'
The 'Mad Axeman', Frank Mitchell, escaped from Dartmoor Prison on 12 December 1966. Escape is, however, a far too

dramatic word for what really happened, since he just casually walked out of the gates of one of Her Majesty's top-security prisons and disappeared into the mists of the moor and away to freedom.

It was another madman, 'Mad Teddy' Smith, who had suggested the caper to the twins. Smith was, amongst other things, a playwright, but his imagination often got the better of him. He had a difficult time telling reality from fiction.

The plan was to break Frank Mitchell out of Dartmoor to protest about his treatment – it would be, according to Mad Teddy Smith, a bit of a media event and it would be good public relations for the twins. The Mad Axeman had already phoned the twins for help and Ron in particular was interested in doing something, especially something big like breaking a man out of the 'moor'.

Frank Mitchell was a giant of a man with big hands, big feet, big everything. He was 37 years old and was serving a sentence of 18 years.

Albert Donaghue and Mad Teddy Smith drove down to Dartmoor and found the designated meeting-place. Frank Mitchell had already been informed of the plans by telephone, since he regularly roamed the moor, given complete freedom by the guards. He was a huge man and had once been certified insane, so no one offered him any argument. Frank Mitchell knew exactly where the telephone box was, where the pick-up was to take place.

As Mad Teddy Smith faked making a phone call, the Mad Axeman Frank Mitchell slowly walked over the hill and to freedom.

Quickly the Mad Axeman got changed from his prison gear into something more suitable, since they were afraid of road-blocks once the escape was known. Soon he was in the car and the three men turned their minds towards London. While they drove they listened to the radio, in the hope of hearing news about the escape and of any police roadblocks. But they heard nothing; nothing, that is, until they were already safely in London and on home territory. The escape was a complete success.

But the twins had underestimated the newsworthiness of the story. For once Ron Kray's sense of media manipulation had let him down.

Mitchell wrote a letter to *The Times* protesting his harsh treatment at Dartmoor Prison and suddenly it was all turning into a farce; gradually it became a nightmare.

The problem for the twins was that the whole underworld knew of the escape and of Ron and Reg's predicament. It looked as though they were losing their grip – their reputation was on the line.

To keep Frank Mitchell happy at the Barking flat, the twins brought in a hostess, in the shapely form of Lisa Prestcott. The Mad Axeman fell in love with her, something that no one could have anticipated. And that only complicated an already complicated situation.

Something had to be done and quickly. Frank Mitchell wanted to escape and to take his hostess with him, but what would the twins have to say about that kind of a scenario? Their answer was the gun!

According to Albert Donaghue at the trial in 1968–69, the twins decided to cut their losses by getting rid of the Mad Axeman once and for all. They just didn't know how to handle the situation, so their solution was to kill the problem by killing Frank Mitchell.

Donaghue was told to get the Mad Axeman outside the flat and into a van. Mitchell didn't like the idea of going anywhere without his new love, but he was persuaded that she would follow once he was safe and out of the country.

Unknown to Mitchell there were three other occupants in the rear of the van. The hit-men were already in position and armed. They were Alfie Gerrard, a South London villain by the name of Gerry Callaghan and 'Hard Man' Freddie Foreman. None of the three were members of the Firm since the twins wanted to keep the outcome a secret – at least from their own gang. To be seen actually disposing of a problem in this way would have done nothing to enhance their reputations.

Mitchell got into the van, which was parked on the Barking Road. Inside he was told to sit by himself on one side of the van, opposite the other three men. As the driver, Albert Donaghue, drove off, the first gunshots rang out loud and clear from the back of the van.

Mitchell wasn't dead, so the three unloaded their guns into the huge man. He was still groaning as another bullet entered his brain. The Mad Axeman Frank Mitchell died at the hands of his 'rescuers'. Lisa Prestcott, back inside the flat, heard the shots and was convinced that they would then come after her. But no one paid her much attention. Donaghue stopped the van and got out. He couldn't stand the stench of death. He walked away from the van, half expecting to be killed himself. But it didn't happen.

Later Donaghue reported back to the twins that the job was done. I have heard it said that Reg Kray wept when he heard the news. The date was 24 December 1966 – Christmas Eve.

When Nipper Read pulled Lisa Prestcott in for questioning about the Mad Axeman, after arresting the twins in 1968, the police car drove towards Tintagel House and away from the area of Scotland Yard. Fearing that she was being abducted by Kray henchmen wanting to kill her, she pulled herself free from her captives and almost threw herself off one of the many bridges over the River Thames. Ultimately, though, she was convinced by the policemen that they were genuine and they continued the ride.

Donaghue was later asked by the twins to deliver £1,000 in cash to Freddie Foreman as a payment for the killing. Recently Foreman has openly admitted to killing Frank Mitchell, but since he has already been acquitted of the murder, under UK law he cannot be tried again for the same crime. So a guilty man still walks the streets.

In this way the Krays arranged another killing in 1966, but this time they didn't pull the trigger themselves. They were being openly encouraged by the US Mafia to use hit-men, something that didn't exactly appeal to their sense of honour and respect. To the Krays, men should be men; and they should be seen to be so.

'What actually happened to Frank Mitchell?' I asked Ron Kray recently, on one of my regular visits to Broadmoor.

'I like to think of him peacefully settled in Australia or South Africa,' replied Ron Kray, head downwards and peering into his lager.

I thought at the time that this was a somewhat peculiar way in which to reply to a question. But now that I have learned the facts about the case, I can understand why. Even now Reg Kray will not own up to his part in the killing. And now that Ron Kray is dead, he will have no more questions to answer.

In the eyes of a psychologist Ron Kray's behaviour is called 'splitting'. In his case, being a paranoid schizophrenic, this is understandable – he has replaced the bad thoughts about Frank Mitchell with a vision of what could have happened. This is a typical schizoid defence mechanism – the traumatic event becomes an internal object, thought or phenomenon – it becomes split off from the conscious side of the mind, the ego. Bad thoughts or events or acts are denied or repressed in favour of something that is more acceptable to the ego.

The emotional implications of the killings drive this 'splitting' of the mind for both Krays. Their anxieties are too much for the ego: thus the splitting from reality to unreality. In the world of the Krays there is a fine line between the truth and make-believe; between the image and the fact.

As time went by, Ron Kray antagonised his twin brother so much, by mocking him over his inability to kill, that the inevitable was sure to happen, sooner or later. This was to be the ridiculous stabbing to death of Jack 'The Hat' McVitie later on in the new year.

The Murder of Jack 'The Hat'

The date was 28 October 1967 and for Reg Kray it was time to kill Jack 'The Hat' McVitie, a small-time villain and pill-taker who had borrowed money from the twins. In a way he brought about his own death by agreeing to kill Leslie Payne, their one-time business manager. Payne was no longer with the Firm and the twins thought that he would most likely talk to Nipper Read, who was closing in fast on the Krays. In the end McVitie didn't commit the crime, but he kept the money. And Leslie Payne, on hearing that the Krays were after him and intent on settling the score permanently, squealed all he could to Nipper Read and told him all about the sordid details of Kray 'long firms', Mafia dealings, protection rackets and so on.

Ron had been urging his elder brother to commit the ultimate sin ever since he, Ron, had openly shot and killed George Cornell. They were, after all, twins and Reg had a duty to kill, just like his brother.

Reg had been drinking all day, still in a terrible state since the suicide of his wife Frances, back in the early part of June. He hadn't been able to get over her death and now, once again, no one had any control over Ron, who could easily manipulate his brother's feelings.

Previously during the summer Reg had had fits of drinking which ultimately led to trouble in the form of a shooting or two. The first was a friend called Frederick. Now if he does that to his friends, then his enemies had better watch out. Poor Frederick had some time back said something not too nice about Frances. This, after a bottle or two of gin, made Reg crazy with a capital 'K'.

Unable to drive, he got one of the Firm to drive him to Frederick's house and a woman with a cluster of children opened the door. First there was the compulsory shouting and calling of names, then there was the scuffle, and finally the shooting. But poor drunken Reg Kray could only wound his friend in the leg.

He was quickly bundled into a car and off they drove, back to a safe house where Reg could sleep off the effects of the booze.

Charlie Kray, on hearing the news, drove over to Frederick's house and took care of the unfortunate man. A friendly doctor was called in and the patient was put to rest, in his own bed, alive and relatively well.

Shortly after this incident, Reg was involved in another shooting, where he again wounded a man.

'You can't kill anyone,' was the scornful remark made by his brother Ron, who already had his button. Ron was relentless; he kept up the pressure day and night. Soon Reg had to give in.

Tony Lambrianou and his brother, Chris, were sent out to find Jack 'The Hat'. The twins had set up a story about a party at a friend's house in Hackney and the Lambrianous were told to find their target and drive him over to the flat. On arriving at the flat, Tony Lambrianou parked his Ford Zodiac nearby and together with his brother led their intended victim down the stairs and inside the basement flat. Ron Kray was there waiting for them as Jack 'The Hat' McVitie pushed past him, asking for wine, women and song. Ron Kray was not in a good mood. 'Fuck off, Jack,' he told him; not exactly the words of a man intending to kill someone. Jack McVitie didn't get the drink, he never saw a woman, but he did end up acting out his own swansong.

To everyone's surprise Reg Kray took out a gun and fired at Jack from point blank range. No one could miss from that distance, but the gun failed. Reg even tried pulling the trigger again. It was really making a farce of his openly attempted murder. Just why Reg deemed it necessary to kill McVitie is difficult, if not impossible, to say. It may have been due to his brother's constant nagging or it could have had something to do with his psychological imbalance after the death of his wife, Frances. Or possibly it was all about reputation. And then maybe it was the booze doing the killing.

Members of the Firm were there that night, but the vision of seeing Reg Kray in that kind of belligerent mood was not normal. It was, on the other hand, expected of Ron. They could only stare in disbelief.

When the gun failed Jack 'The Hat' McVitie began ranting and raving; quite natural under the circumstances. He even thrust his hand through a window, trying to escape.

'Be a man, Jack,' said Reg Kray.

'I'm a man, but I don't want to fucking die like one,' was the reply from a now terrified small-time crook.

The Lambrianou brothers, Ronnie Hart, Ronnie Bender and some young boys who had come along for the party, could only look on as Ron urged his brother to finish the job. He kept taunting Reg, winding him up, trying to pull all the strings. The pressure on Reg Kray must have been intense.

Eventually Reg snapped. He grabbed a kitchen knife and stabbed McVitie in the face. He stabbed him again and again. Soon there was blood all over the carpet, blood flowing everywhere.

Still the gang members stared in horror, not believing or understanding what they had witnessed. No one had expected a killing. No one thought Jack was worth it. But no one prevented it.

Tony Lambrianou was told to get rid of the body and Albert Donaghue was asked to redecorate the flat. Even after a thorough job, the police managed to find blood six months later when they found out about the killing. Again, when Nipper Read took the twins and their brother Charlie into custody, people began to talk. It was only then that the real details of the murder came out into the open.

At the time of the killing of Jack 'The Hat' McVitie, Charlie Kray was safely home in bed. It was a rude awakening when he too was charged with getting rid of the body. It was ruder still when he was convicted and sent to prison for ten years.

The killing of Jack 'The Hat' McVitie, more a ladies' man than a thug, was meaningless and stupid. Reg Kray had nothing to gain from such an action and everything to lose. In the end it brought him 30 long and miserable years in jail.

'They were arrogant, brazen killers,' said Nipper Read after the trial. Indeed they were found guilty of terrorising the whole of the East End of London.

As a paranoid schizophrenic Ron Kray must take much of the blame, but the nature of twins must also have something to do with the equation. This topic is explored in chapter six and even after all these years it appears that we all still have much to learn about the Krays.

Mob Deaths
It wasn't only the Krays who were good at killing. The US Mafia also showed a flair for the dramatic murder or two.

The top Mafia bosses who did business with the Krays

mostly met with untimely deaths, generally with a bullet in the head. It was commonplace then, as it is now. You don't retire, you get retired!

One of the best Mafia friends that the Krays had was Angelo Bruno. Being a member of the US Mafia's *commissione* he was a man of power, like the other bosses Sam Giancana and Vito Genovese. It was Bruno who first used the Krays in London to act as minders for his casinos and clubs. It was Bruno, too, who was incidental in getting the Krays hired for protecting US singers and performers when they toured the UK. It was no coincidence that he shared bodyguards with Frank Sinatra. And it was probably Bruno who suggested the Krays when the Mob in New York needed to get rid of stolen US bearer-bonds.

Angelo Bruno was to end his days with a bullet in his head, while sitting in his car in a Philadelphia suburb. The boss of Atlantic City and Philadelphia was a powerful man. I believe he still is.

Recently, on 6 November 1997, three men were arrested outside a city bank. They had been in talks with the bank regarding a loan that they wanted, to be guaranteed by $800 million of US treasury bonds, which they had in their possession. One of the men was from Taiwan, one was from the USA and one was English.

They were caught by a team from Scotland Yard who were working closely with a US secret-service agent, here in London. The bonds were believed to be forgeries. Money fraud where borrowing is used to fund drugs and other laundering businesses is high priority within all major police forces around the world. These loans provide a much-wanted supply source of cash. It would appear that money laundering, as practised by the Krays, has not stopped. It flourishes here, today, in the City of London.

Another Kray pal was the Canadian Mafia boss, Don Ceville. He was the first one that Leslie Payne went to see in Canada regarding the importation and negotiation of stolen US bearer-bonds. Like his friend Angelo Bruno, he ended his days with a bullet in the head. He was finally found some years ago buried in a peat bog, just a little way outside his beloved Montreal.

Even 'Crazy Joe' Gallo and his boss Joseph Colombo ended up with holes in their heads in the early '70s, while Tony 'Ducks' Corallo got away with 99 years in Leavenworth.

And Eddie Pucci, Bruno's right-hand man and bodyguard to Frank Sinatra himself, was shot and killed on a golf course in Chicago shortly after the Krays were arrested by Nipper Read. The killings continue to this day as one by one the old guard are replaced by the young pretenders. The fact is, though, that they don't pretend any more.

Even Sam Giancana was shot and killed by a pal while cooking his favourite meal. Nothing is sacred to the Mafia!

The Case of the Brighton Peer and the Death of Leslie Holt

In May of 1964, Leslie Holt set up a meeting between Lord Robert Boothby and Ron Kray – the topic of conversation was a project in Nigeria that the Krays were interested in getting Boothby involved in, on a charitable basis.

Leslie Holt was a well-known cat burglar and former boy boxer. It was in his boxing days that he had met Lord Boothby and they became 'good friends'. This homosexual relationship was kept secret from most people, because of the law of the time. But Ron Kray, himself a homosexual, knew of the relationship and wanted to exploit it to the full.

When the project in Enugu, Nigeria, came up in the spring of 1964, Ron Kray met Ernest Shinwell, the son of Lord Shinwell, whose dream child it was. Lord Shinwell and Ron Kray had dined at the House of Lords – Lord Boothby was to be another feather in Ron's cap and, potentially, a good image builder in the eyes of the media.

Holt was one of nine children from an East End family. As a young boy he was sent to reform school and here he developed an interest in animals and boxing. He was dashing, popular and to many, glamorous. It was at a boxing match that he had met Boothby and a relationship developed immediately.

Holt introduced Lord Boothby to crime, prostitution and

gay clubs. Holt was bisexual and had an affair with Boothby; one that was to last for many years. Meetings took place at Boothby's flat in Eaton Square – they tried to keep their meetings secret, but Ron Kray knew . . . exactly what was going on.

Ron needed a figurehead for the African scheme and he had decided that Boothby was the right man for the job. Through Leslie Holt he set up a meeting with Lord Boothby at his London flat. Together with him on this day were Boothby's lover Leslie Holt, photographer Bernard Black, who was there to record the event for posterity and Mad Teddy Smith, another homosexual gangster and a friend of Labour MP Tom Driberg.

They discussed the Nigerian project and Boothby told Ron Kray that he would think about the plan. A few days later, however, Boothby telephoned Ron to tell him that he didn't have time for the project in his busy workload.

Black took many photographs that day in 1964 and on 12 July of the same year, he handed a complete roll of photographs to the *Sunday Mirror*. Previously in the day the newspaper had run an article headed 'Peer and Gangster', where they didn't name names but hinted at a homosexual relationship between a well-known peer and a top gangster from London's underworld. Black was after some easy money.

However, later on that same day he had a change of mind and asked for the photographs back. He pleaded that they were not his to sell, but it did no good. The *Sunday Mirror* refused to hand them back.

On the following Tuesday, 14 July 1964, Sir Joseph Simpson of Scotland Yard issued a statement in *The Times* saying that he had asked the Yard to look into allegations recently made in the *Sunday Mirror*, allegations regarding orgies and homosexual conduct between a peer and a man with a criminal record. There was also talk of clergymen being involved.

The *Mirror* followed up the story on Thursday 16 July, with the heading 'The picture we dare not print', where they added lots of detail to the bones of the story, but again without divulging the names of those involved.

However, on 22 July 1966, the German magazine *Stern* came right out and named Lord Boothby as the peer in the story and Ron Kray as the gangster.

Lord Boothby, who was on holiday in France at the time, telephoned his friend in London, Tom Driberg MP. They were in a mess and needed help quickly. The help was to come from none other than Prime Minister Harold Wilson.

Boothby had always been fond of boys. He had once said: 'I'm not sure if I like the boys better than the girls, or the girls better than the boys.' He was a well-known bisexual even at university, but his charm normally kept him from trouble. Apart from boys, his favourite hobby was gambling, bringing us once again back to Ron Kray.

Ron wined him and dined him in the West End of London, introducing him to many young boys who caught the eye of the peer. Ron once told a poor young man: 'You will go home with Mr Boothby. You will do anything Mr Boothby wants. Or I will hurt you badly.' There are no prizes for guessing the result.

Boothby frequented the casinos owned by the Krays and still carried on his relationship with Leslie Holt, who was always at his side. That is, whenever he was not out carrying on his trade as a cat burglar. Boothby couldn't understand why he couldn't stop, but Holt did it for the fun of it and just wouldn't stop.

The relationship between Boothby and Ron Kray isn't difficult to understand. Boothby always lived on the edge, he loved excitement. And Ron Kray gave him plenty of that. He also gave him gifts, apart from boys.

Harold Wilson was a worried man, since he knew all about the stories involving Tom Driberg MP, one of the elder statesmen of the Labour Party. Driberg was a homosexual who had a peculiar side-line in setting up people for robberies. And he got a cut of the takings for all his hard work. Driberg was also involved in the African business.

Harold Wilson assigned Gerald Gardiner QC and Arnold Goodman to the task of getting both Driberg and Boothby off the hook. Their solution was for Lord Boothby to write a letter to *The Times* denying all the allegations. This was published on 1 August 1964.

It worked and Boothby even got £40,000 from the *Mirror* in compensation. The case was over and both men could sleep easy at nights, together with their 'boyfriends'.

Leslie Holt continued to visit at Eaton Square and Mad Teddy Smith continued his relationship with Tom Driberg. Nothing had changed, other than the *Mirror* losing a lot of money. If they had continued the fight, they would surely have won. But then this was a political game.

Lord Boothby was, however, having second thoughts. The visits to Ron Kray's pad at Cedra Court continued and he still enjoyed the orgies, but he gradually became aware of the media and was convinced that a complete change was required.

Although he had been married, Lord Robert Boothby was not very keen on women. The only one who had taken his fancy was Dorothy Macmillan and she just happened to be the wife of the Tory Leader, Harold Macmillan. But even this didn't stop her having his child. So with one miserable marriage behind him, and one impossible relationship with Dorothy and the child to conceal, he decided to get married again.

The wedding was the media highlight of the year and Leslie Holt became the first victim of the marriage – he was barred from Eaton Square. And so the story ended – well almost.

'It was all down to Wilson,' Boothby told friends later. 'He got me out of it.' But he still managed to meet Ron Kray secretly and carry on their mischievous games of 'pass the boy'.

So Boothby ended up with the compensation money from the *Mirror* and Ron Kray ended up with the notoriety that the media had so gratefully handed him on a platter. He was now a household name, just like Lord Boothby.

Some time later Charlie Kray was looking around for some ready cash when the twins were once again in trouble with the law, this time over extortion. He paid a visit to Lord Boothby at his Eaton Square flat and asked him for a loan of £40,000, just the amount that the peer had recently been handed by the *Mirror*. 'Sorry, dear boy,' said Lord Robert Boothby, 'it's all gone.' Boothby had gambled it all away in a matter of months.

Mad Teddy Smith was also getting himself into trouble, by being involved in an extortion case with Ron and Reg Kray. Leslie Holt, who was also implicated, got away in time. This dangerous liaison between high life and low life carried on for some time, but gradually it faded; in the end it died a miserable death.

Holt then teamed up with a Dr Kells, who found clients for his cat-burgling skills. These robberies continued for a number of years, until Scotland Yard caught on to the two men. The doctor knew that the police were on to him and hadn't decided what to do when Holt inadvertently gave him the solution. Holt had some trouble with one of his feet and Dr Kells offered to operate on it for him. It would be no trouble and wouldn't take long.

Holt died on the operating table in 1979. The doctor was tried for murder, but acquitted. The man who had introduced Ron Kray to Lord Robert Boothby, the man who is pictured in all the photographs taken at Eaton Square, was dead – another victim of injustice.

No one knows what happened to Mad Teddy Smith; he disappeared in 1968, shortly before the arrest of the Krays. There were rumours at the time that Ron had killed him. Perhaps we will never know for sure.

Lord Boothby died with his reputation almost intact. It is only now, after his death, that the whole truth is being heard for the first time and his true relationship with Dorothy Macmillan and Ron Kray is being documented. Dr Kells died of a heart attack only a few years ago. So justice was finally served after all. Ron Kray died in Broadmoor in 1995, although his legend still lives on in the East End of London. And Reg and Charlie Kray are still alive but in prison.

The case of the Brighton Peer is a web of intrigue and deceit. It was covered up by the Prime Minister of the time and led to the abandoning of the case against the Krays. Because of certain statements made by Scotland Yard, the case against the twins was put back more than two years. The police had issued statements denying investigations into the

Krays and their underworld activities. The Krays were free of the press too: no one would touch them – the media were scared of more court cases like the *Mirror*. The Krays were free to do as they bloody well liked. And they did just that.

Lord Robert Boothby must be laughing in his grave at all the fuss he has caused in his lifetime. He lied about the whole thing and got away with it. He danced with the devil, cheated him and succeeded. He dared to live out his devious life in the full glare of the media and was never caught live on camera again.

In 1964 he was featured on *This is Your Life*. There was no Dorothy Macmillan, no Mad Teddy Smith, no Leslie Holt, no Ron Kray or Bernard Black, the photographer who took those amazing black-and-white photographs. Boothby had a black-and-white existence – partly open to public scrutiny, partly hidden from prying eyes. But he, like Ron Kray, had learned to manipulate the media and he did it to great effect. It was a sad day for journalism when he died.

The Case of the Magic Bullet

When it comes down to sheer luck and being able to escape the malevolence of Ron Kray, then we have to mention George Dixon. Dixon was a small-time criminal, more a hanger-on than a true member of the Firm, although he had been involved with the Krays for a time and was usually welcomed by the twins. However, he had made a few inopportune remarks about Ron and homosexuality; not something that everyone was talking about. Not, that is, in front of the man himself. Ron had therefore barred him from all Kray establishments.

Now most men would have thought themselves lucky, not being cut up at the pig farm or thrown into the sea or into an open grave. But George Dixon just couldn't take a hint. He heard that Ron Kray was at The Regency Club in Stoke Newington and decided to have it out with him once and for all. It was almost the last thing he ever did. On charging into the club he made directly for Ron Kray, who was sitting with some friends at a table in a corner. He then insisted that Ron tell him why he had been banned from the clubs. Now seeing that this was only a short time after the Cornell killing, when Ron had shot dead the Richardson henchman in cold blood at The Blind Beggar, this was not a good idea.

Ron, however, was in a good mood and not in any shape for a battle of words. He therefore slowly pulled out a gun, aimed it at Dixon's head and fired at point blank (here we go again) range.

Dixon stood there motionless. So did everyone else in the club.

Nothing happened, apart from a slight 'click'. The gun failed to fire. It was George Dixon's lucky night after all. Instead of firing again, to the relief of the customers in The Regency Club, Ron Kray simply pulled out the dud bullet and gave it to Dixon as a souvenir.

The story isn't clear as to whether or not George Dixon was ever allowed back into a Kray establishment, but after treatment like that would anyone risk an unlucky bullet? Whatever Ron Kray had ever done before in his criminal career, that evening he made George Dixon's day!

Murder Incorporated

When the banker A.B. Cooper took Ron Kray on a guided tour of New York in April of 1968, one of the hottest topics of conversation and discussion between the top Mob bosses and Ron Kray was the idea of setting up Murder Inc. in the UK. All the Mafia families were involved, throughout the USA, and Frank Ileano of the New York Colombo family outlined the whole set-up to Ron. It would be a simple matter to organise Murder Inc. in England and Ron and Reg Kray would get all the contracts and therefore all the money. The key was to get outsiders in to do the killings. The Krays would become even more powerful with the backing of the Mafia. They would be true allies.

Ron thought much about this idea and presented it to his brother Reg when he returned to the UK. There was also the promise of more bearer-bonds and that too represented substantial earnings for the twins.

Ron had already, during the summer of 1967, tried various

ways of killing people. The idea of Murder Inc. was nothing new to him, but somehow he just couldn't pull it off. There was always a problem. Perhaps that problem was A.B. Cooper.

It was Cooper who had supplied the machine guns and hand-guns – even the crossbow that is now housed in Scotland Yard's Black Museum. He even provided the syringe hidden in a briefcase. But none of them worked – or none of the killers did their job correctly. It was Cooper's idea to kill President Kaunda and other political leaders for money, naturally. Ron made his own hit lists but we cannot be sure how many he actually killed. Needless to say that many of the old Firm disappeared at that time, including Mad Teddy Smith (many were convinced he had been killed by Ron).

Cooper was also behind the diamond mine in South Africa that never materialised.

A.B. Cooper was the common denominator but Ron never wised up. Reg was never keen on the stuttering American; neither was Charlie. 'Who could trust a guy with the initials ABC?' Charlie once told me. How true.

But the strangest attempted killing was yet to come. After the trip to New York A.B. Cooper was once again flavour of the month; he could do no wrong. So when Cooper suggested to Ron Kray that they should kill a Maltese nightclub owner by the name of George Caruana as a favour to the US Mob, Ron naturally said yes. It was his way of thanking his American cousins for their hospitality.

Cooper brought in a man from Scotland to do the killing, but yet again it all went wrong. There was either a hex on Cooper or there was some other explanation. Cooper never told Ron and Reg Kray that he was working for the American FBI as an *agent provocateur*. He never told them that he dealt directly with Nipper Read's boss, Du Rose, at Scotland Yard, and that he was actively trying to get proof for a murder conviction that the Yard were trying to hang around the necks of the twins. And he never told them the real reason for killing Caruana.

When the Krays were sentenced in 1969, it didn't take long for the Sicilian Mafia to arrive in the UK to take over the drugs trade. The Mafia family that came here were called Caruana, part of the Caruana-Cuntreras Syndicate. Now it would really have been a coup for Cooper to kill off a Caruana Mafia boss for the FBI and simultaneously also to get enough information on the Krays for Scotland Yard to put them away for ever. This would leave the double-dealer Cooper in the clear and he could take over the bearer-bond deal himself since it was lucrative indeed. Remember, Sicilian Mafia often used Maltese passports to enter the UK. It is not surprising that they still do.

So was this the real reason for the intrigue surrounding the attempted Caruana killing? Perhaps we will never know. But the arrest of the Krays in May of 1968 put an end to any thoughts of establishing a Murder Inc. From then on the Mob handled things themselves.

The Krays were a machine; a 'firm' of loosely connected individuals who all worked for a common cause. This cause was the advancement of Ron and Reg Kray, in any way possible. Killing was just one way of keeping discipline in the ranks and of maintaining fear in the minds of their customers and associates alike. This feeling that the Krays were always there and able to pounce at any time, day or night, kept everyone in check.

It was only after the shooting and killing of George Cornell that the twins decided to have a break together. This was indeed a rarity; even when they visited Enugu in Nigeria they never went there together as the terrible twins. But they were enjoying a honeymoon period, due to the killing, so they took a trip down to Spain's Costa del Sol and across to Tangiers to spend a week with that old gangland boss Billy Hill. They were entertained day and night and thoroughly enjoyed themselves. For a short while they weren't worried about business back home in the UK. And socialising with a respected villain such as Billy Hill was a prestigious happening for the Krays.

The reaction to the Cornell killing by the entire East End community was to confirm their status as gangland leaders; men who did their own dirty deeds and got away with it. They felt comfortable and safe. They were top dogs – the 'Kray Twins'.

4. STARS IN THEIR EYES

'Judy Garland made us welcome at her party,' said Reg Kray, reminiscing about the old days at the height of the Kray empire. 'In the early hours of the morning she sat there on the floor and broke out into song – all her old songs.'

He had been used to mixing with the great and famous US showbiz personalities, sent over to the UK with just a little help from their friends, the Mob. When the Mafia in the USA wanted their pals to get the best protection and assistance that money could buy, they always turned to the Krays. But Judy Garland was different to the rest.

'I took her to parties in the East End,' he told me. 'I liked her.' When Frances died, it was Judy Garland who came to the rescue by offering to let Reg stay at her home in Hawaii. Reg was shattered that his wife had taken her own life and he was almost prepared to give up a life of crime for Judy. Reg Kray still had pleasant thoughts about these times, long ago. He had stars in his eyes.

The Krays had always made a habit of meeting the rich, the famous, the notorious. From boxers to film stars, from athletes to politicians, from singers to songwriters. They had mixed with them all, or almost. To hear Reg Kray talk of the stars they met was like listening to *Who's Who* on cassette. Boxers such as Rocky Marciano, Joe Louis, Sonny Liston and Muhammed Ali; singers and entertainers such as Sophie Tucker, Joan Sutherland, David Essex, Frank Sinatra, Nat King Cole, Billy Daniels and Johnny Ray; politicians such as Tom Driberg, Manny (Lord) Shinwell and Lord Boothby; actresses such as Joan Collins and Barbara Windsor; actors such as George Raft, Robert Ryan, Richard Harris and Lee Marvin. The list is endless.

But was this all planned as in some kind of grand scheme? Or did it just happen?

Ron Kray, affectionately known as the Colonel, had always imagined himself as the Al Capone of English crime. He even dressed like him. To reinforce this image he had photographs taken of himself, suitably dressed, with celebrities of the time. This was an out-and-out effort to make himself a celebrity by association.

No one was spared the camera trick. Lord Boothby said yes, to his regret; this was the start of 'The Case of the Brighton Peer'. Christine Keeler said yes, and in doing so created inadvertently a connection between John Profumo and Ron Kray. Henry Cooper said yes, although he has always denied meeting the Krays. George Raft said yes, many times, but then he was getting paid for it by the Mob.

The Krays, and in particular Ron, made a serious attempt at creating larger-than-life images of themselves by being photographed and being seen out and about in the company of 'stars'. He was into image-building even before the marketing and PR companies in the City even knew it existed. No other criminals have been able to emulate this extraordinary feat.

The Krays were the first gangsters in the UK genuinely to seek media attention. They were mesmerised by fame – it was to Ron in particular a reason for being alive. Ron Kray considered himself the best at what he did. Whether it was slicing someone up with a cutlass or a sword, or charming celebrities at his clubs, he thought big and aimed high. To Ron, mixing with stars was the norm; no low-life mediocrity for him.

Although they met showbiz folk of all kinds and sizes, there were not many who made a lasting impression on the Krays. One man who broke all the rules was George Raft.

'Where is he?' asked Ron Kray as he descended the stairs leading down to the Colony Club. Reg and Charlie followed after. The Colonel always led the way.

'He's here,' said Big Eddie Pucci, one of the Mafia's best

bodyguards and the man who handled Mob business in London. 'You'll be meeting him soon.' Eddie chased after the Krays into the plush surroundings of the club.

The George Raft's Colony and Sporting Club, to give it its full title, was the latest invention of Meyer Lansky, who had assembled a syndicate of fellow well-connected mobsters to establish casinos in the USA and overseas. The man who oversaw the gambling was the best man in the business, Dino Cellini, and the manager was to be Alfred Salkin.

Since the Colony Club was not yet open for business, there were all kinds of workmen and delivery people at the club trying to get it organised for its grand opening night. And that was the reason for inviting the Krays.

The Mafia knew well that the Krays were the people to talk to in London if they wanted the right kind of protection for their establishments; this was bread-and-butter work for Ron and Reg Kray – even Charlie sometimes got in on the act.

The month was March and the year was 1966, and George Raft had just been given a 12-month visa for entering and working in the UK. Initially he did some boxing commentary for US television, but the serious business was with the Mob. He was chairman of the club, with a flat in Mayfair, a Rolls-Royce, a chauffeur and even a dog. His job was to see that the punters had a good time. He was good at it.

His movie career had long been over and at 70 he was no spring chicken, but he was a tremendously fit person who enjoyed people's company and was well suited to the job. He had previously worked at clubs in Cuba, but this was his first posting to London. He too wanted to make a good impression.

The four men walked across the red carpeted floor, past all the paint pots and boxes and into the bar. There, at a huge oval table, sat the star. Amidst all the confusion he was immaculate and just like his movie image. As the Krays and their American friend approached, George Raft rose to greet them.

'I hear that you will be working with us,' said George Raft as he shook hands with Ron Kray, who was first with an outstretched hand. They greeted each other warmly like old friends and soon that is exactly what they were. Ron and Reg

Kray had just found a new subject for their incessant photo-shoots, and they had also found a new friend.

Eddie Pucci had already explained the deal to the Krays, that they would be receiving a share of the profits for their involvement. That suited them nicely. It was a great new club in Berkeley Square; plush, posh and sweet poetry to the Krays. This was just the kind of image that they were looking for and it was handed to them on a platter by the US Mafia. All three Kray brothers enjoyed their time at the Colony Club. They were introduced to all the high-flyers of the day, both home grown and imported. And all the stars came out to meet George Raft. Joan Collins was a frequent visitor, so too was Sylvie Burton. They came in their droves to meet the ageing idol.

On one particular evening Charlie Kray was having a quiet drink with George Raft, over by the bar. Charlie had just arrived and needed to whet his whistle while he settled into his normal routine. This was mixing – with drinks or with people, it made no difference to Charlie. He wanted a good time and he knew that George Raft could give it to him with ease.

'Come and meet a few of my US pals,' he said casually to Charlie Kray. 'They are over at the tables.' The two men made their way into the gaming room, fully fitted with plush carpets, velvet wallpaper and golden chandeliers. Soon George Raft spotted an old friend.

'Charlie,' said the actor, 'let me introduce you to Charles Bronson.'

Charlie Kray welcomed the American to the UK and to London. But before he could engage him in further conversation George Raft had seen another friend from across the pond.

'And this is Richard Jaekel,' he said. Charlie once again put on the style; instantly he felt taller than his normal six feet. But again he was dragged away by his host to yet another table where some guests were hard at work playing roulette.

'Another couple of pals for you to meet,' said George Raft. 'This is Telly Savalas and Donald Sutherland.' Charlie's hands were beginning to wear a bit thin but he played his part well, as usual, and drinks were ordered all round.

'There are plenty of you here tonight,' said Charlie. 'It's like an invasion, what's going on?' He looked at the two actors in eager anticipation.

'We're makin' a movie,' said Telly Savalas. 'I believe they're gonna call it *The Dirty Dozen.*'

Later in the evening actors Lee Marvin and Robert Ryan came to the club to play at the tables and to socialise, that great game enjoyed so much by George Raft himself. That, he often told people, was his purpose in life. No television for him. But then that was his job and the US Mafia expects every ex-film star to do his duty.

And this he did, right up to the time he was refused entry into the UK by the Home Office. They said he was undesirable, but the 'powers that be' let all Raft's old Mob pals into the country, just the same. It was only the amiable actor who was refused admission to the UK. Why this happened is still a mystery, but when it happened the Mob just carried on its business as usual. George Raft died in Los Angeles and never again visited our shores. Ron and Reg Kray were denied meeting their good friend ever again, something that also confirmed their hatred of authority in this country. They couldn't understand it, so this reinforced their hatred of the Old Bill.

George Raft had toured all over London with the Krays, visiting boys' clubs and boxing tournaments, even inviting ex-world heavyweight champion Rocky Marciano along with him to see the youngsters at work in gymnasiums and sporting clubs. He was always a great hit, with his Rolls-Royce parked outside and with his uniformed chauffeur; and he never caused anyone any harm. He may have been employed by the Mob but he was pure Hollywood.

It was through the clubs and the Mob business that the Krays met all the stars of show business. Artists such as Lucian Freud, brother of Clement Freud, who frequented Esmeralda's Barn along with actress Honor Blackman and magician David Burglas. I remember at this time, back in the '60s, being asked by David Burglas if my twin brother and I were available for shows in London. The idea was to put one of us in a box, all tied up, only to produce the other one from behind a screen and call it all magic. Naturally, the twin would be released from the box to show that it was just a trick, but I often wondered if he had ever asked the Kray twins to do the box trick with him, especially after I found out many years later that he was performing at Esmeralda's Barn when he invited us to join his show. It is still an intriguing thought.

Also at the 'Barn' were Phil Everly of the Everly Brothers, Eric Clapton and the Walker Brothers. Diana Dors was also a good friend of Charlie's and he even took her along to visit Ron when he was in Broadmoor. The talent was everywhere, even at the Wellington and the Cambridge Rooms, just off of the Kingston Bypass. Ronald Fraser was a regular; so too was Richard Harris. The celebrities of the day liked to rub shoulders with the Krays – it added some spice to their lives. After all, they played villains on the screen and here they were with the real thing. It may have been good for character study, but the image presented to the public and the police caused some sleepless nights in high places.

When Barbara Windsor had trouble on the set of *Sparrows Can't Sing*, she turned to Charlie Kray for help. Joan Littlewood was worried about a gang of dockers who were asking for protection money from the film company, but Barbara phoned her boyfriend Charlie Kray at The Kentucky Club, on the Mile End Road, and he soon put an end to their threats.

Joan Littlewood accompanied Barbara Windsor to the club one night to thank Charlie and the twins for getting her out of trouble. Meeting the famous lady was thanks enough for Ron Kray, who never let such a moment go by unnoticed. They all enjoyed the evening so much that Joan Littlewood asked Ron and Reg if she could use the club as a set for the film. She needed a club for the final scene, a celebration in a nightclub, and The Kentucky fitted the bill admirably. Ron made a joke about shooting in the club and it was all agreed. And then she told the twins that the première of the film was to be in the East End of London at the cinema just across the road, and that Lord Snowdon and Princess Margaret were to be the top guests. On hearing that Ron had a cunning plan. 'We'll throw a party afterwards,' he told them. 'We'll have a great time.'

Ron's plan was to get all the guests to the club after the première, including the Snowdons, but in the event they couldn't stay on for the party. But all the other stars crossed the road to the club and even Roger Moore came along for the fun of it. George Sewell, an old friend of Charlie's, was there; so too were James Booth, Joan Littlewood and Barbara Windsor herself. All their old friends came as well to meet all the celebrities of stage and screen. Lord Effingham met Roy Kinnear, Ronnie Knight was introduced to Hard Man Freddie Foreman (who was later tried for the murder of the Mad Axeman Frank Mitchell) and the twins had a ball.

It was fast becoming second nature for the twins to hob-nob with the jet set of the time and they took to it like a duck to water, especially Ron who enjoyed the extravagance and outrageousness of everything theatrical. It was all a show to him and he excelled at it. Even his orgies at Cedra Court, his home in the mid-'60s, were filled with famous names. Tom Driberg MP was often there with his good friend Lord Boothby and a bunch of boys. So too were pals Mad Teddy Smith and Leslie Holt, both of whom were involved in 'The Case of the Brighton Peer' (see chapter three). It was a clandestine meeting place for many up-and-coming homosexuals, and others, who partied the nights away to the amusement of one and all. Ron Kray had at last found a set that he could feel comfortable with.

The image presented by Ron and Reg Kray was of businessmen in complete control and they played that role well, when it suited them. At other times, however, they were still the vicious thugs that had risen from the ashes of the war, dirty and evil, with financial gain on their meagre minds. They could change in an instant, most unpredictably, especially Ron with his twisted paranoia. When they fought together they were invincible, they were their mother's favourite children, they were 'special'.

All of the Kray brothers were accomplished boxers, with Charlie Kray even fighting for the Royal Navy. Both Ron and

Reg were schoolboy champions and later they all boxed as professionals, even appearing at the Royal Albert Hall together on the same bill. Only one brother, Reg, won his fight that evening, with Charlie losing on a knock-out and Ron being somewhat typically disqualified for unsportsmanlike conduct in the ring. Reg Kray in particular was an extremely good prospect and many in the boxing business had high hopes of seeing him as a major contender one day. And remember they were still only 16 at the time. But it was not to be and the boxing world's loss was the criminal world's gain.

Through their boxing they met many celebrities of the day and apart from Rocky Marciano, who was a very close friend of George Raft's, they met many other Mob-connected ex-champion boxers. One such man was Joe Louis, one of the greatest heavyweight boxers of all time. Through their pals across the pond they got to hear that the champ was having a hard time financially, so they told the Mob to send him over to London and they would see that Joe had a good time and did some demonstration and exhibition matches. They toured all over the UK, visiting both north and south. On one particular trip to Manchester, they almost got Joe Louis into a lot of trouble with the law.

Ron and Reg were staying at the same hotel as the ex-world heavyweight champion, together with some close friends including Joe Pyle and Johnny Nash. Reg was afraid that the local police were trying to fit them up with guns, or 'shooters' as he calls them. The Krays actually asked Joe Louis to go to the railway station to check their luggage for firearms, just in case they were right in their suspicions. This he did, eventually finding nothing, but it did reassure the Krays who boarded their train with nonchalance. The big man had repaid a debt of gratitude, something that would stand him in good stead with the UK's greatest gangsters.

Another man who thanked Reg Kray for his life was yet another ex-world heavyweight champion, Sonny Liston. Reg drove him back to his hotel from the Cambridge Rooms one evening, while quite intoxicated with alcohol. Sonny Liston kissed the pavement as he got out of the car and thanked his lucky stars that he was still alive. Still shaking from the experience, he swore never to ride with Reg Kray ever again. The boxer may not have known it at the time, but Reg is quite short-sighted and doesn't like to wear spectacles. I remember hearing one incident concerning Reg and a double-decker bus; the bus won the argument and Reg ended up in a big hole in the ground. But Reg didn't care, he just went into a car showroom, connected with their protection racket, and drove out in a brand-new American car. But he still didn't wear his glasses.

One of the best-ever British boxers that they both enjoyed meeting was the boxing champion Freddie Mills. They would often visit Freddie Mills at his club and drink to past victories. There has always been much speculation that the twins were responsible for the death of Freddie Mills, but I have not come across any damaging evidence that would confirm this fact. But I do know from Charlie Kray that there were rumours that Nipper Read was going to arrest the ex-champ for the 'Jack-the-Stripper' murders. Prostitutes in the East End were being found killed all over the docklands area, but no one was ever prosecuted for the murders. Before the police had a chance of questioning Freddie Mills he had already committed suicide by shooting his brains out in a car. The Beatles immortalised the event in one of their songs, but the real truth will probably never be known in full. One fact did emerge, however, when it came time to read the will. Freddie Mills died almost broke, so it certainly did look as though he was being blackmailed for something more than just running a nightclub.

When Nipper Read wrote his book entitled *Nipper* in 1991, together with James Morton, where he mentioned the Kray case in utmost detail, he suggested that no such arrest was imminent in the Jack-the-Stripper case. But anyone who knows the history of boxing in the UK and the involvement of Nipper Read in the Boxing Board of Control, knows that he would never disgrace the name of Freddie Mills, one of the all-time greats of British boxing. And, in any case, Charlie Kray may have been wrong about his involvement. It was all a long time ago and memories can play tricks on the most astute of villains.

Many other boxers got the Kray treatment, including that great champion Henry Cooper. Cooper has always gone out of his way to deny any involvement with the Krays, even suggesting that he had never met them. This is quite wrong, since I have many photos in my possession of the twins in the company of Henry Cooper, but I can understand the reasons behind this denial. He never had any business involvement with the twins at all and no one can stop anyone taking photographs in public places, so being a well-known boxer and celebrity he was bound to get Ron Kray's photo treatment. Henry Cooper was and still is, a twin. He, unlike the Krays, understood the difference between notoriety and fame and he was keen to protect his public image. He knew all of the twin tricks and how being a twin can be an advantage, if used in the right way. This knowledge enabled him to outwit the Krays and he never succumbed to their power games.

Ron Kray, on the other hand, didn't give a damn about how he achieved the cult status of a celebrity; he longed for public recognition at all costs, and was prepared to do anything, even murder, to get it. Reg was drawn into this twilight zone by the sheer force of his twin brother, a force that he would never truly overcome.

Ron and Reg Kray, with their brother Charlie in tow, looked after visiting American celebrities when they toured the UK. This was done through that jovial giant Eddie Pucci, a man whom they first met through their old Mafia pal Angelo Bruno, the boss of Philadelphia. Eddie arranged all the showbiz deals for the Krays, even including on one occasion sending Nat King Cole's wife over to London for a shopping spree. Ron Kray met her at the airport, took her all over London to Harrods and the other famous stores, even King's Road in Chelsea, and he loved every minute of it. It may seem strange for such a violent and paranoid crook like Ron Kray to be acting as a guide for the wife of an American singer, but Mad Frankie Fraser is doing just that now so Ron, as usual, got there first. This simply shows the other side of Ron Kray, the good as opposed to the bad. The schizophrenic disability that he was forced to carry with him would make him seem human one minute and downright mad the next. There was a good, a bad and an ugly side to his nature that would change in an instant along with his mood swings. But when it came to protecting the stars, he was totally reliable.

When Judy Garland came over to the UK it was generally Reg who looked after her. She appeared to be most vulnerable at this stage of her life and would cling on to Reg's arm in almost any given situation. Maybe it was because of her drinking and her own bouts of depression that made Ron stay away, or it may have been the favouritism shown by Judy towards Reg. As a single man Reg took well to her show of affection, but it was certainly embarrassing for him after he was married to Frances. He became very reluctant to be embraced by Judy Garland in the presence of his wife or in the presence of photographers. But he continued to take Judy to the East End and to Chelsea, where she sang her heart out until the early hours of the morning at various night-clubs. Reg even took her along to some of his local East End pubs, with Judy Garland singing songs on request. She was a favourite of all three Kray brothers and they have talked and talked about her over the last 30 years. Even at the trial back in 1968–69 Ron Kray shouted at Lord Justice Stevenson, 'I could be dining with Judy Garland, instead of being stuck here in the Old Bailey' – something that he obviously wished he was doing at the time.

Johnny Ray was another favourite of Ron Kray's. It may have been because they were both gay and drawn together because of that common trait, but as with Lord Robert Boothby, it was probably because they both enjoyed the company of young boys. Remember, homosexuality was a criminal offence in those days and something to hide. Thank goodness that times have changed and that we are more tolerant in this latter part of the 20th century.

Entertainers such as Errol Garner were frequent visitors to The Stork Club, and Reg was surprised to hear that he couldn't read or write music. But it didn't matter to the Krays, they weren't much for reading themselves. They all enjoyed the club scene, which was remarkably drug free at the time. But that has all changed now and drugs appear to be the norm, although the twins themselves never dealt in the illicit substances. Some say today that things would have been very different in the UK now if the Krays had not been put away back in the '60s. True, they didn't deal in drugs, but the Mafia were very keen on influencing their decision in this respect. Maybe the lure of the stars would have persuaded the twins to import cocaine, heroin and crack through their Mob pals; maybe they would have resisted these pressures. But this is all pure speculation.

Barbra Streisand, Billy Daniels, Frank Sinatra and Tony Bennett; they all paid respects to the Krays. The twins from the East End of London had made it; they were household names who could command respect, if not for their business dealings, then certainly for their money. But it wasn't only these foreign showbiz names that entertained the protection of the twins. British home-grown celebrities also flourished under their wing. 178 Vallance Road was not the kind of place where anyone would expect to see showbiz stars – well, it wouldn't be if it hadn't been the home of Violet and 'old man' Charlie Kray. Ron changed that by introducing his mum to Edmund Purdom, who was an up-and-coming film star at the time, with a highly popular television programme behind him. Ron took him back to see Violet in her East End home, where he was introduced to all the neighbours. And he wasn't the only celebrity to visit the terraced house in Bethnal Green.

Sophie Tucker was a regular visitor who popped in from time to time to talk to her good friend Ron Kray. Ron was openly homosexual and a most charming person when he wanted to be and when his psychiatric illness allowed. He would entertain these visiting showbiz folk in the living-room, while mum made the tea. They would talk until the small hours, with Ron giving good advice just like a marriage guidance counsellor or your friendly financial adviser; he was well respected for his judgements, another fact that would seem to have disappeared over time, overshadowed by the darker side of his character.

Because of all their connections in film and theatre, it may appear obvious that the Krays found much time for audience participation, both in the clubs and at the theatre. Lionel Bart was a friend who invited them to all his shows in the West End, even inviting them backstage to meet the stars afterwards. This happened regularly and, once again, gave the press a host of photographic opportunities. Photos appeared in the newspapers of the time so regularly that every policeman in the country could identify Ron and Reg Kray on sight, something that greatly pleased the twins. Here were two hoods who openly sought publicity without thought to monetary gain. They even posed for photographs free of charge. David Bailey didn't ask them to pay him for the famous photos that he took of all three Kray brothers – he didn't dare. And they didn't ask for payment from him. After all, his photos helped to establish their own immortality. They are still today some of the most famous photographs ever taken and they have stood the test of time. Everyone knows the Kray brothers, not necessarily because of their deeds, but because of these photos. Indeed it is surprising to find so many good photos of Ron and Reg Kray still around in the archives. They haven't lost their popularity even now.

One surprising fact to come out of my investigations into Kray preferences, pastimes and hobbies was the enjoyment both twins obtained from opera. Reg and Frances, even on their honeymoon, found time to take in La Scala in Milan, where they saw Renato Sciotto in *Madame Butterfly* and when they returned to London they all went to see Joan Sutherland at the Covent Garden Opera House. Whether they did this for the music or for the chance of meeting the stars cannot be established, but it does show a willingness on the part of both twins to seek the brighter and lighter side of life. The world could really have been a good place for the twins and their brother Charlie, one that they could have enjoyed to the full. But they have never lost their own fame, indeed their notoriety has gained through the years with t-shirts, films, books and even records made of or about them. Their celebrity status is assured and history will tell their story for years to come.

It is not therefore surprising that Ron and Reg Kray have been in contact with celebrities and sports personalities throughout the '70s, '80s and '90s. Just because they were banged up in jail was no reason for their pals to forsake them. After all, if the Mafia could stay in touch, then their showbiz allies could show a little respect. Over the years this has mainly been in the form of letters which have assured the Krays of everlasting friendship and assistance. They have been censured by the authorities, but nonetheless it has been possible to recommend go-betweens to handle deals and to maintain connections. The unfortunate thing for the Krays has always been that they will not forego control by letting others organise and negotiate on their behalf, so this limits the deals that they have been able to do and the old contacts that they have been able to maintain.

Once, when I was visiting Reg Kray, he told me about his good friend Don King in New York. King is, as you may know, the manager of the ex-world heavyweight boxing champion Mike Tyson, but King's other claim to fame is that he is well connected with organised crime – the Mob. 'If you ever need to get around in New York, then he's your man,' he told me, quite casually. 'You know, it can be dangerous over there.' I felt as though he was trying to sell me insurance. Or maybe he would call it protection?

Throughout these past 30 years the Krays have waged media war, with incessant displays of loyalty appearing in the press from old friends, and articles telling all about their good and charitable deeds, all performed in the name of decency. Gary Bushell has constantly told us in *The Sun* of how it was always safe to walk around in the East End when the Krays were around. Maybe that is true, but you have to ask yourself why. And why should such people have so much control over our everyday lives? The comedian and actor Mike Reid has joined in the celebration of the Kray name, saying that 30 years is too long for murder. When comparing latterday cases with the Kray trial, it must appear illogical that the twins were given 30-year sentences, but as normal everyday citizens, do we really have all the facts about the Krays? And what have we still to discover?

This media hype has served them well and has kept their name alive in the modern television age. It is so alive that we could perhaps be forgiven for calling it a virtual reality life, since we know so little about the facts. The media have trivialised that part of their lives that made them kings of the underworld, in favour of the image so carefully created by Ron Kray – their iconisation as showbiz folk who ran foul of the law and have overpaid their dues.

It is possibly this sensationalism and celebrity worship that has enticed people like Bon Jovi, the rock star, to write to them, or maybe it was just a case of following orders for the singer from New Jersey. It is well rumoured that Bon Jovi too has Mob connections, just like the companies Elektra and Atlantic of WEA fame, but just like in the '50s and '60s it is difficult to tell who controls whom, since no one goes around wearing a badge saying 'I am a member of the Mafia'.

A frequent traveller to see Reg Kray in recent years has been the singer and actor Roger Daltrey. It was through his perseverance that the film *The Krays* was actually produced, since he was the first to show an interest in the project and to start developing a script. Billy Curbishley, manager of the band The Who, which featured Daltrey on vocals, is also a regular, and Daltrey and Curbishley advised Reg Kray on the project, culminating in the deal that secured £297,000 for three jailbirds who were convicted of heinous crimes against the state. So the Krays became even more famous, or should that be infamous, and next time around they want to make £2 million. That is the price they have set on their fame and fortune. And next time they want bigger stars!

Of all the love–hate relationships that Reg Kray has had to endure the most peculiar is that which exists between himself and a certain famous young actress. The fact that he is her brother's godfather has meant little to her at times, but then has been eagerly and actively confirmed by her at other times. It is an on-off relationship without par. The young lady is, of course, Patsy Kensit and her story is told in greater detail at the end of the book where I delve into the love lives of the Krays, seeking that knowledge which explains and analyses the fatal attraction that they all seem to have for members of the opposite sex. Patsy is now apparently again writing to Reg Kray, asking for forgiveness for her sins, since she has recently denied all knowledge of the Krays in major interviews, something that has deeply offended and infuriated the Kray family. In the case of Ron, of course, it was not the opposite sex that had him dreaming at night, but he somehow managed to endure two marriages – to women, so I must include him here.

But why are the Krays themselves 'stars'? Why do we talk of them in the same way we talk about film stars and pop stars and even royalty? I think it all started when they were born twins. Their mother called them 'special' and special they became because of their twin-ness. But others called them special too, so they grew up believing it. Indeed, at school they did well in boxing, winning championships, which again proved that they were special. Indeed, the Kray twins were no ordinary little boys from the East End of London.

Everyone knew them because they were twins, and referred to them as the twins. It was only later that their real identities, Ron and Reg, were used around the area of Bethnal Green. I can hear their mother Violet calling out 'Ron and Reg' in the same voice and at the same time, when addressing only one of the twins. My own experience shows that a mother is not always sure who she is talking to. Even now, on the telephone, my mother can't distinguish between my voice and that of my twin brother. They were stars in their own right even from birth, so it was only natural that they should become stars later on in life.

From my own experience of being a twin, I have numerous stories of meeting celebrities and stars of stage and screen, simply through the fact that I am a twin. One such story includes a popular band of the time that was also known to the Krays. My brother and I were working during our school vacation at Heathrow Airport, back in the early '60s. We were both serving at the bar from time to time and also working in the rear of the premises, making sandwiches. Noticing that my brother Rod wasn't attending the bar, I walked out and asked the first customer if he wanted a drink.

The customer, a young man of about my own age, said,

'We'll have two teas please,' and gave me a rather odd look. Nevertheless I quickly went back into the rear of the premises, only to notice that Rod had just made a new pot of tea. Happily I poured two new cups of tea and went out to the bar to serve my customers. Rod was already there talking to the two lads, who had a rather peculiar accent. He also had two cups of tea on the bar.

The youngsters looked at my brother, and then at me, and then back at my brother. 'Christ, you're twins!' said one of them.

'I've never seen such identical twins in my life,' said the other. They both stood there, mouths open. There wasn't much they could say that we hadn't heard before.

'And I've never seen such identical haircuts as yours,' I said quickly in reply. I now found myself looking at their hair, curiously cut in the same extraordinary fashion. 'But what shall I do with the teas?' I asked curiously.

'Don't worry,' said one of the lads. 'George and Ringo will be along in a minute. They'll have the teas.' It took me some time to translate from the Liverpudlian to Middlesexian, but I got there in the end. We were talking to John Lennon and Paul McCartney and the two they referred to, and who joined them a few moments later, were George Harrison and Ringo Starr. Together they were The Beatles.

We met them quite a few times that summer, along with other top names such as Cliff Richard, who has never outlived his sell-by date, and John Charles, one of the first British footballers to play in Italy. There were many others, who were surprised by our twin-ness; this made us special and gave us a chance to meet them. If we had been ordinary brothers then the chances of meeting such stars would have been greatly reduced. This is just one advantage of being a twin.

I have other such stories of how we met Harold Wilson, one of our great Prime Ministers, and of how we both worked in the film business. Twins seem to meet people and that's a fact. The mere fact of being twins in the '50s and '60s made them different and memorable. They were born with stars in their eyes.

5. MOB RULES

'Frank Sinatra would like to meet you backstage after the show,' said the amiable giant Eddie Pucci. Eddie had been a football player of some repute but to the Krays he was known as one of the best bodyguards in the business. They had first met him when he came to England with Mafia boss Angelo Bruno, who had employed the Krays to look after his gambling establishments in London, and they had continued as associates when Eddie arranged for the Krays to act as protectors for American stars who came over to perform in the UK.

Ron Kray was always excited when his Mafia pals sent over a 'star'. He would wine them and dine them; even take them shopping. But this time it was no ordinary celebrity he had come to meet. It was the one and only Frank Sinatra, a king among men, and he had brought the whole family with him.

Ron, Reg and Charlie Kray sat with their mother and father, Violet and old man Charlie, throughout the performance. They sat in the best seats in the house, the best that Mob connections could buy. And they were absolutely delighted at the invitation to join Frank after the show. Ron, in particular, just couldn't wait.

But wait he had to, since the meeting was not to be. Reports had just arrived at the Apollo Theatre that Sinatra's son, Frank junior, had been kidnapped.

The year was 1966 and this was at least the second successful attempt at snatching Sinatra junior away from the protectful eyes of his Mafia-connected father.

The first kidnapping had taken place at Sinatra's own hotel, the Cal-Nev on the California–Nevada state line, in 1963. Young Sinatra had been performing with the Tommy Dorsey Band at Harrah's Casino on Lake Tahoe, when he was grabbed for ransom money. Sinatra soon recovered his son and most of the money. Exactly how this was done still remains a bit of a mystery, although Mafia involvement cannot be ruled out. And Sinatra was said by many to have organised the kidnapping himself for publicity.

This second time, however, was a college prank. It was of no particular importance at all, save that it stopped the Krays from meeting 'Old Blue Eyes'. The fact that the meeting between Sinatra and the Krays never took place is also of no importance. The fact that it was mooted shows the status of the Krays – all three Kray brothers – in the eyes of the US Mafia. These were allies across the pond, men of substance, pals to be treated with respect.

The life of Frank Sinatra will always be inextricably linked with the Mob. Indeed, for anyone trying to make a name for himself in Hollywood, it was almost impossible not to meet or have dealings with the Mob. They controlled all the film unions, they controlled money lending, they controlled gambling. One of Frank's oldest and dearest friends, Sammy Davis Junior, was always in debt to the Mob. He would borrow for gambling purposes but due to his friendship with Sinatra, was always treated kindly. But the Mob always collect on a debt. It can sometimes be in cash or possibly in other ways, such as a favour or two.

When John Fitzgerald Kennedy was running for President of the United States in 1960, it was Frank Sinatra who organised fund-raising events throughout California and Nevada, including at his own Sands Hotel in Las Vegas and at the Cal-Nev, with his many celebrity pals. But among the stars of the day, such as Dean Martin, Sammy Davis Junior, Peter Lawford and Marilyn Monroe, there were other very special guests, such as Chicago Mafia boss Sam Giancana.

Giancana had made a deal with Joe Kennedy, Jack's father, to get presidential backing for his protection, prostitution, gambling and extortion rackets, after the election of Jack Kennedy to the White House. Sam Giancana wanted to be around to see that everyone had a good time and to make sure that his man was elected to president. To secure co-operation he even had the hotel rooms bugged. If he couldn't get what he wanted then he would release these tapes to the press or elsewhere, wherever it would do him any good and get him the favours he so desperately needed.

Sam Giancana was one of the most important Mafia bosses of all time. He was on the *commissione* – the Mafia's very own trouble-shooting organisation – along with old Kray pal Angelo Bruno and rival supremo Vito Genovese. It was a club for *capos* and the most powerful criminal organisation ever. It still exists.

Frank Sinatra and Sam Giancana were very good friends and close business partners. But even good business partners don't always see eye to eye.

In July of 1962 Frank Sinatra was getting ready to marry again. His intended bride was none other than one of Sam Giancana's most intimate of friends, Marilyn Monroe. Monroe had been going through a bad time and Sinatra wanted to help. But maybe there were other reasons why Sinatra wanted to protect Marilyn. It just may have been that Sinatra knew that the Mob had been asked to silence Marilyn Monroe for good.

Having had close relationships with the Chicago Mob for many years would naturally have made Sinatra privy to many of the Mafia deals. And Mob deals include killings for money. If Sinatra had married Marilyn Monroe just a few days before her death on 3 August 1962, then she might have lived through her ordeal. However, she didn't marry Sinatra and so died on orders from the CIA.

The CIA, FBI and other organisations were all afraid of the knowledge that Marilyn had of their business dealings. Having slept with both Jack and Bobby Kennedy, she had listened to many hours' worth of pillow talk; and that kind of talk can be dangerous. She had to die. Her death was arranged by her close friend Sam Giancana, with orders coming from the CIA. The Mob often handled the dirty business for the government.

The trouble between Giancana and the Kennedys really began when J.F. Kennedy was elected President. When father Joe Kennedy saw his son Jack and family safely installed in the White House and his other son Bobby made Attorney

General, he changed his deal with the Mob. In fact he cancelled it all together.

Sam Giancana actually visited Jack Kennedy in the White House to try to get him to honour his father's debt, but it didn't work. Giancana was barred from ever again visiting Jack Kennedy.

The result was that father Joe persuaded son Bobby to set up a task force and to go after organised crime in a big way. This he would soon regret, since the Mafia are all about honour of a kind. It means that you don't back down from arrangements made in an honourable way. And Sam Giancana was of the old school and an 'honourable man'.

So it was Jack Kennedy who paid the price for his father's double-dealing, when he was shot and killed in Dallas on 22 November 1963. Although there have been many theories about the killing, this author believes that Lee Harvey Oswald was telling the truth when he claimed he was a patsy. He was set up by Sam Giancana, who not only wanted to settle a private score but was also paid by people within the US government who wanted to see a different President in the White House. One with a different attitude towards the Russians and Cuba.

But even this didn't change the attitude of Joe Kennedy. He asked Bobby Kennedy to get Sam Giancana and all of his Mob friends. The problem in those days was that a close friend of Sam Giancana was probably also a close friend of Joe Kennedy, since Joe had dealt in bootleg gin in the old days of prohibition along with the Chicago Mobsters.

It was at this time that Frank Sinatra was barred from visiting the White House. Being a close pal of Giancana's, however, made him a go-between for trying to reach some kind of a deal with the Kennedys. It didn't work and in 1968 Bobby Kennedy was also killed. Some say that it was Sam Giancana who ordered the hit.

Giancana was later to die at the hands of his own people, the Chicago Mob. So it was with many of the Krays' old Mob pals, they all ended with a bullet in the head. All except, that is, Frank Sinatra. He, at least, was allowed to die gracefully and without his boots on!

The Krays first had dealings with the US Mafia when they helped to 'protect' a gambling club in London belonging to Angelo Bruno, the Mob boss of Philadelphia and that den of iniquity known as Atlantic City. This had always been prime real estate for the Mob and rivalled even Las Vegas. The big difference, of course, is that all Mafia families are welcome in Las Vegas, whereas only one family ran Atlantic City. Things have changed slightly in recent years, but not enough to bother the current Philadelphia boss.

Bruno sat on the *commissione* together with Giancana, Genovese and other top-flight Mob bosses. It was an organisation put together by the entire US Mob to sort out any difficulties that might occur, with regard to territories or rights or such. Mob business had strict boundaries; it still does.

Through Bruno the Krays met Sinatra and began acting as bodyguards for visiting US celebrities such as Nat King Cole, Billy Daniels, Johnny Ray and many more. They also sent over many of the world's best-known boxers including Joe Louis and Rocky Marciano, who was a particular pal of George Raft who ran The Colony and Sporting Club on Berkeley Square for Meyer Lansky. By the early 1960s the Mafia were firmly entrenched in London.

Bruno was such a top *capo* that he shared bodyguards with Frank Sinatra, one such man being Eddie Pucci, the giant American ex-football player and good friend of the Krays. Pucci was always with Sinatra when he visited the UK and he accompanied many of the top US stars when they visited these shores.

It was probably Angelo Bruno who involved the Krays in the most lucrative venture that they were ever to undertake – selling stolen US bearer-bonds on the European Undercover Exchange.

With Bobby Kennedy hot on the trail of the Mob in the summer of 1965, stolen negotiable bearer-bonds to the value of some $2 million were burning a hole in safety deposit boxes and other safe places all over the USA. They had been stolen from security deposits by pals of the Mob for a price, and they were ready for sale. The only problem was that they were too hot to sell in the good old US of A.

The solution was to negotiate their sale in Europe, using the Krays as go-betweens. The deal was simple; the Mob gave the Krays the bonds, the Krays sold them and kept half the money for their trouble. They should cover their own costs, however.

Ron and Reg Kray could look forward to becoming millionaires on this deal alone. It was simple, clever and quick. But they weren't clever enough to handle it themselves, so they needed help.

The man they chose was Ron's own business manager, Leslie Payne, and in July of 1965 he took a flight to Montreal in Canada to do the first trial run with the Mob boss of that city, Don Ceville. It was only a small amount of bonds, to the tune of some £25,000 or so, but it was the start of the big time for the Krays. Payne collected the bonds with all their certificates of origin and smuggled them back into the UK in his briefcase, just like a pack of sandwiches.

Ron and Reg Kray were pleased with the deal. It had worked just as the Mafia had said it would, but there were problems with the rest of the securities; they had no paperwork. Certification of origin was necessary if these bearer-bonds were to be sold openly, just like the real thing.

The man chosen to handle these forgeries was an American banker known as A.B. Cooper. Cooper had a small private bank in the City of London; a private bank for private business. Exactly how he was recommended to the Krays is somewhat unclear, but he appeared to Ron Kray, at least, to be the right man for the job. As usual, it didn't matter what his brothers Reg and Charlie thought about the matter; the Colonel was always right.

Cooper was a man of mystery, someone who had apartments everywhere, including London and Geneva. He spoke with an anglicised accent, was almost bald and stuttered badly, especially when under pressure. He had a Rolls-Royce and spent money like there was no tomorrow. He also had a dog. But Cooper's credentials pleased Ron Kray. He said that he had been involved in gold smuggling, weapons deals and money laundering. To Ron he was the perfect choice.

Cooper explained that forging the certificates of origin was no problem at all, but they would have to be sold throughout Europe, without setting up a regular supply source. These could be traced, he explained to Ron and Reg, so couriers should be used to carry the bearer-bonds to the ultimate destination. These destinations were the major banks and exchanges in mainland Europe.

The twins chose their brother Charlie to be the chief courier, much to the annoyance of Leslie Payne, who had done the first pick-up in Canada. He was much annoyed by this decision, but had to toe the line, just like all others in the Firm.

In August, news reached the twins that more bonds were gathering dust in Montreal and the Mafia required collection immediately. The news had come from Gordon Andersen, an old friend of Charlie's from the failed Nigerian business. Andersen had certain business relations with the Mafia boss of Montreal, Don Ceville. He dealt in insurance.

The others selected for a trip to Montreal were Charlie Mitchell, a bookmaker; Bobby McKew, a printer; and Leslie Payne, Ron's business manager. Payne had been there before and could easily recognise the Mafia boss Don Ceville. Anyway, the Krays thought that Payne not being there would appear a little suspicious. They didn't want anything to upset their plans.

The deal was set for early September and the twins asked their brother Charlie to bring the bonds back into the UK in his briefcase just like any other businessman. Charlie was looking forward to visiting Canada, so he agreed.

At the airport they ran into a party of Bunny Girls, who were being trained for work in the newly opened Playboy Club. Charlie thought at first that they were all being arrested, but soon he realised his mistake and settled down to a trip to Canada in the company of these gorgeous girls – what a sacrifice to make!

The trip was uneventful and the party consumed a lot of

booze, as usual. Soon they arrived in Montreal, fresh from their journey and in good humour.

But what awaited them in Montreal was anything but good news. They were arrested immediately they stepped off the plane. Surrounded by red-coated Royal Canadian Mounted Police, they were taken individually by car to the 'Tombs', Montreal's top-flight prison.

They were told nothing but to leave their belongings in paper bags, for collection (maybe) later. Charlie Kray, Gordon Andersen, Charlie Mitchell and Leslie Payne were all put behind bars. Charlie speculated as to the reasons for their arrest but he couldn't figure it out. After all, they had just arrived. They all spent a long and frightening night in the 'Tombs'.

The next day they were all dragged into court but the Mafia *capo* had sent them a lawyer, who argued their case. Gordon Andersen had actually seen Don Ceville at the airport while they were being arrested, so Ceville was fully aware of the precarious situation. The lawyer did her job well and it was agreed that the party would be deported. Again, flanked by the Royal Canadian Mounted Police, they were taken back to the airport and put on the first flight back to London. It was a sorry and humiliating story to tell – one of deceit, confusion and ultimately evasion – but they were all really quite relieved when they were deported. Charlie in particular could imagine spending the rest of his life in that cell, so being thrown out of Canada wasn't such a bad option. The only problem with the whole sordid affair was that he would have to explain the entire charade to his brothers, the twins.

Back in London the Krays held a meeting to determine what had gone wrong and who had squealed to the police. But they couldn't reason it out. Charlie thought that Mitchell had set the whole thing up to try to get the bond business for himself, but no one could be sure. In the end it didn't really matter. A few days later Don Ceville took a flight from Montreal to Heathrow and delivered the bonds personally to Ron and Reg Kray. He had no trouble getting into the UK. It was all a formality.

So the Krays were in business and between 1965 and 1966

Charlie Kray was to travel throughout Europe, collecting and delivering instantly negotiable bearer-bonds for and on behalf of the US Mafia. He got to know Geneva quite well, so too Hamburg, where the banking facilities came in handy. It was all handled legally through the official banking system and the money arrived back in London at Cooper's bank, ready for the twins. Half went back to the USA through Gordon Andersen, but the Krays kept half the takings for their trouble. As Charlie Kray always said, 'It was no trouble at all.'

One fortunate outcome of this ridiculous Canadian adventure was the simple fact that the Mafia in the USA and Canada knew that they couldn't rely on the Krays coming to collect the bearer-bonds. So the Mob were forced to set up safe routes to Europe in order to deliver the bonds in person to Charlie Kray. Because of this, Charlie Kray was the only one of the Kray brothers to deal man to man with some of the biggest names in the history of the Mafia. The chosen routes were to Paris, Hamburg, Geneva, Amsterdam and Frankfurt. For Charlie Kray it was a merry-go-round life, full of leisure and luxury, all paid for by the US Mafia.

A.B. Cooper, the mysterious and silky-smooth banker, arranged for the forgeries, as agreed with the Krays. But Charlie still didn't trust the man, he was too good and apparently had contacts everywhere. This made him a dangerous ally.

After the Canadian trip Charlie Mitchell went back to his money-lending and bookmaking business until his death by the gun at his Costa del Sol home. The murderer was never found.

Bobby McKew inherited a fortune and settled in South Africa, well away from the Krays and the impending trouble with the law, while Gordon Andersen continued the insurance game, acting as co-ordinator with the US Mob. None of these men were ever tried for these crimes. In fact none of the Krays were ever convicted of dealing in bearer-bonds and the deals continue to this very day.

Charlie Kray's life was now full of wine, women and lots of champagne. He travelled all over Europe and enjoyed the rich and pleasant lifestyle together with his pals from the Mob.

These men from the USA really knew how to live – the best hotels, the best women that money could buy, the best champagne. Have I mentioned the champagne?

But one particular occasion was to become a nightmare for Charlie Kray; one that he would never forget, even with many years in jail with only his memories for company. This was the time he had to burn $250,000 of instantly negotiable bearer-bonds in a dustbin at his mother Violet's home at Vallance Road, Bethnal Green.

It was November 1965 when Charlie Kray received a phone call from his brother Reg informing him that there were bearer-bonds to be collected in Paris. Charlie quickly drove to his mother's house for the meeting in eager anticipation of the Paris trip. Greetings over, they settled down to business and Reg laid out the plan. Charlie, together with Leslie Payne and accountant Freddie Gore, would take the flight to Paris, stay at Claridge's Hotel on the Champs-Elysées, meet the Mafia contacts, collect the bonds and smuggle them back into the UK. It was simple enough, they thought; how could anyone mess it up? And with Freddie Gore bringing them back in his briefcase, they would have enough criminal evidence on Gore to keep his mouth shut.

The three men travelled to Paris as planned. There were no problems on the outward trip – after all it was beginning to become routine. They all knew what they were expected to do and all had agreed the plan.

The meeting with the two 'wise guys' (American slang for Mafia) went ahead as described by Reg Kray back at Vallance Road; there were no mistakes and the bonds were delivered in a plastic carrier bag. The men all then went out on the town, from Pigale to Montmatre and from the Etoile to St. Germaine, with money being no object to any of them. The twins were paying.

Charlie hid the bonds behind a wardrobe in his room and didn't even bother to look at them. He was sure it would be the normal $25,000 to $50,000 worth of bonds, no need to make a fuss. So they all enjoyed their late evening and early morning in Paris.

The following day Charlie Kray dressed and checked out

the bonds. To his amazement there were $250,000 worth, much more than normal. And to think he had left them stuffed behind a wardrobe all night. He then quickly went down the main stairway to the dining-room to meet the others for breakfast. He took the bonds with him in the carrier bag.

'These are yours,' he said to the accountant Freddie Gore, as he handed over the bonds. He was pleased to get rid of them, since a lot of money had always been a problem for Charlie Kray. He didn't know how to handle it.

Gore looked at the carrier bag and asked how much there was in securities. He was startled at the reply. 'What!' he exclaimed at the top of his voice. 'How much did you say?' came out in a whisper, when he noticed that everyone in the dining-room was looking at him.

'I told you,' said Charlie quietly and soberly. 'There are $250,000 of instantly negotiable bearer-bonds.'

Leslie Payne's eyes lit up. This was indeed a windfall. Reg and Ron would be pleased and maybe there would be something extra in it for him. He smiled and continued his breakfast with much pleasure.

'I can't do it,' said Freddie Gore. 'I can't smuggle that back to London,' he pleaded. But the others weren't in the mood for bargaining. It had all been agreed back in Bethnal Green and neither Charlie Kray nor Leslie Payne wanted to change Reggie's cunning plan.

Somehow Charlie knew that Gore would spoil the whole deal, so he asked Payne to take the bonds. He flatly refused. They were not his orders; only Reg could ask him to do that.

So Charlie Kray had to stuff the bonds in his bag in order to bring them home to England and to the waiting hands of his brothers, Ron and Reg Kray. But first he had to get back home.

The taxi drive out to the airport was deathly quiet, there was not a sound from any of them. Gore was sweating profusely, since he knew his cowardice would be reported when they got home, and Payne sat quietly, not wanting to take responsibility for anything. After all, it wasn't he who was in charge of the party, it was Charlie Kray, elder brother of the

Kray twins. Payne was still annoyed about not being put in charge after the first trip to see Don Ceville in Montreal.

Soon they were on the plane and heading home. Charlie Kray kept to himself and consumed even more champagne. Now that is not easy on a short trip like this, but as usual he was good at his work and time passed easily. When the plane eventually landed he only had a short walk with his overnight bag to be out of the airport and then it would just be the taxi drive home.

However, he was stopped at the customs desk. 'Anything to declare?' asked the customs man. What a question for a man carrying $250,000 in stolen instantly negotiable bearer-bonds, all without certification.

'Nothing,' said Charlie. 'If you don't believe me then take a look,' he said as he opened his bag. 'There's only dirty laundry.'

The customs man had just come on duty and regarded Charlie's statement as simple proof of innocence. 'Okay,' he said with a grin and Charlie Kray was on his way. Some distance behind him came Leslie Payne and Freddie Gore, Laurel and Hardy to the Firm; they too walked through the customs check with ease, but then they didn't have anything to hide. But just to be careful, they kept their distance from Charlie and took another taxi back to the East End.

Once home Charlie looked for a suitable hiding-place for the bonds and he quickly found it behind a loose panel in the bathroom. That night he slept well, but he was woken with the sound of the telephone and on the other end was one of the Mafia guys he had met in Paris just a few days earlier.

'They are too hot, Charlie,' said the man. 'You had better get rid of them as fast as you can.' The urgency in the man's voice told Charlie that it was all true enough, not just a bad dream.

Charlie's way out was to burn the 'hot' bonds in a dustbin in his mother's back yard. He counted them one by one as he threw them into the bin. 'One thousand, two thousand' – it never ended. To Charlie it was as though he was throwing his life away, or at least part of it. He cried. Not even a cup of tea helped the situation.

But the Mafia were true to their word and they continued

to bring over small carrier bags which they exchanged for large amounts of cash. The business was good and the twins made a lot of East End dosh out of the deal.

After the George Cornell killing in March of 1966 the Mafia were beginning to have second thoughts about using the Krays as collaborators in the deals involving the instantly negotiable bearer-bonds. They were actively looking around, searching for new partners – they were actually considering setting up operations themselves, even though Europe was far from home base in the USA. There was also a kind of protocol to observe and respect with regard to the Sicilian Mafia who rather looked on France, Switzerland, Germany and Holland as their own restricted territory. As usual with our European partners, the UK was always regarded as a special case.

Some limited amounts of bearer-bonds came through normal channels during the summer of 1966 and the early part of the following year, but by the end of 1967 the flow of dollar bonds had all but completely dried up.

To resume good business with the Mob, Ron Kray decided that a trip to New York was necessary. The bonds represented good money to the Krays and he could meet the *capos* and cement otherwise strained relationships. Ron wanted them both to go to New York in the spring of 1968, but he also added that it didn't matter too much if Reg decided not to go. He would just go by himself to meet the illustrious bosses of organised crime.

Reg couldn't believe what he was hearing. 'It's a trap,' he said. 'You can't do it. We have prison records. We can't get visas.' Reg was adamant that it was all pie in the sky, but Ron wasn't finished.

A.B. Cooper had already suggested to Ron Kray that the prospect of going to New York was not as far-fetched as many would imagine. He said that he had contacts at the US Embassy in Paris who could arrange for all the necessary documentation. Cooper would take care of all the paperwork – passports, visas, tickets – all Ron had to do was to sit back and enjoy the trip. Cooper said he would even arrange for high-level meetings with the top Mob bosses in New York. Ron had nothing to lose and everything to gain according to Cooper.

'If I want to go to New York, then I'll fucking go to New York,' was Ron's reply to his twin brother. Discussion completed.

While Ron was all for it, Reg was not at all sure about the whole reasoning behind the trip. 'I'll stay home and take care of business,' he suggested to Ron. It was no good arguing with Ron, the Colonel always got his way. The argument in the flat at Braithwaite House, Shoreditch, had lasted long enough for both men and walls have ears, so once again Ron Kray had made a decisive decision. It was one, he thought, that would change his life for ever and in a way it did just that.

Reg stayed on at his parents' flat while Ron returned to his country retreat, The Brooks in Suffolk. His parents Violet and old man Charlie were staying in the Lodge House for the weekend so he would soon be able to tell them both of the good news. Their little boy was going to America!

It was all set. At the beginning of April 1968 Ron Kray, the underworld boss of London, was heading for New York for what he was sure would be a historic meeting with Mob bosses. With him were the banker A.B. Cooper and an old school friend called Dickie Morgan, who was good fun for Ron to have around since he made him (Ron) laugh.

The trio flew from Heathrow over to Orly Airport just on the outskirts of Paris and took a cab to the Frontenac Hotel, just off the Champs-Elysées. It was an uneventful flight, with the normal light conversation. Soon they were unpacking in their rooms.

Cooper told Ron that it was too late to go to the US Embassy that evening so he suggested that they all go and have dinner with an old friend, who spoke perfect English and had many contacts in the criminal world. Ron was pleased to meet someone – anyone. It was a convivial way of passing the time in Paris (although I would have thought of something just a little different myself) and Ron was always interested in new ideas.

The evening went well, with Ron and the Frenchman

doing most of the talking. Soon they were back at the Frontenac and ready for a nightcap. Ron was not tired but he was keen to be in good shape for the trip to the Embassy, so they all retired early that night.

The following morning was D-Day; it was now-or-never time for Ron Kray to find out whether or not he could gain admission to the United States of America. Cooper was sure that he could handle it but Ron wasn't too sure. Even if he couldn't get a visa it was still a holiday and the expense wouldn't break the bank. It was a no-lose situation for Ron Kray.

They took a cab from the hotel and drove directly to the US Embassy. The driver pulled up outside and the three men got out and started walking up the steps. 'Impressive aren't they?' said A.B. Cooper, referring to the uniformed US Marines standing guard outside.

But Ron was more interested in their ceremonial swords. In fact he stopped for a moment to inspect the troops, much to the dismay of his companions. The inspection over, a smiling Ron Kray entered the building with Cooper leading the way. After Ron came the jovial Dickie Morgan. To Morgan it was all a laugh, so he took everything in his stride. He played follow my leader.

Cooper led the way through the corridors, finally coming to a stop at an unmarked door. He didn't knock, just walked straight in. At a desk sat a lone woman, who didn't appear to be expecting them. 'I've come to collect visas,' he told the woman, who was eating a sandwich. 'For my two friends here,' he added, pointing over to Ron Kray and Dickie Morgan. She began to argue that it wasn't possible to issue visas right away and that if they had been ordered in advance they were not ready so could they come back in the morning. This didn't please Cooper, who began telling all sorts of stories about sick relations in the USA and how important it was that the three men get to New York as soon as possible

It worked and within half an hour the visas were issued. Ron was overjoyed. Dickie Morgan had something to look forward to, a visit to the USA. And A.B. Cooper could breathe a sigh of relief. They partied the night away in celebration. But first Ron had to make a phone call back home to tell his brother Reg that Cooper had succeeded in getting the visas, just to gloat a little. Reg told him again that it was a set-up but his younger brother didn't believe him. Even if it was, he thought he could control it.

The next day was one full of bright hopes for new beginnings with the US Mafia and Ron asked Cooper for all the details of meetings that Cooper said that he had already arranged. Highest on Ron's list was meeting Meyer Lansky, who had set up The Colony Club with his pal George Raft as chairman. But already Ron had won. He was on his way to the USA, to New York and to places that he had only previously been able to dream about. Already he had beaten the system.

'We are meeting little Joe Kaufman at JFK,' said A.B. Cooper. 'He has arranged hotel rooms and will be taking you to meet the *capos*, Ron.' Cooper was feeling smug, since he had done what to many was the impossible: he had arranged for a convicted felon to get a visa for the USA. No one could take that away from him; it would do his prestige in the UK a lot of good.

Joe Kaufman and his wife Marie were very good friends of Charlie Kray and his wife and they had even spent some holiday time together in Spain. Joe Kaufman had often been to London on business on behalf of the Mafia, who used him as a courier for bonds and also for passing on messages, and Ron had met him on many occasions. Kaufman was to be trusted and Ron was pleased to be meeting an old friend.

Ron's mind began to wander as they neared the USA. He had already met Tony 'Ducks' Corallo, a top lieutenant in the Lucchese family from Brooklyn, when he was over in London scouting for locations for new clubs. Maybe he would be on Kaufman's list. Then there was Lansky, a very important fish to Ron Kray since he had connections everywhere within the Mafia, even Las Vegas which he had helped Bugsy Siegel set up as the gambling Mecca of the USA. Then, of course, there was his old pal Angelo Bruno, the Philadelphia godfather who also ran Atlantic City. He was surely high on the list too. And of course there were all the celebrities that he had met in London, sent over by his good buddy Eddie Pucci. Whoever he would meet in New York, Ron Kray knew then that it was the new start that he so eagerly wanted.

It was probably fortunate for Ron at this time that he never knew what had happened between his brother Charlie and Tony 'Ducks' Corallo back in London only a few months earlier. I am sure he was never told about the incident but I see no reason for leaving this small detail out of the story. When Corallo was in London he told Charlie Kray that he had a small present with him from his boss in Brooklyn. Charlie was in a good mood and in a somewhat patronising way told the man that the twins only wanted their friendship not gifts so Tony Corallo never gave Charlie the present. He took it back with him to the USA. Oh, the present you ask? What was the present? Well . . . it was a suitcase full of money – some $50,000. What a proper Charlie! When it came to making stupid mistakes Charlie Kray made them big time!

But this little event didn't occur to Ron Kray as the plane came in to land at JFK Airport, since he didn't even know about it. So he was sublime in his innocence for once.

'Now don't say too much going through immigration,' said Cooper to his fellow travellers. Ron and Dickie Morgan nodded – they wouldn't have known what to say anyway.

The plane landed and the group disembarked and strode through the immigration as though they owned the place. The only question Ron was asked was if he could support himself and a quick flash of rolled-up dollar bills soon showed the immigration officer that he most certainly could take care of himself, even in a place like New York.

'It was all fixed,' said Cooper to his friends. 'The Mob had planned it that way.' Whether this is true nor not, Ron didn't worry about it. He had arrived in New York City and that was all that mattered. He had won the game and now he would make history.

Little Joe Kaufman met them at the airport, just as Cooper had said he would and they all headed east towards Manhattan in Joe's luxury limousine. The trip to the Warwick Hotel was noisy to say the least but Ron was enjoying every minute. He loved the pace of the city, he took in all the sights and he smelt the smells of the city streets. He felt comfortable.

The visa was for a seven-day stay and the first night they spent with Joe Kaufman and his wife, Marie. It was an informal dinner at an exclusive restaurant, mainly 'wise guys'. It was a place to make connections and Kaufman was a regular and therefore treated with respect. It all helped to impress Ron Kray. Kaufman was chatty and gave Ron a message from Angelo Bruno. Bruno couldn't make it up to New York, but he would be pleased to see Ron in Philadelphia or Atlantic City if he had the time. Ron was pleased to hear from the Philadelphia godfather so soon after his arrival. Everything was looking good and Ron could start to relax, feeling that he was in the right place at the right time.

'I'm trying to get hold of a good contact I have in the Colombo family,' said Joe Kaufman. 'It's a little difficult but I should be able to reach him by tomorrow.'

Ron ordered another drink. There was no need to thank 'Little Joe', after all, it was only business.

The following day Joe Kaufman phoned Ron Kray to tell him that he had set up a meeting with Frank Ileano, a lieutenant in the Colombo family, somewhere in Brooklyn. Ron wasn't bothered where it was just as long as he met a Mob boss. Kaufman was as good as his word, he had managed where Cooper hadn't succeeded. In fact Ron Kray and Dickie Morgan hadn't seen much of Cooper after that first evening out with Joe Kaufman. He told Ron that he was trying to reach contacts but he apparently wasn't very successful. Ron didn't care, he would soon be discussing big business with the Mob and that was the main point of being there.

It was on the second day that Joe Kaufman collected Ron Kray from the Warwick Hotel and drove out along 5th Avenue towards Brooklyn. Dickie Morgan was sent on a shopping spree along with some of Ron's dollar bills so he couldn't overhear what was said in the car or at the meeting. On the way out the two men chatted about the Gallo brothers, Kaufman's friends in the Mob and the people who had arranged for the meeting at a house in President Street, a sleepy area of Brooklyn. 'Crazy Joe' Gallo was a feared gangster of the old school, having gotten his 'button' many years earlier. The other brothers were just as dangerous, but Larry and Al Gallo didn't have the reputation that their brother enjoyed throughout the USA.

The meeting at President Street, near Prospect Park, started a little coolly for Ron Kray. He was asked to wait until his credentials were checked out with Angelo Bruno and this took some time. He had to wait in silence as the Mob went about their business; this was not easy for a man like Ron Kray but he did his best and soon the Mob boss appeared. He was in good humour since Bruno had spoken highly of Ron Kray. It is always good to have friends in high places.

Discussions started almost immediately. These talks covered almost every aspect of Mob business, from protection to prostitution, from drugs to murder, from stolen bearer-bonds to gambling. They discussed it all and built up a friendship of sorts. Even the Gallo brothers relaxed and gave advice to Ron Kray on setting up Murder Inc.

The next few days Ron had many meetings with Frank Ileano and 'Crazy Joe' Gallo, all over New York, so there was even sightseeing included. Things were going well, until Frank Ileano sprung a bit of a surprise on Ron Kray

'You are being followed by the FBI,' he told Ron Kray. Ron just couldn't believe it but he knew that the Mob had their way of knowing things. But why would they be following Ron, he had only just arrived in the country? Frank Ileano had read his mind. 'They must have had a tip-off,' he said quietly.

Dickie Morgan had said previously to Ron that he thought they were being followed, but Ron didn't want to believe him. Now he knew it to be true. But the Gallos had arranged the meetings in secret, throwing off the FBI tail so Ron could meet with Frank Ileano in the peace and quiet of New York's Little Italy. He enjoyed the food and the chat, everything was just fine.

Ron Kray and Dickie Morgan had lunch with Rocky Graziano and Tony Zale in Greenwich Village and they both

ABOVE: Ron and Reg Kray fighting each other. Their mother put a stop to that, and soon they were fighting the world
RIGHT: Reg in the ring at the Double R Club in 1957

ABOVE: Reg and Ron with their mother Violet
BELOW: The three together (*left to right*): Reg, Charlie and Ron

Ron with Terry Spinks and Sonny Liston (*above*) and
Joe Louis (*below*) – 'His hands were big, his feet were big,
everything was big'

ABOVE: Ron with showbiz pals Barbara
Windsor, George Sewell and James Booth
TOP LEFT: Lord Boothby, Ron Kray and Leslie
Holt (the man who set up the meeting at
Boothby's London flat)
BOTTOM LEFT: Lord Boothby and Ron Kray at
the start of the 'Case of the Brighton Peer'

ABOVE: Judy Garland visits her friends Reg and Ron in London during the swinging '60s

TOP LEFT: All three Kray brothers with Rocky Marciano and their Mafia connection, George Raft

BOTTOM LEFT: Ron with 'good friend', singer Johnnie Ray

ABOVE: Charlie Kray with his parents. The David Bailey photograph of all three brothers is on the wall in the background
LEFT: Reg and his wife Frances

appreciated the company of these boxing champions. They met other friends and associates the Krays had done business with back in London but they couldn't get to meet Meyer Lansky. Lansky didn't want to be seen in the company of Ron Kray since he knew all about the FBI. But he did pass on his best wishes through Joe Kaufman. Tony 'Ducks' Corallo also had to bow out for the same reason. Ron Kray was just too hot to handle, not unlike his times in the East End of London.

Cooper was still a scarce commodity, always proclaiming that he was working on his contacts but continually with the same result. 'He's stuttering more and more,' said Dickie Morgan. 'What's he got to be nervous about?'

But Ron had already been successful in his own eyes. He had met with a top Mob boss and had in-depth discussions. The rest was party time and he enjoyed it all along with his old and new pals.

The Murder Incorporated system intrigued Ron Kray. He learned all about *Omerta*, the Mafia's code of silence, and about the idea of putting as many people as possible between yourself and where the action was to take place. This would mean giving verbal orders to one associate, who would then pass them on to another and so on, *ad infinitum*. This is the buffer system used by the Mob to distance themselves from events such as killings. But Ron Kray was always a hands-on kind of person – he loved getting his hands on a knife, a sword, a gun, a machine gun and the like. It was difficult for him to understand how he could build up respect if he worked the Mafia way. It worked for the Americans but could it work in London?

One evening Ron phoned his brother Reg back in England. He told him of the meetings with the Colombo family and about drinking with old pals, he left nothing out. Reg was pleased for his brother, but then asked about A.B. Cooper. Ron told him straight that he hadn't seen much of Cooper but that it didn't matter since he had achieved so much in such a short time. He had beaten everyone, even the system, he told him.

'That reminds me,' said Reg. 'Nipper's looking all over for

you.' He was referring to Nipper Read of Scotland Yard who was working overtime back in the UK trying to collect evidence against the Krays. It was unusual that Ron Kray had been out of the news, so Read was getting anxious. Ron, however, was delighted.

The *pièce de résistance* was the news that Kaufman had managed to do a deal on more bearer-bonds. So the lucrative bond business could be started up straight away. This was indeed good news for Reg; it made the whole affair worth while.

The rest of the time passed with partying and sightseeing with the Mob. Ron Kray had truly achieved everything he had set out to do but without the help of A.B. Cooper. Ron was beginning to have serious doubts about the man who had worked the visa deal so sweetly. Could there be another reason behind these events and if so, what? His only regret was not being able to meet with Lansky.

Back home in the UK Ron Kray was treated like a king in the East End. It was party-time all over again for the returning hero. But once again Cooper did his vanishing trick and made like a tree – he went straight on to Paris. Reg wasn't surprised. In fact he was pleased, since he didn't really want the man around. Cooper had a knack of spoiling Reg Kray's fun.

Shortly after Ron returned to London the Krays were all arrested. On 9 May 1968 Nipper Read sprang his trap and caught them all, but he didn't have all the proof he needed until much later. But with the twins behind bars the rats started to leave the ship; they sang one by one.

The Krays never had a chance of putting Murder Inc. into practice and they never received any more of the bearer-bonds from the Mob. Kaufman did come over to the UK with $25,000 of stolen bearer-bonds for delivery to Cooper but he was arrested with them on him, so no new deals went through. The twins, however, never knew about the bonds, it was supposed to be a secret deal for the banker.

There has been much discussion about the exact nature of A.B. Cooper's involvement. At the trial he admitted that he was working for the FBI and he certainly did pass on information to Du Rose, Read's boss at Scotland Yard. But he also contrived to kill people and it was only due to the stupidity of some of the chosen assassins that he was never accused of murder. In fact the visa office at the US Embassy turned out to be the head office for the FBI, European Division, so no wonder there was no sign on the door.

The Krays came so close to setting up a Mafia-style operation in the UK, but in the end it was their own code that let them down. They wanted the world to see them as untouchables, kings of crime, but it was Nipper Read who delivered the winning punch and knocked them out cold for 30 years.

Read's was an outrageous gamble but it paid off. With the Krays behind bars people started talking and soon Scotland Yard had enough on the twins to put them away. There would be no more trips to the USA for the Kray twins, no more visits by Mob gangsters to see their pals the Krays in the UK, there would be no more bearer-bonds to launder for the Mob – or would there?

'If you need help in New York,' Reg told me recently, 'I'll put you in contact with an old pal of mine, Don King.' The real connection between King and the Krays is probably historical and based on boxing, but as Mike Tyson's manager (or is that ex-manager?), King is pure 'wise guy'. So even behind bars the Krays have had their admirers and pals within the Mob.

Joe Pagano, a particular friend of the Krays, was a top hit-man for the Genovese family, one of the biggest Mob families ever; the twins were very sad when he died some years ago. They said publicly that they had lost a true friend.

In the end the Krays will only be known as home-grown British gangsters, but they came so close to being mobsters on the big scale, with business operations on both sides of the Atlantic. With only a little more care and attention to detail they could have made it. As it happened they had to do their own killing (or at least some of it) and so they became victims of their own sense of foolish pride. No one has come close to emulating the Krays; perhaps no one ever will.

6. TWINS

One in every 50 people in the UK is a twin and approximately one-third of these are identical twins. Society presupposes that twins are special since it is a natural phenomenon. We know it occurs in humans as it does in animals but we do not understand why. That makes it special. The Kray twins therefore by definition were special, just as their mother Violet always maintained. The problem with the Krays, however, is that one of the twins, Ron Kray, was a paranoid schizophrenic and a homosexual, which distorts all the academic research and brings us right back to basics. So what are twins?

Our knowledge of identical twins is very sparse. Because there aren't many twins: available for research purposes, even though some recent television programmes have suggested otherwise, this tends to make investigation difficult if not impossible. How can a researcher or investigator get a statistically viable sample to work with to enable substantial evaluation of results?

Generally, the only matter scientists can agree on is the origin of twins: how cells divide to form two identical individuals (in outward appearance anyway). But still they don't know why. Instantly we have a problem. We see a pair of twins, as in the case of Ron and Reg Kray, but they are two different people. They look the same, they behave the same and society tends to treat them the same. But twins are individuals!

History has treated twins in many varied and interesting ways. Sometimes they have been regarded as cherished individuals, sometimes hated. They have been considered as godly apparitions, but also as the personification of evil. They have been killed and discarded and they have been worshipped and pampered. The world of twins can sometimes be a dangerous world indeed.

There are stories of Castor and Pollux, and Romulus and Remus from Roman history, and even great writers such as Shakespeare have examined some of the myths surrounding twins, for example in *Twelfth Night* and in *The Comedy of Errors*. Plautus used the mystery and secrecy of twins in *The Menaechmi* and *Amphitryon*. And in more recent years Dumas exploited their mystique in *The Man in the Iron Mask* and Patrick White in *The Solid Mandala*. Even Bruce Chatwin wrote about a pair of farming twins in his Welsh story *On the Black Hill*. So why are we so interested in twins? To understand we must start at the beginning, by defining what twins are from a scientific viewpoint and that means looking at the egg.

When the cell divides and becomes two individual new cells the result is mono-zygotic twins. These are so-called identical twins as if they were cloned. Ron and Reg Kray, especially in earlier years before Ron's illness changed his features, were typical mono-zygotic twins. Often one is right-handed and one left-handed. One may be quiet and unassuming, the subordinate twin, the other the leader who makes up all the rules. It is not necessarily the elder twin who becomes the dominant of the two; in the case of Ron and Reg Kray it was the younger, Ron, who was the stronger willed of the two and dominated both early childhood and later adolescence.

When the cell splits into two like cells the genes are also divided, so each is a real copy of the other. The main difference is that chromosomes do not split – they simply go with one or other gene and that is why twins have different personality profiles. This cannot be seen from the outside, in the way of facial features, bone structure and such, but can be witnessed in behavioural patterns and mental ability. Reg Kray was the organiser of the two, who liked everything in its place; logical and orderly. Ron Kray, however, was the dreamer who looked at each day as a chance for fame and fortune; the adventurer. But in Ron's case this was also accentuated by the fact that he was afflicted with schizophrenia. It was only later when paranoia also set in that his condition caused the whole family and the Firm much discomfort, since he became uncontrollable. His brother Reg, the control freak, could not control him. Not being able to go against his brother, he made the only decision that was possible for him – he joined him in his madness.

Science cannot tell us much about the illness that confronted Ron Kray as far as his twin behaviour was concerned. His fits of extreme jubilation and deep depression do not reflect his twin-ness. He was a sick man and his brothers did all they could to protect him. Personally I found Ron Kray to be a very charming man who could tell a good story with wit and guile; a man who knew he would never be free, even though he loved to talk about all the travelling he would do when he got out of Broadmoor. He was a true gent in the best East End traditions. He was also a mean thug who killed at least one man in his time, but history will probably forgive him his transgressions and put it all down to paranoid schizophrenia, which so surely was the case. His story is a twin story, of goodness and badness, and of his own twin's efforts to help, no matter what!

When I first went to visit Ron Kray in Broadmoor in 1992 I was a little reticent. I had heard all the stories about the twins and I was about to meet the mad one of the two. Charlie Kray had arranged the meeting where I was to talk to Ron about a possible future film on the Krays. The previous film released in 1989 and called *The Krays* had been a success and the twins were looking for more money, so I was called in to provide a plot.

The trip to Broadmoor was just like any other trip to Broadmoor, an area I knew well because I have family who live near by. I hated the drive but I had promised to make the trip so I felt obliged to keep the appointment. And that is what it was, an appointment to meet the most notorious gangster in the country.

Through the front office, through the maze of locked doors

conveniently opened for me by one of their over-sized guards, along the paths and through more doors and I was there in the meeting hall. It was not a nice place, a little old and shabby for my liking, but the pleasantness of the staff made up for all of that. Over at a table, along with some hospital friends and his wife Kate, sat Ron Kray. I approached the table and Ron stood up to greet me.

'Nice to meet you,' he said slowly and kindly, as though he really meant it. And then he stared right through me with those intense deep-set eyes of his as he reached out his hand in friendship. I had been warned about those eyes and I had been warned about that fierce handshake, so I was almost prepared for what was to happen.

We shook hands vigorously and I said hello. 'I have heard a lot about you,' I said confidently, staring into his eyes. Strangely I felt immediately at ease with the man, no sign of nerves or doubt. 'By the way,' I said. 'I am also a twin.' That was it. I had obviously said the right thing.

'I knew it,' said Ron Kray. 'I knew we'd get on all right when I saw you at the door.' He continued to shake my fragile hand with what looked like the utmost of pleasure and I am able to confirm here and now that indeed, when he found it useful, Ron Kray had one of the strongest and most overpowering handshakes that I have ever experienced. And I consider myself no slouch when it comes to having a strong grip.

I was relieved. The journey to Broadmoor was worth while after all. But then I knew we'd get on. That 'twin thing' is like a magnet, it draws people together; only twins can really understand twins.

'Sit down,' he said, smiling a wry smile. 'What do you want to know?' That was it. The ice was broken and we spoke like long-lost friends, trying to make up for lost time. We each recounted stories only twins can tell, of mistaken identity and jokes played on the unsuspecting. Ron was very articulate and funny with it; he could certainly tell an amusing tale.

We were now ready to begin serious discussions and I was keen to get into some of the twin stories in a more detailed and absorbing manner. My first choice was obviously a good starter. 'Tell me about the escape from Long Grove,' I asked. I had already heard about it from Charlie but I needed the inside story if I was to use it for publication purposes or a film.

Ron looked at me with delight written all over his face – he was enjoying every minute. His eyes sparkled as he began to explain about the experience. 'It was all Reggie's idea. He told me about it some weeks before when he came to see me and I was ready,' he replied, all keyed up and ready to go. 'I wore a blue suit and waited for him in the visitors' room, where we could talk and have a cup of tea.' The plan was indeed simple: Reg would walk into the room, put his overcoat on a chair and then sit down with Ron, who would have a photo album with him which they would look at and laugh about, just like any other visiting day. Ron would then pick up the overcoat brought in by Reg and leave his spectacles on the table before asking to be let through to the main corridor outside the secure area on the pretext of getting the tea. Ron would simply take on the identity of his twin brother Reg. Reg would put on Ron's spectacles and Ron would continue walking through the long corridors of Long Grove Asylum and to freedom. It was a plan that only twins could devise, using their uncanny similarity to great effect.

In June of 1958 Ron Kray had had enough of life in Long Grove Asylum. He had been treated kindly by the doctors but not by the other patients. 'They're all mad in here,' he told his brother Reg. He wanted out and that meant using the six-week rule that was law at the time. This stated that if a patient was to escape and could stay at large for more than six weeks without committing any crime, then on recapture he would be sent back to the prison where he had been serving his sentence to serve out the remaining period of that sentence. In Ron's case a stretch of 12 months. At least then Ron would have a time for release from his incarceration whereas in the hospital he could be held there indefinitely.

Reg and an old friend by the name of Georgie Osbourne drove to the hospital on the busiest Sunday of the year. This was no coincidence, since Reg had as usual done his homework well. They left the Lincoln by the gatekeeper's cottage, in full view of anyone at the gate, and proceeded to walk into the grounds and along the path leading to the main doors of Long Grove. No one realised that there was another car, a Ford, parked near by but out of view of security at the gate, where three men sat patiently for the return of their favourite patient. These men were Billy Nash, Bernie King and Mick 'The Hammer', and they were all old friends of Ron Kray's.

The twins greeted each other in the visitors room as planned. They were both wearing identical blue suits as planned. And they began the charade of studying the photo album as planned. It was so far working out well for the twins. Ron put his glasses down onto the table, with Reg picking them up and putting them on in a very casual manner. There was no rush, no haste, no panic. Ron rose from his chair when the security people had their backs turned and picked up the coat. 'I want to go and get some teas now,' he said as he neared the only door to the room. 'Can you unlock the door for me?' he asked confidently. A man looked at him from outside the room. Through the glass in the door he looked like one of their regular visitors so there were no problems. He had seen the man before and he always went to get the teas. Ron was let through into the corridor as Reg sat with Georgie Osbourne and laughed and joked about the photos in the album. They were also joking about the success, so far, of the cunning plan to free his twin brother.

'What did it feel like to be free again?' I asked Ron, trying not to get too caught up in the euphoria of the moment. Ron had confirmed everything that Charlie had previously told me, and more, so the story was really taking shape in tremendous detail.

'It was incredible,' he told me. 'I had a long, long walk down the gravel drive to the main gate. I thought it would never end. And I was getting so hot in that bloody overcoat, but it was all part of changing places, so I had to put up with it. There were people all around the gardens but nobody noticed me. I walked out through the big gates and found my friends sitting in a car waiting for me.' He was smiling. It appeared somewhat strange to see Ron Kray smiling since I had already heard so many tales of his vicious character and of the terror he induced in people. But here was a man enjoying himself by telling a story of the old days and how he enjoyed it.

Reg and Georgie Osbourne stayed on until somebody realised that a switch had taken place, but they couldn't hold him since he was not a patient at the hospital. Reg and his pal walked back along that same gravel driveway to their car and drove off as though they were just off on a Sunday's drive in the country. The plan had worked in every detail – the only problem now was to keep Ron in hiding until the six weeks were up.

At first Ron was kept in a caravan in the Suffolk countryside but he didn't like it too much. It was just like being in prison. So he persuaded Reg to let him come to London. This was not a problem since they had numerous good hiding places and friends who would help to conceal Ron, so there shouldn't have been any difficulties. But there was one problem that no one had thought of; Ron was an ill man and he needed medicine.

While Ron continued to take the tablets prescribed at Long Grove he didn't have bouts of depression and was easy to handle, but six weeks was a long time and the pills in his possession would not last that long. Reg had to do some hard thinking and so too Charlie. They even thought of getting their own medical opinion and taking Ron to see a specialist. But before the pills ran out Ron managed his own twin trick. 'How did you do that?' I asked him.

'I just walked into the pub, sat in a chair normally reserved for Reg and ordered his favourite drink. Everyone thought I was him,' he joked. He really did enjoy these twin tales. 'Someone even asked me how Ron was doing. So I told him that Ron was doing fine. I didn't tell the man that he was talking to him.' Again he laughed about his reminiscences. These were the good old days and that was all he had left, his memories.

Other tales followed of how they used to use each other's driving licences. For example, if Reg was on the run from the police or wanted for questioning he would take Ron's driving licence with him to prove he was Ron. Ron did the same when it suited him. They could swap places with ease, something that came in handy when it came to alibis. But Ron's story of Long Grove was not finished yet.

When the tablets ran out Reg and Charlie got their second opinion and the doctor diagnosed paranoid schizophrenia, something that needed urgent attention and constant medication. But fortunately for Ron the six weeks were up and when he returned voluntarily to Long Grove they sent him straight back to prison to serve out his time. So the plan had worked well, they had cheated the system and soon Ron would be a free man. Being a twin certainly did have its advantages for Ron and Reg Kray.

Through those sessions with Ron at Broadmoor I came to learn much about the way being a twin affected both their lives. They were competitive, each trying to outdo the other, whether it was boxing or business. At one time Ron even asked for protection money from a club that was part-owned by Reg, one that he had taken on while Ron was inside. This was not the attitude of a compliant twin. Ron was aggressive by nature but he knew instinctively that his twin would always stand by him in a fight or a court of law – it made no difference to the Kray twins. Their brother Charlie could never come between them and he never tried, he knew better.

Ron and Reg Kray were then and even now after Ron's death always will be twins. The memory lives on of those 'terrible twins' who dominated the underworld in the '50s and '60s, and I am sure their stories will be told for many more years to come.

The phenomenon known as twins consists of both mono-zygotic (identical) twins and di-zygotic (fraternal) twins. The Krays were mono-zygotic, as previously stated, and the behavioural patterns of such twins has been researched and studies undertaken at the Institute of Psychiatry in London. The Institute began a few years ago to study the development of twins through their twin register but results are inconclusive since the research started only recently with infant twins and not with adult twins who could relate and recall real-life incidents. Time alone will tell if this research is of any use or whether they have missed the boat. After all, twins have been used for research purposes for many years, including by the evil Dr Mengele.

Back in the time of the Third Reich Dr Mengele took twins from a variety of ethnic backgrounds and performed experiments on them to determine the effects of gas, poison, injections of toxic substances and so on. The vast majority of these twins were of Jewish origin. The Krays also had a Jewish background although they were influenced by gypsy and other ethnic stock. They were lucky that they were born in the UK and not in mainland Europe.

Mengele would take one twin and inject a poison and use the other twin as control for the experiment. He would then cut up both and see the results. Since he reckoned that the insides of the twins would be the same, he thought he could determine the success of the drug. This was a very crude experiment but thousands of twins had to suffer in this way. And all in the name of science.

This leads us on to a tricky topic, that of cloning. This has been performed recently in the UK, for example Dolly the sheep. Scientists can perform these experiments on a daily basis and the results will be the same time and time again. It is now possible to clone sheep so when will we be able to clone people? Twins are the nearest we can get to clones but they are not pure reproductions, since all the tests show that two individual twins have two different psychological profiles. These profiles can be distorted, however, if one or the other has an illness such as schizophrenia and that is the problem with the case of the Krays. Ron was a paranoid schizophrenic and so out of control with regard to the rules. But then he never paid any attention to the rules.

Research is being carried out all over the country on sets of mono-zygotic (identical) twins to try to determine the depth of such human characteristics as telepathy, extra-sensory perception (ESP), language abnormalities (for example, in the case of the so-called 'silent twins'), thought patterns and processes and many, many more topics of interest, especially in the field of medicine. So cloning itself is only one area of twin study and this has been developed mainly in the field of genetic engineering, where doctors and scientists are now able to clone to order, so that identical embryos can be produced for fertility treatment. This could mean that one embryo is used initially, so one or more could be kept in cold storage for use later. This would then produce a family of identical children. The question is really whether or not this is justifiable morally and scientifically and many fear misuse of knowledge in genetics.

Dr Jerry Hall of the George Washington Medical Center is just one scientist experimenting in genetics and cloning. He splits the egg to produce exact copies of embryos which are used in laboratory conditions for implantation, retaining one or more embryo in case they are needed later. If, for example, the child dies, then a new child with exactly the same looks can be born to the same mother, an exact replacement. It is a dangerous game and many fear the knowledge gained in this way. It can so very easily be misused, as in the case of Dr Mengele's experiments.

Other scientists fear this experimentation and talk openly of 'family farming'. 'The public feels uncomfortable with meddling in the life-producing process,' warns Dr David Meldrum, of California's Center for Advanced Reproduction. 'They will see this as one more step along a slippery slope.'

So nature supplies us with natural twins whereas science produces clones in a more unnatural way. But here we are dealing with 'what you see is what you get' and this is only the outward appearance. We are still left with the internal problems of twins such as schizophrenia and other mental disorders where the chromosomes have been infected or mutated for one reason or another. If science produces clones with mental disorders maybe the world will turn away from this method of scientific research. Only time will tell.

Dr Susan Blackmore at the University of the West of England in Bristol has researched twins for some time with regard to telepathy. But again the results are inconclusive. However, any twin can relate stories of telepathy; this is not uncommon. Even in the case of the Kray twins there are incidents where Ron and Reg were in contact mentally if not physically. These cases are generally put down to having the same genes, and gene research appears to be telling us that our physical and behavioural attributes are determined by these genes alone. Culture and social class, it would appear, have very little to do with our development. If this is the case then the development of twins cannot be changed, even if the two are kept apart for a long time. In the case of the Krays then, Reg could not have changed Ron's way of being even if he wanted to. It is all decided by our genes even before we are born. Dangerous ground indeed since it means that Reg would have killed anyway and didn't need the encouragement of his brother. There will be no one else to blame since our genes predetermine our characters.

Violet always talked of the telepathy between her boys; even their letters revealed similar thoughts and thought patterns. 'If I got a letter from Ron, then I would soon be getting a letter from Reg full of almost identical plans and points of view,' she would say. 'It was uncanny, but they always said the same.' Any twin will understand this since it occurs almost randomly throughout their lives.

The telepathic sympathy between twins is something that we hear about on a regular basis but proof is difficult to establish. Dr Blackmore has not been able to show telepathy between twins although she is aware of all the stories. But these stories cannot be verified although for twins themselves this is not necessary. I myself have such a twin story, one of telepathic thought travelling long distances to reveal the mental and sometimes physical state of the other twin. My story goes as follows: when I was living in Copenhagen, in Denmark, back in the early '70s, I had a terrible night tossing and turning in my bed which resulted in me breaking out in a cold sweat. Before anyone says that I must have been enjoying myself with female company let me explain the reason for my difficulties. I was having a nightmare concerning my brother.

He was in pain and I couldn't help. I felt helpless and hapless. It was awesome. When I woke in the morning I immediately telephoned my brother in Salisbury to tell him of my experience, since I thought I was going mad. 'Are you all right?' I asked cautiously, not wanting to appear a right prat and silly with it. He then, without any prompting, went on to explain about the treatment he had only had the previous day to extract a wisdom tooth, treatment that had left him in terrible pain. 'It was the worst night's sleep I have ever had,' he told me. At last I could breathe a deep sigh of relief. I wasn't going mad after all.

Language is an often quoted topic when discussing the phenomenon of twins. Most twins appear to have their own special way of communicating with each other and the Krays were no exception to this rule. The twins only had to give a certain look for the other to realise what they were thinking. Reg and Ron understood their own sign language and their own body language, something that is only really now beginning to be understood, especially in the field of business. The Firm always talked of their lack of visible communication – it wasn't necessary to talk to each other since they instinctively understood the other's thinking processes. This is something that accentuates the difference between twins and ordinary people.

Others can't understand it and so it becomes something to fear. The Krays used this to their advantage on more than one occasion, such as the fight with the dockers in a pub on the Mile End Road. Everyone in The Regal knew that the twins were going to meet the dockers but Ron and Reg never talked about it. They seemed to know what was going to happen and didn't need to openly communicate with one another. When the time came for the meeting they simply put down their cups of tea, straightened their ties and walked out of the billiard hall. Not a word was spoken. Even when the time came to fight, they didn't need a coded message or sign; they knew it was the right time and that the other would join in immediately. They beat off the dockers using fists not words and walked home to see their pals at The Regal. Silence, it would appear, is a language of communication between twins.

But are the genes to blame? Or is it just that twins have already found a friend even before they are born? They have nine months together in the womb to establish firm relationships and not even a mother can break that bond. They can't talk to each other during this period so they must develop some other way of communication. Call it instinct or call it telepathy, the difference is the same. Twins are hard to deal with because of this sixth sense. Two people who look the same and don't need to talk to each other to understand how the other feels pose a bit of a quandary. It isn't only the sight of two identical people that threatens; it is also the lack of communication that exposes witnesses to the paranormal. It all makes 'outsiders' fearful and the Krays were indeed feared by everyone.

Probably the most interesting research in twins that could considerably help us today is the work done in the USA at the National Institute of Health in Washington by Dr H. Clifford Lane. Here he has chosen twins with an unusual characteristic, one is heterosexual and healthy whereas the other one is gay and HIV positive. He has been studying 12 sets of twins, all taking part in this pioneering hospital project. Because their genes are identical, doctors hope to cure the sick twin through replacement treatment. The HIV-positive twin is bombarded with billions of healthy cells taken from his mono-zygotic counterpart. 'We are optimistic that this could lead to a positive advance in the fight against AIDS,' he has repeatedly said. Research is not yet finished but so far so good. So there may yet be a cure for AIDS, all through the study of twins.

The strange fact that makes the above research possible is the coincidence that there are at least 12 sets of twins in the USA that fit the bill for the research programme. So is it then normal for one twin to be heterosexual and one homosexual? The simple answer is that we don't know. And then again what is normal? There could be so-called normal heterosexual twins just as easily as twins where both are gay. There are no research details that would conclude anything of this nature. The only conclusion is that the similarity between twins is all in the genes – it is nature and not nurture.

Ron Kray being a homosexual created a curious picture. He was both macho and gay, both a twin and a separate individual, both a crook and a philanthropist, both generous and greedy. The study of Ron Kray is an extensive look at both background and history, whereas Reg Kray would appear to present a more normal picture of your everyday male. Whether or not these contradictions also apply to him is pure speculation. But twin research shows that the genes are there and it seems that nothing we twins can do will change the nature of our make-up. Twins are tied to each other by an invisible bond, one that will always take the strain of the ups and downs of such a close relationship and one that will always be there, even in death.

Medical faculties all over the world are studying physical and mental similarities between mono-zygotic twins to try to determine whether or not these twins have the same weaknesses, the same strengths, the same disorders. It is also important and interesting to note that even in death Ron Kray was a tool for such study – his brain was removed before he was buried and taken away for research purposes to Cambridge University. The problem here was, however, that no one saw fit to tell the Kray family and that is a diabolical and disgusting thing to do. So the authorities let Reg Kray bury his twin brother not knowing that Ron's brain was missing. When the brain eventually turned up Reg had to have the coffin dug up and the brain put inside, once again reunited with its owner.

Meanwhile the research also continues at the Minnesota Center of Twin and Adoption Research in the USA. Professor Thomas J. Bouchard has for many years carried out research using twins that were separated at birth. Here he has proved once and for all that nature beats nurture every time. The genes would appear to have the upper hand in all statistics and no matter what the social background of the families that the twins enter, however dissimilar, the twins develop in an almost identical way. This would tend to indicate that no matter what the sexual preference of the twins or illness that one of them may have, their pattern of life is determined even before birth through their genes. So, in a way, it was quite inevitable that Reg should kill someone after his twin had killed George Cornell. So Jack 'The Hat' McVitie was just in the wrong place at the wrong time. Destiny took control.

The Krays were never, to their knowledge, involved in any academic or medical research other than being scrutinised in various recent papers and books by sociologists such as Professor Chris Jenks and Dr Dick Hobbs. But maybe Violet Kray could have benefited from the knowledge gained since 1978 by the twin organisation here in the UK, known as the Twins and Multiple Births Association. TAMBA helps parents to understand the needs of twins, especially in infancy. The peculiar fact is that all the twin books available concern themselves only with infants; there is no guide to twins in adolescence. I for one would like to see this undertaken immediately. Maybe then we would begin to understand how the Krays, through their twin-ness, came to dominate crime in the UK. There were other brothers in crime, whole families even, but no twins – until the Krays.

Dr Hobbs suggests that 'when issues emerged from beyond the parameters of these concerns, then offences were committed that the police could no longer ignore'. The concerns in focus were trouble, toughness, smartness, excitement and autonomy and when the Krays altered these boundaries because of Ron's homosexuality and mental illness the police had to arrest them both. But the study of twins tells us that genes and genes alone are the decisive factor in the development of twins and that illness and sexuality play only a minor part. It does, however, appear almost certain that if Frances, Reg's wife, had not succeeded in her third attempt at suicide, then Reg would have been able to stop his brother from totally dominating his life. It wasn't only the actions of the twins, therefore, that changed their lives; it was also the actions of all the main protagonists, including their own immediate family.

'The symbolic core of the Kray enticement, and clearly

central to their own sense of identity, purpose and belonging, is their very "twin-ness". This birthright multiplied by the privations of working-class, 1930s, East End life rendered their survival and maturation into adulthood if not remarkable then at least not commonplace,' says Professor Chris Jenks. So also in a sociological sense, this twin 'thing' was at the heart of the twins' success – and downfall. He continues by saying that 'the personality development and public persona(e) of twins is very different to that of non-twins. Infant twins charm and attract attention of other mothers in the street . . .' as in the case of their mother Violet when she was out walking the twins in their pram. 'They create a halo through the synergy of their needs, demands and delights; they fascinate others through the verisimilitude of their hairstyle, their eyes and their matching outfits – they both mirror and contain like facing bookends. Their significance is simultaneously ancient and modern,' Jenks says. Again we have the paradox of complexities that is twins, so how can they be expected to grow up to feel like any other normal human being? The fact is that they don't and they can't be expected to be like any so-called normal person. They are indeed special and they will always remain that way.

Some twins would like to be like any other ordinary man or woman, while others accept their similarity such as in the case of the film *City Slickers 2*, where Jack Palance, who plays Duke, looks in the mirror every morning to see the face of his twin brother Curly, who died in the first *City Slickers* film, so he is with his twin even after death. I wonder if Reg Kray has the same experience when he shaves every morning? Any twin will know what I mean.

'These same traits,' says Professor Jenks, 'in adult twins are appealing, but not in the same ways. They can arouse the vicarious appeal of a "freak show", people sharing physical features, mannerisms, and wearing the same clothes – these are all transgressive and thus threatening images stalked by the conceptual menace of clones, cyborgs and replicants.' These trends and traits are present throughout the lives of the Kray twins, where their later lives were virtually dominated by power in the form of violence and the fear of violence. The following, taken from *The Kray Fascination* sums up the complexities and confusion of identity that twins alone must carry with them throughout their lives:

> In adulthood the identicality generates a confusion between the natural and the intentional, the compulsive and the wilful. The tension contained in this confusion both conceals and discloses a monstrous power that is experienced externally but sourced wholly within the dyad. The ultimate and particular power exercised by twins is that of exclusion, the symbolic rebuff that is generated by 'oneness' manifested in the cryptophasia [private language] identical twins often assume; a community of inner sanctum that defies all and any other membership.

Reg Kray summed this all up with the wreath to his brother laid on the grave at the cemetery in Essex. It said simply: 'To the other half of me.' He even placed a painting of himself and his brother on the grave to symbolise their oneness and constant companionship. Unfortunately the souvenir hunters do not respect any man's private wishes and feelings of sadness in bereavement: as soon as the gathering was dismissed at the graveside, they swooped and stole the painting laid there with such precision and sense of loss by Reg Kray himself. He had been allowed out of prison for the funeral but he was not allowed to see his twin when the illness took hold. He had pleaded with the authorities to let him visit his sick twin brother in the hospital at Ascot, but permission was refused. Ron's dying thoughts would have been with Reg; it is such a pity that the two couldn't have been together at the end. Alone now for the first time, Reg was left in his prison cell to grieve alone, to remember the good times and the bad, to reflect on the past and the possible future, and to think about burying his twin brother Ron.

Chris Jenks also notes that:

A further intimidation that is presented to the collective by the experience of twinning is the threat of loss or abandonment of identity and purpose. The real secret of twins which holds our imagination is their fusion of free will and the tacit disregard for the achievement that is our individual difference. We may struggle to constitute our own characters through experience but the very oneness of twins is utterly dismissive of that struggle.

True, there is a dual feeling of common purpose within the two individuals that tends to make them very supportive of each other. And this can be both helpful and advantageous. When I need to talk or think or reflect, for example, my brother is there to advise and the discussions can be deep and intense. There is no room for anyone else in these discussions or arguments or disagreements, no 'outsiders' are allowed. But ultimately we will make our own final decisions and these can be varied indeed. There is no need for a common purpose or a similar way of doing or achieving things. We each have our own way and often take choices at different ends of the spectrum. But this only brings us closer together, since we realise the individuality of the other. It unites with a common singularity of purpose and diversifies with the assistance and acceptance of the other half, and both polarise simultaneously. Another paradox.

The twin-ness alone cannot constitute a basis for their existence, but it complements the emergence of the Krays as a feared duet within their own particular society. Their social and geographical detail helped to form their mindsets, and this together with their appearance in the timescale of things, in the 1930s, provided the background for their dominance within the criminal fraternity.

Complementarity was itself complemented with opposite polarity, providing contradictions to the norm. As stated earlier, Reg was generally dominated by Ron, but Ron was the younger of the two. As boxers it was Reg who dominated with his stylish and effective boxing, compared with Ron's rough and tough tumbles in the ring, which reflected his street fighter image. Reg was a businessman first and foremost. He would have liked to have continued to drive his Mercedes to the West End as he did back in the '60s; he was even planning on an office in a plush part of London, just like the Richardsons. His perspective was wide and he had a clear vision of the future within the world of glamour, business and sport. But Ron was the psychotic who could not leave his brother alone. Ron wanted to win at all costs and he never gave in to sound common sense. Even as a child he thrived on his tantrums and this, for him, became a way of life. This was his control mechanism and guns and swords became an extension of that control. To him it was like a fix by which he could maintain control over people and events. These unconscious thoughts from his early days came to dominate Ron Kray as they did his brother Reg. Ron, and Ron alone, made the decisions that mattered and those decisions were to haunt him to the grave. They still haunt his twin brother Reg.

> Their seeming capacity for parthenogenesis enabled an almost seamless tapestry to emerge comprised of contradictory, pathetic and incommensurable images. The 'many' Krays were irreconcilable to the Twins themselves and to their burgeoning public. They became gentleman/thug, philanthropist/extortionist, respectable/low-life, calculating/unpredictable, kind/ brutish.

These words from Professor Chris Jenks sum up the thoughts that I myself have had through the years regarding the Krays. There are too many contradictions in their lives, too many similarities and too many paradoxes for anyone other than the Krays. Theirs was a special life and the story still continues. Theirs was a metamorphosis into image and they lived through image. Today we understand the idea of 'celebrity', through film, music, television and so on, but back in the '30s, '40s and '50s this was still an almost unknown phenomenon, apart from the American films that so greatly influenced the twins themselves. But the Krays changed all of that. They became twins of mythical proportions and lived their lives through a sense of mythology which made icons out of killers.

7. MYTH OR MYTHOLOGY

Recent events, such as the death of Diana, Princess of Wales and the trial of Louise Woodward in Boston in the USA, have brought about an intense debate regarding the media and the reporting by the media of these tragic incidents.

The words 'synthetic media attraction' have been used frequently in this debate, suggesting that there has been an over-exploitation by the media solely for the purposes of making money out of it. The televising of trials and such, even parliamentary proceedings, alters the perceived nature of justice; emotion takes over from reason. Sentiment is the key, with enthusiasm whipped up by the press and television alike.

These tragic affairs attract sympathy. People become emotionally involved and a feeling of solidarity takes over – we allow our prejudices for the one side of the debate to dominate. So is this a legitimate human response or just tasteless drivel with little or no regard for the truth?

Now with 30 years in jail, Reg Kray comes in for a similar scrutiny. Why, people ask, should he still be behind bars when others who have committed much more serious offences (in the eyes of the general public, at least) are already free after much lesser sentences? Have we become sympathetic towards Reg Kray, with the apparent loss of memory regarding the violent offences he undoubtedly committed?

To many Reg Kray has become a kind of Robin Hood figure – an icon. He carries on his charitable work from inside prison and contributes regular articles to the media, provoking even further discussion. Colleges have named societies after the Krays, football teams have asked for Reg to be their manager. So have we forgotten the truth, in favour of exploi-ted emotions? And if these emotions have taken over completely, how do we consider today the rough justice performed by Justice Melford Stevenson when giving Ron and Reg Kray at least 30 years each in jail?

Does human virtue then rest on emotion? And, if so, is it right that the media should have such a great part to play in our perception of justice? People are after all vulnerable and no one lives in isolation. But the law should be seen to be just, without emotion entering the fray. The cold and merciless system of justice, therefore, is tempered by human emotion. But in the case of the Kray trial, did this factor work against the Krays and not for them?

Certainly in recent years there has been much controversy surrounding the Krays. We have been inundated with books (sorry, here is another one) and with films and gossip, so has society changed through this revolution within the media? Are we becoming more compassionate with a higher regard towards feelings and emotion as a balance to the cold heart of the law? Is this the reason why we appear to remember the positive sides of the Kray experience, although there do not appear to be many of these at all? Or is it simply that Reg Kray has been so long in jail that the majority of the country, and certainly those of the younger generation who were not even born at the time of the trial, have forgotten the events of the '50s and '60s? But does forgetting mean forgiving? This emotional tug of war continues.

So, is it all a media illusion? And, if so, then who is responsible for it? Do we really know or understand the Krays and should we know or feel the need to know all about Princess Diana and Louise Woodward? This apparent need to know could be considered a reaction towards the harshness of modern society with emotions taking over. Right or wrong does not matter any more – it is all about what we perceive as being right or wrong.

This emotion, however, leads us to making irrational judgements on the basis of philosophical and romantic associations. The need for empirical proof flies conveniently out of the window. The science of law requires proof but the verdict of emotions comes from within and is therefore biased.

Can we then really be manipulated by the media through mass hysteria? Does superstition become a popular culture, replacing old rational values? Certainly journalists manipulate, but then so do those who leak stories to the press. Even Ron and Reg Kray have used the press to their own advantage.

This dissatisfaction with reasoning and the leaning towards emotion and sympathy, even towards villains, cannot by definition be subjective. This is a very dangerous and difficult area of debate since we get down to one common denominator: who controls whom? The will of the people is important but it must not override the truth – this surely must be sacrosanct.

The truth is also objective. The academic élite in the universities also manipulate. But here it is mainly emotion in the form of passion that drives you on. It is the emotional search for truth that is the guiding light. There is no conflict.

Heart over head is an urge towards irrational behaviour. They are opposites. They deal with different values – the one blinded by rationality, the other blinded by emotion.

At the heart of all of this controversy is the actual justice system that we have in this country. It is one of sides – the defence against the prosecution. We learn to listen to both and then to make up our minds. But how can this not be emotional? Our judgements are made on what we perceive to be the facts and not necessarily the truth. This is part of a far wider debate and I will not delve into this subject matter. The adversarial system has throughout history caused many men and women to be sent to prison quite unjustly. Even in the case of the Krays the sentence of 30 years does appear to be unjust – some might say emotional.

Ronnie Biggs, that fugitive from justice living reasonably well in Rio de Janeiro in Brazil, has been pardoned by the Brazilian authorities. His case is over 20 years old so he has been allowed to stay in Brazil. This precedent would be dangerous to take on board in this country, however, but it does show a certain compassion. Feelings towards crimes and those who commit those crimes have changed to a degree.

This is possibly something that the British judiciary should contemplate further.

To understand how the Krays have tried to influence the media to their own particular advantage we have to go right back to the beginning. And the beginning is Hoxton, a much deprived area of the East End and close to the haunts of that well-known villain Jack the Ripper.

'The twins' tale is and always will be inextricably bound to the signs, symbols, rituals and folklore of London's East End' – so says Professor Chris Jenks. His argument stems from an analysis of the types of media necessary for sustaining myth within a social memory, one that organises the past in a symbolic and selective way. He divides the main media types into five categories: oral histories; written records; images and the pictorial; actions and rituals; and finally social framework of space. Although he says that the Krays are just as much about psychic space as social space, 'the confinements of the East End have helped to develop cultural mnemonics through geographical realignment. Selective memory then creates an illusion of history, establishing these larger than life figures through metaphors of grandeur and power. The myth takes control but only when the main protagonists are themselves worthy of such status, through their own mythogenic prowess.'

This is most clearly seen through written and pictorial representations, something that the Krays were all too aware of in the heyday of their nefarious careers. Starting in their boxing days, the twins soon learned that fame meant power and they thought they could create that power not through the ability to discuss and organise, but through the sheer forcefulness of their fists. They were becoming famous in their own village-like area of the East End of London, using this initial step up the ladder of fame as the basis for their thinking. They became known as twins, boxers, tough guys and ultimately gangland bosses, and they used these written and pictorial records to full effect. Ron with his camera always at hand, Reg with his ability with the pen. They helped to create their own image and the media did the rest.

Nothing illustrates the myth of the Krays better than the funeral of Ron Kray. He made every front page in the country, ousting the death of Lord Lovat, the wartime commando leader, from the pages of most newspapers all together. Even the television was full of the event with film footage of the cortège with all the Rolls-Royces and the glass-sided hearse, pulled by six black horses. The stars were there to pay their tribute among the 60,000 crowd, who thronged and longed to see Ron being taken away to his last resting place.

Most of the crowd wouldn't have recognised the Ron Kray who had died but they would easily have recognised the images created by photographer David Bailey, who helped to immortalise the Krays. They are today the images that the media use when describing gangsters and when the comedians Hale and Pace needed a couple of villains for their sketches they naturally chose the Krays. Unfortunately this also creates another image, one with comic overtones, but the Krays were no comedians. This selective memory process is thus enhanced by the media through film and through written recordings, such as the stars who always plead for the release of Reg Kray. They cannot compose a 'big picture' in this way, since they only look at certain aspects of the lives of the Krays. So the myth is enhanced through this social history of remembering.

It is important to note that it is not only the Krays who came in for this treatment – even the policemen who were trying to catch them have now become famous. Such is the case of Leonard 'Nipper' Read, who may not have been so well known today if he hadn't captured the Krays. The image of the detective became one of a specialist whose image was boosted still further by the activities of the Krays and the subsequent prosecutions. This, according to Dr Dick Hobbs, has given an élite status to Scotland Yard, no matter what methodology they use and no matter how much they bungle along. It is dramatic and bizarre in every detail, finally culminating in the portrayal of the fight between good and evil, where both sides become part of the myth. This dramatic fight which saw the imprisonment of the Krays changed their activities from normal everyday life to one of remarkable achievements through the use of fear and the threat of violence.

The case of the Krays had everything, says Dr Hobbs, 'including the hint of police corruption, murder, homosexuality, madness, show business personalities, politicians and the aristocracy. All these cases were presented as a series of dramatic confrontations between good and evil in which the police possess the preponderance of resources, skill and virtue.' For sure, the police were more inclined to go after the big fish than to use a net to catch small fry. The detention of the gang leader was the way ahead for the officers at the time. And some would say that it still is.

But the Krays were not always corrupt and criminal by nature, although they were forced to hear stories of the well-known gangsters and petty crooks of the Mile End Road from their father, who cherished these memories and fantasies. He filled the heads of his twins with these outrageous tales of bygone days; no wonder their imaginations knew no bounds. They grew up with the myths of 'Jack the Ripper' and the boxing heroes from the East End who everyone idolised. They also knew that they themselves were special because their mother had always told them so. And they could certainly trust their mother, couldn't they?

So when the Second World War came to a close they were in the right place at the right time. They were already famous in their neighbourhood and they wanted to be known all over the country. It was Ron Kray more than his brother Reg who had this need for fame. Whether he thought it would hide his homosexuality or at least disguise it in some way, no one can say for sure. But he was convinced by the films of the day that if you projected an outer image of some magnitude then you would soon inwardly become that character. Throughout his life he always tried to live up to his own creation: the Colonel.

But the myth really only came into being when the Krays were sentenced to 30 years in jail, with brother Charlie getting 12 years for getting rid of the body of Jack The Hat. Charlie Kray himself doesn't really fit into this myth – he is only there by association. He has always said that he had to create his own life despite his brothers, but in reality he has tried to live his life on the back of his brothers' success and, normally, with their money.

The simplicity of the paintings and poems created by Reg Kray show his own selective memory. He chooses to paint childlike pictures, depicting normal everyday life, although his life was by no means normal or everyday. His world today is one of poetic description where he has attempted to recreate history to protect his ego. He has blotted out the violence and the bad deeds in favour of the charity and kindness that he and his twin showed to many in the East End. Just like Ron, he could not face up to the reality of their deeds – they camouflaged them to create the image they wanted, one they could live with. It is a world of make-believe just as it is a true tale of historical achievement. This is the image, one of faction, that is so commonly portrayed in the newspapers of the day, where his show business pals argue the case for the release of Reg Kray.

Gary Bushell, writing in *The Sun*, is always calling for the release of Reg Kray. He remembers the good old days of the nearly crime-free East and West Ends of London, but here again we have the use of selective memory. Others, such as Mike Reid the comedian and actor, have voiced the same opinion. Talking of the days when he was a 22-year-old comic doing the rounds of the pubs and clubs, he said: 'We were introduced after a show at the Rising Sun in Bethnal Green and I was left with a lasting memory of them as absolute gents.' I wonder what the relatives and descendants of George Cornell and Jack The Hat McVitie would say?

And still the tributes and the good wishes pour out from all those well-wishers who, with compassion in their hearts, advocate the release of the most well-known gangster in Great Britain. 'Locked in to crazy sentences', said the *People* recently. 'Freedom day for a Kray', said another. And yet others report on the good deeds the twins have performed for various charities and good causes all around the country. When seven-year-old Sean Williams was brutally murdered recently Reg Kray sent the family a letter of sympathy, which they quite naturally cherish. Although I am a little cynical about such behaviour from Reg Kray, his letter did help to ease the suffering of the parents and therefore should not be ridiculed as a callous gesture just to get publicity. In his own way I truly feel that Reg believes he is doing some good and it is good to know that he has the well-being of others in mind. But don't forget the truth about the Krays!

So newspaper coverage has magnified the Kray myth. 'Publicly polite, patriotic, devoted to their mother and dressed in sober suits, the Krays developed an uncanny double act replete with controlled menace; it spawned a whole genre of fiction, and gained them a cult following,' said the *Telegraph* on Ron's death. This is a far more objective view of the legend of the Krays, full of death and violence and intrigue. The balanced picture, however, is not the stuff of myths.

Keith Waterhouse, writing in the *Daily Mail* on 20 December 1993, was concerned about the current status of children's books from Puffin, with all the violence of a blockbuster Hollywood film. Clive King, the hugely successful author, told him that authors were told to use simple sentence structure and tabloid-style headings, catering for 'the couch potato child surfeited with violence on the little screen who Puffin obviously believes can't be persuaded to look at a book unless it is sensationalised and written in short word-bites'. Mr Waterhouse uses the suggestion of *Charlie and Reggie Kray Meet the Borrowers* as an example of this category, which symbolises and reinforces the myth. Puffin, he says, tells of the violence that is around us in these modern times and that we cannot hide from children. This is, of course, true, but wouldn't it be nice to see this childlike unawareness extended, even if it does seem simplistic? After all, there is plenty of time for growing up.

No matter what happens from here on in, the Krays will be there for ever, imprinted on our minds in one way or another. The film helped to create a new generation of youngsters with extravagant and, some would say, outrageous views on the Krays. They have become working-class heroes and are still idolised in many parts of the East End where they are now icons of the establishment – that same establishment that they tried to corrupt. Despite the inaccuracies of the film and the short memories of some of our journalistic commentators, the Krays will always be gangsters, but the myth is now firmly in place and it will take a whole bookful of revelations to change that contrived impression. But maybe even that isn't enough.

8. MUSIC MAFIA PLEASE

This chapter is somewhat sensitive in nature and I have therefore decided to give all those characters directly involved in this Mob-controlled music company suitable pseudonyms. These names are chosen completely at random and do not signify any greater or lesser importance within the company; their role will become clear, however, within the text. Other protagonists and suggested executives, who refused to take up or gave up their posts in the company well before the Mob's involvement became clear are mentioned correctly, as are Charlie Kray and the old Firm godfather Joe Pyle.

I do not intend to whitewash anyone's involvement nor exaggerate anyone's actions. This is simply the truth, the whole truth and nothing but the truth. But then truth can sometimes be misperceived or misrepresented – some may call it selective memory on the part of some of the main characters, but ultimately I must take responsibility for the words and descriptions.

Those outside the company and artists who performed for and with the company are included and named. It would be silly and dishonest of me not to relate the stories as completely as possible and to attempt to do this with totally fictitious names could be seen as making a mockery of the presentation of this most sordid tale. And sordid it most certainly is, with devious actions and mischievous deeds all done for the sake of the attainment of both money and power.

No libel cases please from anyone I mention here or describe in my own colourful way – you know who you are and you don't really want the entire truth to come out, do you? This is a fairy tale of scorn and revenge, of threats and promises, of dreams and nightmares. It all started back in

1986 when an investor in a new music company, known here as Mr Investorman, became involved and embroiled in the violent and turbulent clash between the Mob in New York and the company chief executive here in the London.

'I don't know what to do. I'm going crazy!' Billy J. Kramer was close to tears as he spoke with Mr Investorman on the phone. 'He's going to get a gun and kidnap my children if I don't behave!' The '60s legend and a pal of The Beatles was in complete disarray. He wasn't used to being threatened but in his present company he was having to get used to it. He wanted out!

'Hang on a minute,' replied Mr Investorman, holding the phone tighter to his ear. The noise from the other guests in the bar made listening a precarious thing. 'Is this the same person we are talking about?' Mr Investorman couldn't believe his ears but there was obviously trouble in the air; that was why he was hastily asked to come down to The Swan public house in the New Forest in order to discuss the uncertain nefarious situation with Mr Easyliving. Normally a placid and pleasant businessman, Mr Easyliving was going through a hard patch – wife trouble, girlfriend trouble and now trouble in the music marketplace.

Billy J. Kramer hung up. He wasn't going to say any more. Maybe he had already said too much. The thought of losing his children to a psychopath made him freeze with fright.

'What on earth was that all about?' asked Mr Investorman. He still couldn't understand what was causing all the furore, but in fact there was no easy answer.

Mr Easyliving sipped at his beer. 'They have rejected the proposals,' he said nonchalantly but with just a hint of bitterness. He stared deep into his glass, as if trying to predict the future. He was motionless, even his eyes didn't blink.

'I still don't get it,' said Mr Investorman in disbelief. 'Who has turned it down?' He too reached for his glass. He was out of his league and he knew it. But he still wanted an answer.

'The Americans,' replied Mr Easyliving at last. 'They will not invest the $2 million they agreed.' Again he tried to hide his face in his beer but he didn't succeed.

Mr Investorman stood quietly for a moment, not knowing what to say. Like Mr Easyliving, he had invested a lot of money in the company; it was only start-up capital, since the rest was to have come from a private investor in the USA, but things hadn't been good lately and he would sorely miss the £15,000 investment he had already made. His family life was suffering because of it; it had not only cost him money but also a lot of his time.

'You can call Mr Moneygrabber, if you don't believe me,' said Mr Easyliving, looking up from his crouched position at the bar. He had already been on the booze for some time and was rapidly nearing a state of self-induced nausea. He had already accepted the situation and knew that he had lost.

Mr Investorman grabbed the phone once again and called Mr Moneygrabber, the main man in the set-up and the one who had organised the deal. Was this the right time to confront Mr Moneygrabber? Could he expect a cordial welcome? Would there be unforeseen circumstances or well-qualified excuses to endure? He didn't have long to wait for his answer.

'Why don't you just fuck off!' screamed Mr Moneygrabber into the phone. 'If there is any fucking trouble from you then I'll pick up your children too!' That was it. Billy J. Kramer was not lying about the paranoid behaviour of the chief executive officer. Mr Investorman's worst nightmares were coming true. He hesitantly and slowly placed the phone down on the bar and reached over for his half-empty glass of warm beer. He didn't really want to drink or drown his sorrows, he wanted to get even. He had never felt so angry before.

Mr Easyliving was still propping up the bar; soon the bar would be supporting him. 'I told you so,' he said in a feeble voice. 'He's gone mad!' He was right and nothing could change that. A few drinks more and more detail began to emerge about the music company mainly set up by Mr Moneygrabber.

'And do you know who the money was coming from?' asked Mr Easyliving with a sigh of dejection. He once again drowned his sorrows with a pint of lager.

'How the hell should I know,' replied a by now shaky and

much angered associate. And then, when his mind was clear and his patience torn to tatters, he added, 'Who was it then?' He had to have an answer as if it would in some way help.

'It was to have come from the US Mafia,' whispered Mr Easyliving. No one else in the bar could overhear them and the whispering was just for the hell of it like in some old American gangster film.

Mr Investorman stared in amazement. His mouth dropped a little as he tried to comprehend what Mr Easyliving had said. So he now found himself in bed with the Mob.

'It was all a con – a way of laundering Mob money,' said the freewheeling Mr Easyliving. 'All set up by Charlie Kray.' The words flowed as the drinks went down. Soon the entire story was out in the open. 'And if he tries that stuff with me then I'll show him a thing or two. I've got a gun too!' This was only added for good measure but if nothing else it made him feel good.

Mr Investorman didn't want to believe it but in his heart he knew it to be true. There had been many unexplained recent events and all attempts at getting answers had been fruitless. Now it was all so clear. The situation was both humiliating and intimidating – and neither sat well with Mr Investorman.

Mr Easyliving had had enough grief for the evening. He turned to an attractive young lady standing by him at the lonely bar and proceeded to drown his sorrows in her lovely blue eyes. He didn't want to talk about it any more. It was all over and done with as far as he was concerned.

It was now time for Mr Investorman to leave. He had heard enough, he had seen enough, he had drunk enough. But the drink hadn't helped and he knew that it was once again decision time. He walked out of the bar that night in complete and utter despair. He was in deep contemplation as he breathed the cool night air – at least he was alive. The question was whether or not he would stay that way. But either way, he would never see Mr Easyliving or his money again.

'Let me introduce you to the rest of the board,' said Mr Moneygrabber, as he showed Mr Investorman to his place at the bar. Somehow they always met in public houses or bars, never at the office, but Mr Investorman didn't mind visiting some of London's best-known pubs; it was all so new to him. 'This is Mr Recorderman, who is in charge of record production for the company,' he began. They both shook hands warmly before Mr Investorman was dragged away towards the next board member.

'And this is Mr Friendlybanker, in charge of finances,' he continued as Mr Investorman once again extended his hand in greeting. He thought how useful it could be to have a friendly banker on the board – things were looking up.

'Nice to meet you,' said Mr Investorman, wondering if he would be able to remember all the names. He had no need to worry – the majority of detail here comes from his vivid memory, some 12 years after the event. Somehow telling this story made it a little easier for him. It had caused him much heartache and pain through the years, but his business was now back on track and he could relate events in a clear and concise, if cynical, manner.

'Hello,' said another associate at the bar. 'I'm Mr Easyliving. What do you want to drink?' He was the last but not least of the strange bunch of people that made up the company known as DeFender Music Inc.

And they were a wild bunch too – a record producer who looked more like a bank robber, a banker who had previously worked in Italy and an engineer who was just along for the ride and some easy money. Some would have called it the crazy gang.

Discussions that night ranged from artists to offices. Mr Moneygrabber had found some good offices, or so he said, on the Mile End Road in the East End of London. This didn't strike Mr Investorman as anything out of the ordinary since he had never worked in London and didn't know the difference between East and West. But he was soon to find out. And Mr Moneygrabber gave everyone some tapes of the first artists, all of whom were from the USA. He had only recently received the tapes from an investor in New York who wanted to create a new multinational record company and DeFender Music was to be the name of the UK company, with the American holding most of the shares. He had an investment to make of some $2 million, so all involved were happy and satisfied with their future prospects.

The discussions continued into the early hours of the morning at the pub near Waterloo Station. It was handy for all concerned who had to travel to London for meetings, and the recording studio was just around the corner. It was all very cosy and comfortable – good artists, offices, studios and such. What on earth could go wrong?

And it didn't go wrong – well, that is, not at first. In fact it could have been very successful indeed, even without the money from the USA. But Mr Moneygrabber wanted it all and he wouldn't take advice. When it came to crunch time he opted for his crooked pals and the use of threats but for now he just kept this as an option, held well in reserve. After all, why use the stick of violence if you can get what you want the easy way – by friendly persuasion using money as the carrot?

The summer months of 1986 saw the development of the company and the introduction of a man who was supposedly the contact between the UK operation and the investor in the USA. That man was Charlie Kray. He was the key to the whole success of the company, no matter what other kinds of investment the chief executive officer, Mr Moneygrabber, could conjure up on behalf of the company. His was a key role, but it was put to the other associates as more of a consultant position than a direct executive function.

Mr Investorman had a brother, Mr Managerman, who had a band. The band's name was Shogun and their music was a kind of heavy rock, somewhat in the style of Bon Jovi. They were good, very good, and Mr Moneygrabber had his eye on them as a key part of making his fortune. He pestered Mr Managerman to let him take over the management and filled his head with stories of being invited on tour in New York and the rest of the world, playing at all the great venues.

'I'll get you into the big time,' he told the band. 'We'll get agreements drawn up and we'll cut an album at the studio.' The band were immediately taken in by the man with all his talk of superstars such as his old pal Ozzy Osbourne. He was a good talker when it came to getting what he wanted. Mr Managerman gave in to the pressure and let the band sign to the company. No signature, no album. They were hooked.

The studio lay just off the Waterloo Road and the band rehearsed and finally recorded their album. Unfortunately Mr Moneygrabber had chosen a pop producer by the name of Steve Tatler to do the recording and an engineer of little talent by the name of Paul Gadd. Paul had, however, another claim to fame; he was the son of the pop star Gary Glitter. It was a shame that the lad looked like his father.

The record turned out to be rather disappointing but it drew the attention of Jet Records, who came in and signed the band to their label. Unknown to Mr Investorman, the deal was an arrangement set up by Don Arden of Jet Records, another man with Mob connections, and Mr Moneygrabber, who was apparently owed a few favours. It was beginning to get nasty.

But all the outward signs were promising and Mr Investorman still had faith in the project. This, as it turned out, was a big mistake. Nevertheless, when Mr Moneygrabber suggested buying some records from Ireland Mr Investorman was interested. He had purchased records by the band Black Sabbath before and this deal was sweet; only 45p a disc and as many as he wanted. He could get a whole container for £15,000 cash and he could sell them for £1 a disc. Not a bad profit for anyone.

The deal was all set and Mr Moneygrabber introduced Mr Investorman to Patrick Meehan, the ex-manager of the band, who would handle all arrangements. A briefcase full of crisp pound notes was handed over at a pub in Wimbledon and the shipment was to be sent to France for collection well away from the UK. Mr Moneygrabber was on hand to confirm arrangements and the three men enjoyed a hearty meal.

Patrick Meehan told Mr Investorman that he could get as many records and cassettes as he liked whenever he wanted them. They could be shipped anywhere in the world and with eight titles to choose from there were enough to make a shipment to any foreign distributor. Mr Meehan didn't intend paying any royalty to Black Sabbath, who were due money on the deal. What they didn't see couldn't hurt them, he told Mr Investorman. He had obviously done this kind of deal before so he knew all the tricks of the music trade. The only thing that truly interested him was the money.

A few days passed and no news had arrived from Ireland. A week passed and there was still no news. Two weeks and more passed and still there was no news from the plant in Dublin. Mr Investorman was beginning to get a bad feeling about the whole deal. He quickly got in contact with Patrick Meehan, who told him of a delay in Ireland. The pressing plant was owed a lot of money by Mr Meehan and apparently they didn't want to let the records go. They wanted a further sum of money. After a brief conversation with Patrick Meehan, Mr Investorman and his brother Mr Managerman drove to Heathrow Airport. Here they met Patrick Meehan who was going with them to Dublin to sort the whole mess out. Introductions were made and the three men made their way to the Aer Lingus desk.

'Can you get the tickets?' asked Mr Meehan. He said he had forgotten his credit cards, but the two brothers didn't believe him. They were prepared for this kind of trick and told him flatly that he, Patrick Meehan, had to purchase the tickets one way or another, otherwise they would start legal proceedings against him for the £15,000.

Suddenly Patrick Meehan found his credit cards and before long they were airborne on the way to Dublin. The flight didn't last long and they were soon at the airport, waiting for the director of the pressing plant to come along and collect them for the ride directly to the plant. Soon he arrived and presented himself as Robert McGratton, boss of Carlton Productions of John F. Kennedy Drive, Naas Road, Dublin 12. If anyone would like it, I also have the telephone and facsimile numbers.

Mr Investorman knew that the trip wouldn't work out when he made a joke about being picked up in a Mazda 323. The fact was that they drove in a Rolls-Royce but no one apart from Mr Investorman and his brother understood the pun, based on a television advert. Soon they were at the offices of Carlton Productions and Robert McGratton showed them all the records standing in a huge warehouse, all boxed up and ready to go.

'I'll need another £15,000 before I'll release the goods,' he told the brothers. Mr Meehan just stood and stared. It was all part of a devious scheme devised between Patrick Meehan and the manager McGratton to try to get more money from the punters, who were obviously not used to such company. And all in the name of money.

'And don't try any monkey business,' he told them. 'I'm connected with the IRA!' Well, that was just what they didn't want to hear. Robert McGratton was a wealthy man with a farm in Canada, a house just outside of Dublin, and a Rolls-Royce for entertainment purposes. He was also a frequent visitor to Lansdowne Road to watch the internationals. When it came to hospitality, Robert McGratton was very free with other people's money.

The brothers had a quiet talk and agreed to think over the deal. They didn't like McGratton or Meehan; it was just a typical con as far as they could see it. But they were in so far they just couldn't give up without a fight. But the IRA were a different kettle of fish to some locked-up English jailbirds. Soon they were all three back on the plane heading towards Heathrow. The trip had been a complete waste of time. But the question still remained: what to do about the money already paid over? On the way back, Mr Investorman put on his thinking cap and suddenly he had a cunning plan.

'Charlie, can you help me?' he asked Charlie Kray, as soon as he got to the office, located just off the Mile End Road. Mr Investorman had decided to fight fire with fire; if he was being cheated then he would cheat the plant in Ireland. 'Can you fix me up with a dodgy letter of credit?' He explained all about the wasted trip to Ireland and about Patrick Meehan and his accomplices; he was angry and he wanted to get even, but he needed help.

'No problem,' said Charlie Kray. 'I'll arrange it straight away.' Soon Mr Investorman and a banker from the City were talking about arranging for a fake letter of credit to be sent to Ireland in exchange for the goods. It would cost another £500 but it would do the trick. It was a great idea, but would it really work and would there be any repercussions in the way of a bullet in the back or a few broken legs? It was all getting a little tricky and Mr Investorman needed time to consider his options.

Mr Investorman said he would think about the deal and talk it over with his brother and this he did as soon as he could. Mr Managerman ran a pub and the two brothers talked over the deal one weekend while quietly getting drunk. Their conclusion was that it was just another way of getting money out of Mr Investorman, as news was beginning to reach the other members of the board about quiet meetings between Mr Moneygrabber and Charlie Kray. It all looked just a little ominous.

Before Mr Investorman could make a decision, however, he received a phone call from Mr Easyliving to come down to the New Forest and meet with him. He had some urgent news about the company.

That was when Mr Investorman learned about the Mafia business and was threatened by Mr Moneygrabber. So not only did he lose his investment in the company, DeFender Music; he also lost a £15,000 deal on Black Sabbath records through the crooked dealings of Patrick Meehan and Robert McGratton. 1986 was not a good year for Mr Investorman. Another deal like that and he could have been bust!

What clinched it for Mr Investorman, however, was the fact that a few new directors joined the board of the company. These were some old friends of Charlie Kray's, for example, Joe Pyle, an old Kray Firm member and a friend who also had good connections. This was quickly becoming a Kray firm project and Mr Investorman knew that all his decisions had been the wrong ones. How he wished he had never heard about any business with these people.

The other board members didn't like the inclusion of these known gangsters either and the ever-increasing involvement of Charlie Kray in particular. It was not the kind of project that they had all signed up to but things just got out of hand. When the new associates were introduced to the existing board members one evening at the local pub there was a bit of a bust-up, with Mr Moneygrabber trying to assert his authority in front of all concerned. Some of his decisions annoyed Mr Investorman who just had to speak out against proposals. This quickly received a rebuke from Mr Moneygrabber.

'You agree with the proposals, or you're out. You can fuck off!' Mr Moneygrabber was sniggering when he sat down. At that moment Mr Investorman got up, took his coat and walked out of the pub but not before he told them all that they would one day regret their actions. He now hopes that by telling me the story he can set the record straight. But the whole saga of DeFender Records didn't stop there.

Don and David Arden, father and son, and CEOs at Jet Records, were having trouble with the Inland Revenue but still somehow they managed to clinch a deal with CBS in America to release the next Shogun album – even though David Arden was later sentenced to six months' imprisonment. The band, under the leadership of Alan Marsh and Danny Gwilym, worked hard and eventually the album *31 Days* was released. It did well in Europe and the USA and Alan and Danny even got the chance of going to Los Angeles to record with legendary producer Bob Ezrin. The single was a real rock ballad classic called 'Voices from the Heart'. They followed this success up with the Meatloaf tour in the late '80s where they were cheered on and off the stage by rapturous fans and were really on the way to world fame. But naturally Mr Moneygrabber and his pals had to foul it up once again.

Because of his shady dealings in the USA Don Arden was forced to be wired for sound when trying to get incriminating evidence on Mob pals. He was heading for a long stretch in jail if he didn't co-operate with the FBI so he did what any snitch would do – he wired himself up, delivered his friends and saved himself. But CBS were aware of all the problems and didn't want any further business with Jet Records. So Jet folded and Shogun's career stopped as abruptly as it had started. They were so near yet so far.

To get some of his money back Mr Investorman, when he heard of Jet's demise, made a deal with Arthur Sharp, who was in charge of finances at Jet Records. This enabled him to drive round to the back of the premises in Portland Place and load up records at some kind of silly cost, paid for in cash which went straight into the pocket of the hard-working Mr Sharp. In fact he did so well with the deal that he came back for more. There must be some kind of irony here in the fact that some of the records were featuring the ex-Black Sabbath singer Ozzy Osbourne. It certainly seemed poignant at the time and Mr Investorman enjoyed the joke. In fact he laughed all the way to the bank.

Other board members were taken on to try to secure capital investment into the company but eventually even Mr Producerman had to give up. He went back to his bank business or whatever he did. But he too lost a lot of hard-earned money, even more than Mr Investorman.

As for Mr Easyliving and Mr Bankerman, they too got out before there was really any trouble. They had witnessed the problems faced by Mr Investorman and didn't want to get too deeply involved with Mr Moneygrabber, especially when they learned of the Mob deal in New York.

Someone told Mr Investorman that Mr Moneygrabber and an associate even went to New York to try to collect the money from the US Mafia. They didn't succeed and the company folded. Even the Mob didn't trust Mr Moneygrabber and his DeFender Music Inc. set-up.

Charlie Kray had tried to smooth things along with the Mob without being directly involved with the company, just like he had been back in the good old days of the Kray 'empire'. It was just another of his nice little earners that went sour. Mr 'Fixit' had lost that magic touch. Some would probably say that he never had it in the first place.

A few relevant facts did emerge after the closure of the company but these didn't really shock Mr Investorman. Patrick Meehan, the man who took his £15,000 and wanted another £15,000, was actually a member of the company – he was on the board of DeFender Music. And another board member was a well-known Mafia man in the pay of the New York Mob. This man, by the name of Arthur Mogull, owed the Mob some £2 million and would do anything to clear his debt and keep on living. He had previously worked with Warners, Capitol Records, MCA and United Artists, so at least his credentials were good enough. Even more Mob pals came out of the woodwork, including the company's American accountant, who had set the company up in the USA. Eli Kopelman was just another wise guy in a web of deceit. There were more bankers and more crooks and criminals – and even more illicit companies designed to skim off the profits and to clean the laundry.

It was all about dirty money and dirty tricks. But it failed due to the sheer stupidity of Mr Moneygrabber. DeFender Music Inc. could have been a well-established company by now if Mr Moneygrabber hadn't been so paranoid. Just like the Krays, he didn't trust anyone but himself and he couldn't even do that. He was no businessman and couldn't organise efficiently and plan for the future without thinking of his own pocket first. The company just ran out of steam. What could have been a dream-come-true became a torrid nightmare.

Some years later Mr Investorman came across his name in another shady Kray deal but that really is another story. He was a man of ill repute and with a sordid history, who deceived his way to a living at the expense of innocent people. But unfortunately his kind are everywhere, so reader beware.

Shogun broke up and went their separate ways but I have learned through the grapevine that their old *31 Days* album, originally released through the ill-fated Jet Records, plus the Bob Ezrin version of 'Voices from the Heart', is shortly to be rereleased. Since all the rights have reverted to the writers, they feel that they are entitled to issue the product on a new CD and I for one wish them well. They were just another bright band ruined by an unscrupulous manager and this is a familiar story in the music business. Mr Investorman and Mr Managerman would also like to send their best regards.

9. STILL WHEELIN' AND DEALIN'

In the summer of 1992 I went to visit Reg Kray when he was a guest of Her Majesty in Nottingham Gaol. The talk among the brothers had recently been films, and in particular the making of another 'Kray' film. The movie *The Krays* had done well through Rank Film Distributors, not that the twins had had much pleasure in the project. So this time around they wanted full control and much, much more money.

'I want £2 million,' said Reg Kray impatiently, but then everything Reg says is tarnished with impatience.

'That could be possible,' I replied. 'But surely you must have made something like that from the first film?' I queried. It was a mistake.

'We got a miserly £255,000,' said Reg angrily, his eyes lighting up like fireworks.

I didn't know what to say. Neither did anyone else. I had gone there with an old friend and someone else who just wanted to meet Reg and have the privilege of conversing with one of the UK's all-time criminal greats. The other guy did the driving and paid for the trip and he even gave Reg a well-deserved 'drink'.

What was even more disturbing than the aggressive tone used by Reg Kray was the feeling that Reg was, somehow, in another world. I put it down at first to being in jail for so many years. But then it dawned on me – he was slowly but surely getting stoned out of his tiny mind on booze. True, he had a glass of orange juice on the table in the meeting hall. But there were guards all around so how could he get the alcohol?

The answer lay nearby where a mother was attending to her baby brought in that day to visit with his or her father, another inmate of Nottingham Gaol. They had brought in the vodka in the baby's drinking bottle, right under the noses of the prison staff.

Reg was still angry but the booze was beginning to get to him. 'I don't want Charlie involved this time,' he said. 'It was all his fault last time. We should have made over £1 million.' Reg went on to explain that originally he had insisted on an initial up-front payment with a royalty depending on the success of the film. This was a clever move but then Reg has always been keen on money. Charlie, however, together with another of the negotiators, Wilf Pine, were in dire need of cash funds. These two conspired to renegotiate the deal with a once only up-front figure of £255,000. There would be no royalty, no further payments, no future millions.

Once again I felt ill at ease. I didn't want to tell him that I knew all about the film negotiations and of the trouble that the twins had had with elder brother Charlie. It wasn't really my place to tell tales. I didn't want to tell him that his brother had been selling off the rights for chunks of money – £5,000 a shot. I also didn't want to tell him that I had invested in Charlie's royalty like so many others. And I certainly didn't want to be the one who told him of Charlie's constant and incessant debt.

The other negotiator, Wilf Pine, was also not someone to be trusted. He had not only once been a bouncer and bodyguard, but also a bankrupt and a man of ill repute. I could also have added that Wilf Pine would do anything Charlie Kray asked him to and much, much more. So in reality the team doing the deal on the film were more interested in their own well-being than in that of the twins. Even before they started their negotiations they were on a lose-lose situation.

'I'm fed up with being ripped off,' said Reg slurping down another shot of vodka. 'We never get what we are owed.'

I was beginning to wonder what Reg Kray thought he was owed but Reg once again intervened. He was unusually intense, probably due to being banged up for all those years and later I found out that this was quite normal for him. For almost 30 years Reg Kray had been all dressed up with nowhere to go.

'And if I find out who has been ripping us off with those Eastenders t-shirts then I'll teach him a lesson or two!' He was fuming. And it was not a pretty sight. Reg Kray was getting very hot and I was becoming quite bothered.

Once again I was beginning to feel the heat. Was it my duty to inform on his old pals? Should I tell him of the deals that were being done in the name of the Krays? Should I spill the beans? Or should I just be quiet and say nothing, shut up and not grass on his old friends?

The meeting was soon over and I was relieved to be leaving Nottingham. It had been a long day. The session had gone reasonably well and the driver talked about Reg Kray all the way back to London. My friend and I were, however, a little thoughtful so we let him talk and the time passed quickly.

I parted company with my two companions and set about trying to get the last train from Waterloo down to Salisbury where I live. I had a short wait but I was soon on the train and heading south-west to Wiltshire. These trips are a little tiring but nevertheless they are necessary, especially when working on business deals and ideas where it is important to deal face-to-face. For that was what the trip was all about – ideas to make money and seeing people who could make things happen.

On the way back to Salisbury I sat alone in the carriage. There was plenty of time to think about film deals, about merchandise and about books. Whatever was going to happen, I had made up my mind: I would not be the one who had to tell Reg Kray that it was his brother, Champagne Charlie, who had done the deals on the Eastender t-shirts. This had infuriated both twins. And I would certainly not be the one to tell him that I was the one who actually set up the deal for Charlie!

On 31 May 1989 a meeting took place at the offices of Gold Mann & Co. at 80 Fleet Street, EC4Y 1EL to determine in contractual form the proceedings regarding the development of a feature film, provisionally entitled *The Krays*. Those present were representatives of the company Parkfield Group plc, Wilf Pine and Nicky Treeby who were acting as agents for

Reg and Ron Kray, Charlie Kray and a solicitor acting on behalf of Gold Mann & Co.

The main points were read aloud in the office, but all that really interested Charlie Kray were the figures that appeared in Clause 3 of the agreement, the one which spelt out the money that the three brothers would receive for the film rights. No one said that they couldn't get paid for these rights. No one mentioned the fact that Ron and Reg Kray were convicted murderers or the fact that Charlie Kray had received a sentence of 12 years for getting rid of a corpse. No one even doubted that fact that they were due payment under the law of the land. But some would say that rewarding murderers is not what justice should really be all about.

The moment came and the solicitor read out the most important of all the clauses in the agreement. For the sake of clarity and since I do not want to be sued for including the wrong information in this book I will now show, word for word, the full details included in Clause 3, the one about the money. It reads as follows:

3.3 To the Kray Family:-

    3.3.1 Within 7 days after the occurrence of the events set out in clause 4.1 the payments due to the Kray Family under clauses 4(ii) and (iii) of the Kray Agreement (and in full and final satisfaction thereof) amounting to £110,000;

    3.3.2 £25,000 within 30 days after the payment pursuant to clause 3.3.1 above;

    3.3.3 £50,000 within 30 days after the payment pursuant to clause 3.3.2 above;

    3.3.4 £50,000 within 30 days after the payment pursuant to clause 3.3.3 above;

    3.3.5 £20,000 within 21 days after the expiry of six calendar months after the calendar month during which the Film is first theatrically released in the United Kingdom.

Charlie Kray's share would be one-third of this total, amounting to some £85,000. Not bad for a villain. And his brothers would each receive the same amount. Naturally enough they would be obliged to part with some of this to their agents, Mr Pine and Mr Treeby, but that would still not be a bad day's work for a couple of crooks from the East End of London.

Naturally the Krays, together with their agents, had to sign a guarantee that they held the rights in the first place. But just how anyone can sign away the story rights to a couple of killings is beyond my own limited knowledge of the law. Don't dead men or their families have rights too? I wonder if they were paid any vast sums of money?

Anyway, the solicitor continued to read out the agreement, clause by complicated clause, but for those present the main points had already been covered. It was the money they wanted and of course the publicity too. There was, however, a minor complication about the payment. Ron and Reg wanted a smaller up-front payment and a fixed royalty rate from the takings. But Charlie Kray and Wilf Pine were in such dire need of cash that they were willing to risk the wrath of the twins to get their hands on some filthy lucre. And remember, Ron and Reg were not exactly in any position to negotiate themselves. There are certain laws involved when doing deals from jail and the Krays were keen to bypass these normal proceedings to get hold of some cash that they could keep for themselves, away from anyone else's prying eyes.

Tales were told and stories invented to convince the twins that this was the best deal possible and they fell for it, deceived by their own brother and his willing accomplice. They wouldn't be getting the millions they were after, but Charlie would be getting himself out of a fix. In the event it still wasn't enough to pay off his debts, since he had already sold these film rights for ready cash; cash that had already gone walk-about.

The real story of the film began back in 1982, when Roger Daltrey and a film company known as Boyd's Co. Film Productions Limited managed to secure a written agreement from the twins for a film to be made about their lives. It was originally to be called *The Kray Brothers*, but things didn't really happen before Bejubop Limited entered the fray and finally started developing a workable script. Roger Daltrey, the lead singer of The Who and a budding actor, had made a good start but Bejubop progressed with the script until Fugitive Films were ready to make the film itself. But again there was just one little snag that had to be overcome – finances. That was where Parkfield came into the picture. The agreement, as outlined above, gave Fugitive Films the money to work with and gave the Krays the assurances that they needed – and of course, let's not forget the money.

But even with the finances guaranteed Fugitive Films ran into trouble. The first thing they did was to run back to Parkfield Entertainment and tell them that they needed more money or they couldn't finish the film. So Parkfield had to put their hands in their pockets once more and cough up another couple of million. In all the film cost some £6 million, which was grossly over budget, but it did very well at the box office here in the UK and even sold well throughout Europe. Miramax, the American company which took the film for the USA and paid about £2 million for the fun of it, took it off the circuit after only two weeks. But later the film did well when released on video in the USA and many television companies took it for late-night showing. So all in all it recouped its investment. Video rights here in the UK, however, were something else since by that time Parkfield Group plc were in liquidation.

Cork Gully, who handled the receivership of the company, were looking to sell the video rights to the highest bidder when I went to see them at their offices in Noble Street in early 1991. At their offices, located right next to the City of London itself, I was shown all the receipts from the film, including details of sales through United Media, who handled the film here in the UK. They hadn't quite reached the £6 million mark at that time, but with the sale of the video rights success was assured, for the film at least. Parkfield, with their unexpected extra investment in the project, went bust.

To try to sort out the rights and the contracts I even went

to see a pal of Charlie's at Pinewood Studios. His office was located right opposite the brand new James Bond set and it was plush and comfortable, just like a producer's office should be. But the man in charge was none other than that old Kray pal Joseph 'You can call me Joe' Pyle. Pal Joey showed me some more paperwork.

I was there simply because I had promised Charlie Kray to look into matters for him. I had seen most of this paperwork before, although I was not initially involved in the original project, but some of it did surprise me and the letters were all headed 'confidential'. Everyone wanted to keep things quiet and when that happens it normally means that someone wants to make money out of the situation. But whether it was the liquidator or the boss of Touchdown Entertainment, as Joe called his company, was not very clear. But I didn't get to see Joe Pyle again because he was caught up in a cocaine bust and sentenced to five years' imprisonment.

In any case the video rights were sold and the film became profitable, but if Ron and Reg Kray had had their way they really would have become millionaires. This would have come in over a period of time, however, but every time it is showed now around the world it does absolutely nothing to fill the coffers of the Kray brothers, which is what it was intended to do right from day one.

'Why didn't you want to meet the Kemp brothers who played you in the film?' I asked Ron once, when I met him in Broadmoor. He looked up and sighed as he reached over for his non-alcoholic beer and his cigarettes.

'Why would I want to meet a couple of wimps like them?' he asked, putting another cigarette in his mouth. A guard came over and lit the cigarette for him and Ron sat back and relaxed. After all, there wasn't much else to do.

'But weren't you interested?' I asked, as curious as ever. Maybe this is a writer's lot or possibly it was because of my own knowledge of Ron and his particular kind of vanity. Surely, I felt, he was interested in who would portray him on the silver screen.

'We got the money and that was all we wanted,' he said in

reply as he continued to chain-smoke the cigarettes I had brought in for him. That was it. Once again it was all about money. But Ron didn't care about the money so why the big deal about getting as much as he could, I wondered. Kate Kray came up with the answer. She told me that Ron didn't care about what money could do for him since he couldn't spend it in Broadmoor. But he did care about the people he could help so he gave it all away. In his own inimitable way Ron Kray was a true philanthropist.

The demise of the distribution company was an event completely out of the hands of the Krays and unforeseen and unexpected by everyone including Ron, Reg and Charlie Kray. By accepting a one-off payment instead of royalties, the Krays didn't get their nice pension every month in the way of a royalty cheque as planned. It was all down to the greed of two men who gave up the opportunity for riches in the future for something here and now, all determined by their own predicaments and outstanding debts. So Ron and Reg would not be millionaires because of the film – they would have to continue to wheel and deal in their own ways to make a buck and to keep the funds flowing in their direction.

As they say, you can choose your friends but you can't choose your family.

The t-shirt deal was simplicity itself. Charlie Kray and I shared an office on the Mile End Road in the East End of London at the time and he had seen t-shirts selling all over London, showing the sights, the Beefeaters, the Horse Guards and such. So he wanted to cash in on the popularity of his brothers and make a buck or two. He asked me if I knew anyone in the business who might be interested in manufacturing Kray t-shirts so I made a few phone calls and quickly came up with a short-list of companies. He told me that the twins would also be getting some of the royalty but then I would say that, wouldn't I? In the end he pocketed the money and kept the whole operation quiet. He thought it was a need-to-know situation and that the twins didn't need to know.

My brother Rod and I went for a stroll one day along

Oxford Street to check out the t-shirt business, which was doing a roaring trade with all kinds of products, such as Eastenders t-shirts and other souvenirs. We could very easily see the possibilities for Kray t-shirts and asked a few of the storekeepers about their suppliers. They were very cagey about giving us any names but when we mentioned the Krays attitudes changed as if I were talking about aliens. It was simply astounding that just a name could have that affect. So, with a little friendly persuasion, one of the traders met us in a pub and spilled the beans about the t-shirt trade. That was all we needed.

I talked to three companies about the proposed deal but we couldn't agree on a percentage that sounded reasonable. So I turned my attentions to a small company run by an old friend from South Africa. He had a good business going and his company, Flash Merchandising, was doing well within the t-shirt sector, which is very competitive indeed. I spoke to Charlie about the kind of deal that I would be looking for in this type of arrangement and we sorted out some royalty rates that he felt the twins would be satisfied with. The rest was, for me, normal business and this kind of business is best handled on the river.

I met my friend, let us call him Gerry, and we sailed in his boat down the River Thames to a quite delightful pub right on the riverbank. After a few drinks we eventually got around to talking about the deal but then we decided that it was too hot for business and we had a few more drinks. It was a marvellously sunny summer's day and the river was the best place to be. But everyone must eat so we ordered some of the best food in the house and went outside to eat and to talk a little business. Actually, the deal was all arranged well before this meeting of minds because it was all negotiated on the telephone and by fax. This jaunt on the river was simply to seal the arrangements and to pick up the contracts. Contracts secured in my briefcase, we sailed back to his moorings and parted company. The rest is history.

Charlie Kray from 1986 onwards was on a pension, as the Krays call it. He was in the receipt of a regular income paid directly to him and he could do anything he liked with it. He was the one who chose not to give any of this money to his brothers and thereby put me in an embarrassing situation that time in 1992 when Reg was talking about the t-shirts. As I said, I couldn't volunteer the information then but now, with the benefit of hindsight, maybe I should have told him that his brother was cheating him out of another fortune.

As for me, all I got out of the deal was a miserable t-shirt, and that was for proof purposes only. It just goes to show that the old saying is quite right: once a crook, always a crook.

But the deals didn't stop there; they just continued. Charlie had tasted success and the trappings of success and I was again asked to perform a miracle when I was presented with a cassette tape. It was purportedly an old tape of Reg talking to some pals over a few glasses of whisky, but there was a catch. It was instantly obvious to my trained ear (I was once a student at the British Academy of Music) that the tape was of recent origin and not old at all. No, no, no, they all told me, it's the genuine article. But I knew different. I did nothing with the tape for a few weeks, waiting for someone to call asking about progress. When the call came I laid it on the line.

'You can tell everyone else that it was made 20 years ago, but don't try to tell me,' I told the man acting as agent for Reg Kray (this was Reg's deal, and no one else, not even Ron or Charlie, was involved). This is how it was with the Krays. They tell you that they support each other but in reality they are helping themselves. The guy on the other end of the phone line didn't know what to say. I had rumbled him and I had rumbled the plan. Finally he had to tell me the whole plot.

Someone had taken a hidden cassette recorder into the prison to record a bogus conversation where Reg is telling stories about the old days. He talked of the Mafia, Judy Garland, George Raft, Joan Collins and many, many more, all crammed into 25 minutes of recording. In fact it sounded very much as though he was reading from a script. They even had him asking for another Scotch. This was all set up to make money out of the lucrative interview disc market, something that I was very good at back in the mid-'80s. I even had my own interview picture discs circulated all over the world and my company, Fotodisk, was a major player in this field.

So the truth about the fake was out but Charlie wanted me to play along with the hoax and who am I to go against the wishes of the Krays. I designed the disc, edited the tape and put the whole production process into motion. It turned out to be a great picture disc, with one of Reg's favourite pictures of himself on the A-side and a picture of the twins on the back. There was no room for Charlie. But when the product was finished and ready to go to the distributor, no one could agree on the selling side, so for six months the records lay on the factory floor. It was just another operation where there were too many cooks (or should that be crooks?) spoiling the broth. A few years ago someone turned the tape into a CD and now it is visible on the Worldwide Web. At last, after all this time, it is available on the Internet.

These deals were always there, be they for posters or photographs, records or CDs, articles for inclusion in various magazines – or books. The most lucrative of all their book deals was the first one, called *My Story*, written by Fred Dinenage for Sidgwick and Jackson in 1988. It is interesting to note here that the actual copyright in the book is held by Bejubop, one of the companies that tried to establish the film *The Krays*. This was possibly to get around the law at the time, which didn't like to see money going to convicted criminals for the sale of rights, be they book or film. But Ron and Reg Kray pocketed a £100,000 advance for their rights, and Fred Dinenage pocketed a sizeable sum for the writing. It did well in the bookshops, reaching the top ten in the paperback lists, and the critics say that it is very well worth reading. But it didn't shine any light on controversial issues such as whether or not they killed the Mad Axeman, Frank Mitchell. Now, of course, we know that they did give the orders for his immediate death and Frank Mitchell was dumped at sea off the coast of Kent. But it still makes interesting reading.

Fred Dinenage had previously worked on a television documentary about Broadmoor and it was here that he had first met Ron Kray, one of the hospital's most illustrious patients. So when it came time to write the book, it was Ron who suggested the TVS man for the job and Sidgwick and Jackson were pleased with the result.

Later on, in 1991, Ron was asked by Sidgwick and Jackson to write another book. He took the money and set about writing some notes for inclusion in the book, using a ghost-writer, but in the end he had to give up the idea. He couldn't think of anything to say! Maybe with the right encouragement he could have complied with the wishes of the publishers, and I for one would have been interested to read the book, but ultimately he had to give them their money back. And believe me, that was not an easy task for Ron Kray.

Reg Kray has written a number of books and has had three of them published here in the UK. By far the best is *Born Fighter*, released through Century in 1990. It is what you would expect from the title and Reg doesn't let the reader down. In recent years, however, he has been trying to interest a publisher in his memoirs of prison life, but I suppose we will have to wait for his parole before anyone takes him up on his offer. But in the right hands it should make good reading, and since I have already had a preview of some of the chapters, I can truthfully say that I think it will certainly pack a punch!

But the book saga rolls on and on and recent newspapers have been carrying reports that a new book will soon be available, written by none other than Reg's new wife, Roberta Jones, or should that be Kray? So she will soon be joining the rest of the family in trying her hand at publishing. But in reality it is just another nice little earner for the Krays. As far as this new extravaganza is concerned, I really don't think that Reg Kray will be saying anything that we don't already know this close to his parole, which could come about any time after May of 1998. But maybe the university-educated new woman in his life has something to say for herself, and I am sure we all await her carefully chosen words with a keen sense of anticipation.

Reg, on the other hand, will continue to give his newspaper interviews for around £1,500 a time and his man-to-man chats for about £200. Other little earners include Kray waistcoats and belt buckles – all adding to the Kray bank balance. He will even sign a photo or two, for a price.

In 1994 Ron and Reg Kray even tried their hands at recording a CD. It used clips of interviews smuggled out of prison along with a jungle beat popular at the time. The boxer, Nigel Benn, put it together with various main artists but it didn't get the right publicity or distribution so the twins' didn't have a hit on their hands. It is strange to think of such tough guys as rave artists when the only time Ron Kray ever talked about a hit-list was when he was working out who to kill next. How times have changed!

The twins, in particular, have used every trick to get publicity and one of the latest crazes is to get a Kray tattoo. Just why teenagers and youngsters should be interested in getting jabbed all over like this is a little bewildering – all those needles only to get a picture of Ron and Reg Kray plastered all over your body. And like the twins, you've got them for life. But it keeps the profile of the Krays right up there with all the other celebrities of the day and therefore it serves its purpose. The Kray bandwagon rolls on.

Perhaps the most amazing story that never came to light during the early part of 1992 was the relationship between Ron and Reg Kray and two brothers from South Wales – Leighton and Lindsay Frayne. The newspapers of the time told the story of two bungling boyos from the valleys who tried to emanate the Krays in both lifestyle and actions. On 3 June 1992 the tabloids pictured the brothers on the front page after they had appeared in Newport Crown Court on charges of robbing a building society in Newbridge, Gwent, of £10,000. The offence had been committed, said Mr Patrick Harrington, the previous July when Lindsay Frayne and a friend, Stephen Cook, entered the building society wielding guns and asking for money.

'Lindsay Frayne held a gun while going backwards out of the door, just like in a TV film,' said Mr Harrington, who was prosecuting the case. He also spoke of sawn-off shotguns and other firearms and condemned the brothers for their actions. Although only one of the brothers was accused of being involved in the robbery the other brother, Leighton, was accused of masterminding the crime. Lindsay, 25, and Leighton, 31, were between a rock and a hard place.

They had appeared in the *People* the previous year posing as the Krays in one of the famous David Bailey photographs and were paid well for their time. This unfortunately fell well into their plans since they were working for Ron and Reg Kray. It was part of an elaborate plan, one that the Krays had instigated as part of a plot to put them back as number one in the hierarchy of British crime. In the end the whole thing was covered up as a bungled attempt at robbery but behind the headlines was the real truth about the deal between the Krays and Leighton and Lindsay Frayne.

The plan was nothing new in the realms of gangsterism – Ron and Reg Kray would use the Fraynes as surrogate gangsters to control the underworld, waiting for their release. When freed from jail, the Krays would once again take up the role of leading UK villains and pay off the Fraynes for their work. The Krays would use all of their contacts to create the right image for the lads from Wales and they would use their muscle and money too. It was simple and it almost worked. What they didn't know at the time was that the police had already started taking an interest in the Frayne boys ever since the days that they were in Cardiff Jail, where they corresponded with the twins. The police knew the kinds of tricks that the Krays could play and they were there waiting for them at the pass to cut off their retreat and to get their men.

It is by no means certain that Lindsay Frayne was involved in the robbery at the building society, but the police were looking for something to hang on the brothers, so this was a good opportunity. Since most of their private dealings were just that, very private, then it was a simple matter to frame the boys from the valleys. The authorities were not bothered about getting them for one particular crime – they just wanted them at any cost. They could see the writing on the wall and it said Kray.

In many ways the boys played right into the hands of the Krays, giving them a good get-out route of the whole deal. If they succeeded then the twins would control the underworld, but if they failed they could call the youngsters a couple of stupid hillbillies, which is exactly what they did. And Leighton and Lindsay Frayne gave them all the evidence they needed. They used to drive to London in an old Vauxhall Cavalier well past its sell-by date, and they would be careful with the money too, eating small portions and keeping an eye on the budget. This was mainly done because the twins were covering the costs and the idea was to make money, not spend it.

The Fraynes also visited Violet's grave, paying their respects to their heroes' mother, and they met Tony Lambrianou, one of the old gang members and the man who did 15 years for his involvement in the killing of Jack The Hat McVitie. They even visited The Blind Beggar where Ron Kray shot and killed George Cornell. It all added spice to their lives but the good life got the better of them. One day when they were at The King's Oak in Epping Forest they bragged about having money, supposedly from the robbery in Wales, and they partied the night away with a stripper and some pals. Unfortunately, one of those pals took some photographs of the lads, photos which are still described as 'top secret' even today. It may be the pornographic content that has made them unsuitable for publication or there may have been an informer or two in the shots. The police had had enough of their antics and the brothers were arrested.

By the middle of June 1993 the brothers from the valleys of South Wales were sentenced to eight years for their parts in the robbery in Newbridge. Their relationship with the Krays stopped abruptly with their arrest, and, apart from a mugging or two to try to protect their image, they were finished, for the time being at least. The guns were real enough and the right intentions were there but they just couldn't pull it off. The Krays had played their cards well and were never questioned by police about the incident but the Fraynes were behind bars and of no further use to the twins. If they were ever going to take over London they would have to find another way.

My own investigations have revealed a plot by the Frayne brothers to kill Reg Kray and to take over the underworld for themselves. The Fraynes, however, got too big for their boots and the arrest for the building society robbery stopped them in their tracks. We may never really know the reason behind the capture of the Frayne brothers but I think we all owe a debt of gratitude to the boys in blue from South Wales.

When it comes to charitable work then Ron and Reg Kray have done their fair share of fund-raising for good and honourable purposes. In the majority of cases, they have used their contacts within the fight game to organise boxing matches with all proceeds going to the chosen cause. Some time ago I was myself privileged to be present at such a charitable event where stars of boxing and television were present. So too were the usual suspects including Charlie Kray, Tony Lambrianou, and Leighton and Lindsay Frayne. Gary Bushell was there representing the press and there was the normal gathering of assorted hoods and cheap crooks.

There they were in their tuxedos, bulging at the necks and sweating like nobody's business. The auction was the highlight of the evening and most of the big London football clubs had supplied footballs all signed by the teams. There were some from Arsenal, from Tottenham, West Ham and so on – they had all put themselves out for the charity and now it was the turn of the guests to make their bids. And they put their hands in their pockets all right and the evening was a tremendous success, enabling the twins to send off a large sum of money to their cause.

This was and still is typical of the Krays, but sometimes the organisers get a little greedy. Since the twins are never present then they have to leave the collections up to old pals and these old pals are all crooks. No wonder they don't always get what is pledged on the night. This has caused many problems through the years, culminating in a recent investigation into charities run and organised by Reg Kray from inside Maidstone Prison. This concerns charity fraud and central to the police enquiries is the use of telephones from inside the prison. Since the prisoners have access to these phones then it is possible for all kinds of crooked dealings to be planned and organised from inside the jail simply by making a phone call.

The Krays have always used these events to further their own causes and to get them the publicity that they crave. But I have never ever been aware of the twins themselves making off with the takings although I cannot say the same about their old pals. Once again their so-called friends aren't doing the Krays any favours. They line their own pockets on the back of sincere desires to help other unfortunate people, especially children. Reg will undoubtedly continue the practice and I am sure that many will benefit from his philanthropic charity work.

10. LIFERS

After being kept in Parkhurst Prison for 20 years, Reg Kray has been sent on a tour of the UK paid for in full by the British taxpayer under the ever-watchful eye of the press. Even now after 30 years in jail Reg Kray cannot feel absolutely sure of ever being set free.

The only sure thing he has had to look forward to was a regular six-monthly trip to Broadmoor Hospital to see his twin brother Ron, who was sent there after attacking a fellow prisoner at Parkhurst many years ago. And now even that is over: finished and done with when Ron died suddenly of a heart attack in the early part of 1995.

But the days of being a 'Category A' prisoner and constantly kept in maximum security are long over for Reg Kray. Now he can look forward to his release in the comforting knowledge that it will one day appear. He has been downgraded in status and shoved around the country in ever-decreasing circles. And now he is on the last leg of the tour. He even has the key to his door with him day and night; he has never attempted to escape and has been a model prisoner.

Those early days were hard. As a Category A prisoner he was regarded as highly dangerous and a possible threat to both the public and to the police if he should escape. Indeed, he was reckoned on as being a possible threat to even the state.

He has suffered all of the hardships that accompany this status, such as not being allowed to mix with the other prisoners and being kept in isolation whilst under constant surveillance (even to the extent of being chaperoned to the toilet by a warder). His visitors and mail have been rationed and restricted, and have been scrutinised by the authorities. The list of restrictions is almost never-ending, but he has handled it well, except for a few bouts of depression. On one occasion he did try to commit suicide.

Ron Kray, isolated in the relative comfort of Broadmoor, had never seen the necessity of keeping fit but his brother Reg has developed into an exercise freak. His daily work-outs have kept him in tremendous condition and today he looks like the aggressive and naturally gifted boxer he was back in the good old days of the Double R Club. This strict routine has kept his brain active and his body lean and mean. No one would want to cross Reg Kray, not even today when he is aged well into his sixties.

So when will he be released? Surely 30 years is enough for anyone? Most 'lifers' serve only a dozen years or so, so why should Reg Kray stay in jail a moment longer?

On 17 March 1995, at the age of 61, Ron Kray died of natural causes at Wexham Park Hospital, Slough, Berkshire. In Ron's case this was 100 cigarettes a day for life. He was rushed to Heatherwood Hospital near Ascot on Wednesday, 15 March, complaining of acute tiredness and suffering from anaemia. He had collapsed earlier in the day in the top-security ward at Broadmoor NHS Hospital that he shared with, amongst others, Peter Sutcliffe – the 'Yorkshire Ripper'.

The following Thursday, 16 March, he was still fighting to get back to Broadmoor, where he could resume his smoking habit, but in the end time ran out and by Friday he was only a ghost of his former self. Having suffered a series of heart attacks, Ron Kray had not been in good health for a number of years and his incessant chain-smoking did nothing to improve things.

He was eventually transferred to Wexham Park, Slough, but it was a trip too far for Ron Kray. He died immediately on arrival at the hospital after another massive heart attack. As hospital pathologist, Dr Mufeed Ali, said, 'He must have died instantly but he would have been in some pain.'

'After being locked up for 27 years he's free at last,' said Reg Kray on hearing the news. 'He beat the system, didn't he? He didn't die in Broadmoor as everyone expected him to.' Reg was playing the game and trying to keep up appearances but inwardly he was appalled that the authorities had not let him see his brother prior to his death. In fact, he hadn't seen him for over nine months, despite having seen him every six months throughout their prison sentence. There was even a possibility that they would not let him visit the chapel of rest but in the end permission was given and Reg was able to pay his last tribute to Ron personally, accompanied by his elder brother Charlie.

The hospital kept everything under wraps. Even the inquest was held in secret. This was carried out by retired Maidenhead solicitor, Robert Wilson, at his West End, Waltham St Lawrence home. It was a brief hearing, by all accounts, with the natural causes verdict being faxed to the coroner's office in Slough. Ron Kray had died from a massive heart attack – natural causes indeed. And the autopsy was performed only 24 hours after his death, which was something of an irregularity. There were numerous complaints about this procedure with even the pressure group Inquest joining in the fray. Barrister June Tweedle, a co-director of the group, said that the inquest should have been held in public. Sentiments echoed by Reg and Charlie Kray. 'Although the coroner does have a great deal of discretion,' she told journalists, 'he does have obligations to tell people who want to be informed. He really has gone beyond the pale.' The Home Office didn't want to get involved even though Broadmoor is a government institution. So there was controversy even after death.

Everyone had warned him about the cigarette problem. A Broadmoor source said: 'We have warned him time and time again that he is killing himself.' And the Heatherwood Hospital at Ascot made it known that, 'He is banned from smoking here and says he wants to leave to have a cigarette. But he is too weak to get out of bed.' The transfer to Wexham Park didn't help. Ultimately Ron Kray killed himself. By the time of his death he was down to a mere shadow of himself at only nine stone.

Reg and Charlie kept up their attack on the authorities in the hope of getting some answers and, I am sure, in the knowledge of getting front-page exploitation from the media. The Krays have always played with a double-edged sword and they continue to do so even after the death of Ron Kray. Every Sunday newspaper in the country had a huge spread talking about the terror twins, the gangsters from the East End of London. They had lists of killings, of deals and of celebrity friends. Even in death Ron Kray was front-page news.

Reg was now the Kray in the limelight. He spoke eagerly with all the journalists, pouring out his soul and displaying the remorse expected of him. 'I didn't sleep much last night,' he told reporters on the Saturday. 'But I forced myself not to think back over all the years because it would have been too hurtful.' It might seem a pity that he didn't think about the pain he and his brother had inflicted on others all those years ago. But these deeds were conveniently forgotten, for the time being at least.

'Reggie is obviously really upset,' remarked brother Charlie on leaving Maidstone Prison, the morning of 18 March 1995. 'But he is coping with it the best he can. He's trying his hardest to get his head round what has happened.'

Prompted further he added: 'When I first met him he was a bit emotional but then he tried for my sake to pull himself together.' There were no frills from Charlie Kray. For once he was telling the truth, the whole truth and nothing but the truth. 'The tragedy about this is that when you are an identical twin you must feel the loss even stronger and I think half of Reggie has died with Ronnie.' Sad words indeed (and I mean that sincerely). For an identical twin the sudden death of one half must be an awesome thing. As an identical twin myself, I can commiserate with him completely.

When the twins were arrested in May of 1968 they were first sent to Brixton together with brother Charlie and other members of the Firm. Even here they managed to have fights with their so-called friends, who had shopped them to the police in return for their own freedom. But they still thought they could survive and asked the Firm to accept the killings in return for payments to their families and good jobs when they eventually got out. No one took them up on their offer and the twins were convicted of the killings. They tried to do a deal for Charlie but in the end he too went down for 12 years. The twins wouldn't admit guilt at any cost and it got them 30 years apiece.

The first 17 years must have been hell on earth for Reg Kray, spent as they were as a Category A prisoner in maximum security in Parkhurst on the Isle of Wight. His only consolation was that his brother Ron was near by. But he had no contact with others so he was left to his own devices with only time on his side. It would have killed many but it made Reg Kray even more determined to serve out his time, and he decided there and then not to try to escape. He would take his punishment like a man even though he was not used to being on the receiving end of punishment.

He spent his time painting and planning, writing and planning, keeping fit and planning. It was the only way he could keep his mind active, let alone the rest of him. It was a lonely world and the time passed slowly. He was moved around a few times to other prisons but the tour normally led back to Parkhurst and the extremes of solitary confinement. Once when he was at Long Larten Prison in 1982 he attempted to commit suicide, but that only got him sent back to Parkhurst with a special note on his file – this prisoner is unstable. But he pulled himself round with the help of his mother, who visited her sons throughout these years, and slowly but surely he could see the years fading away. Another year passing was another year closer to getting out. It spurred him on then and it continues to give him hope now.

Shortly before his final move from Parkhurst they sent him to Wandsworth for a spell in 1986 and he realised that he would soon be downgraded and moved to a more leisurely prison. This happened in 1987 when he was moved to Gartree in Leicester. Reg was past halfway and he was on his way home but there were a few years to overcome first and a few final hurdles to be negotiated. This is when his writing really took off and when he and his brother Ron made a cool £100,000 for their book *Our Story*. Since that day Reg Kray has always been on the lookout for easy money; he has never looked back. The film followed and Reg was kept busy with moves to Nottingham, Blundeston, Maidstone and then Wayland Prison. But all the time he managed to get in a regular six-monthly trip to see Ron, who in recent years had spent most of his time in Broadmoor, a mental hospital in Berkshire.

On 16 June 1991 the front page of *The People* told the story of how the Krays had managed to get rid of the body of Jack The Hat McVitie, when their old pal Tony Lambrianou sold the serialisation rights to his book *Inside the Firm*, published by Smith Gryphon, London. It did nothing to throw more light on the disappearance of the body but it did bring the whole story of the Krays back into the limelight. In reality the book was more about the loose arrangements within the Firm and the story of the Lambrianou brothers than about the twins, but that was the real purpose of the book anyway. It was no tell-tale study of the Krays, since Tony Lambrianou was one of the few members of the Firm who did not turn Queen's Evidence. But Ron and Reg Kray were back on page one where they intended to stay.

The film was well publicised, as was another book by Reg, but the newspapers didn't really pick up on any more Kray stories until they ran an article about Reg and some of his paintings which he gave away for auction so he could help a sick little boy, Paul Stapleton, aged only six at the time. The paintings were very childlike but, since he was trying to help a child to get equipment so he could better handle his muscular disorder, they were very apt and much appreciated by Paul's mother, Stephanie. They show a simple touch in pencil and crayon and the ex-mobster was praised for his actions. He was apparently the only 'celebrity' that had responded to the appeal. He also sent a signed copy of his latest book *Born Fighter* along for good measure. No matter what the real intention of the gesture, Reg's good deed was something that got him to think about others and he started, from then on in, a vast array of charitable events all over the country purely for the benefit of those worse off than himself. For a man so long a Triple A prisoner in Parkhurst it was indeed a charitable thing to do.

In December 1993 journalists could not agree on what made the best Kray story. The *Daily Mail* ran a story about the 29-year-old Lady Alice Douglas, daughter of the Marquess of Queensberry, appearing as a guest actress in a prison Shakespeare company. She was featured on page 23 with Reggie Kray, who somehow managed to get in the shot when Blundeston put on their version of *Macbeth*. *The Sun*, however, had Reg Kray talking a fellow inmate into giving himself up after a hold-up that went disastrously wrong. The fact that the hold-up occurred in Blundeston jail showed the culprit to be a bit of a wally, but it was indeed a brave thing to do since the madman had a knife at the shopkeeper's throat. I am pleased to report that the shopkeeper survived the ordeal. Reg Kray, prisoner no. 058111, enjoyed the play and played according to the Queensberry rules by holding his punches for later in the evening when he really had a chance to talk to journalists.

The early part of 1994 saw Reg Kray move to Maidstone prison in Kent where he embarked on a gearing-down for future release. This was a landmark move for the ex-gangland boss and there was much speculation about an early parole although nothing materialised. But Reg still managed to keep himself in the news by writing to *The People* and calling for Myra Hindley to be kept in jail for the rest of her life. Ron had agreed that Reg should write the letter about the 'Moors Murderer', in which he said that 95 per cent of all prisoners in the country wanted to see her stay in prison and never to be released. 'Let her rot,' he told the newspaper while agonising over her abuse and murder of children.

But Reg was now in full swing and he had an eye for the news. One day he would be asking the Home Office to make him a university lecturer so he could tour the country with his show and the next he would be organising a rave. Then it would be talk about a new house or two and then a series of billiard or snooker establishments spread all over the country. There was no end to his plans and his release from prison was looming ever closer.

But the world of Reg Kray took a turn for the worse in the

spring of 1995 when his twin brother Ron died in hospital after he had been rushed there from Broadmoor complaining of a heart attack. He had lost one half of his persona, the crazy half. This mono-zygotic twin was now just an ordinary person – like any other mere mortal. His world had changed for ever.

Ron Kray had spent the last 20 years of his life in Broadmoor, an NHS hospital for mentally disturbed patients. He escaped the high walls of Broadmoor on 17 March 1995 by dying as a result of his constant smoking. It was his joy and it was his downfall. No one killed Ron Kray, he killed himself; the bullet didn't get him but the smoke did.

Ron Kray was sent to Durham Prison in 1969, separating him from his twin brother Reg, who was allocated Parkhurst. There is no good reason why they were split up and soon the authorities had cause to regret their decision. Ron Kray was a most unruly prisoner and caused the governor much concern. So much that in 1972 he was sent to Parkhurst to join his twin, who they thought could control him. They were wrong since Ron Kray could never be controlled without proper medical supervision.

More fights followed and Ron became a problem to the governor of Parkhurst. Eventually he was sent to the mental hospital Broadmoor in Berkshire, where he could get the required medical and psychological treatment. It had taken the authorities seven years to admit that Ron Kray needed treatment for his schizophrenia, something that Long Grove Asylum knew back in June of 1958. So why did they send a man suffering from chronic paranoid schizophrenia to an ordinary prison? The question has never been answered and it is impossible to access Ron's files at Broadmoor because of the extreme secrecy of the institution.

So Ron was now in a safe environment where he could be cared for and supplied with the necessary medication to give him a normal existence, even though it was still behind bars. But Ron Kray, like Reg, had sworn never to escape. He had no problems with the sentence other than he thought it was too long and a waste of time, but he had the same problem with authority that he had had in the days of his military service. His treatment at the hands of the prison service, therefore, must have seemed very harsh indeed since the man was ill and in urgent need of the correct treatment, something that no prison could offer him. Broadmoor gave him the breathing space that he needed and he settled down quickly into the moderate regime of the establishment.

Ron Kray from this time on thought almost entirely of his friends and of those he could help. This may be a little difficult to understand but as he told me many times, 'I have everything I need in here. What do I need money for?' So he gave it all away and that is why on 17 March 1995, when he passed away, he died penniless. His only luxury was his designer clothes and his well-decorated room, nothing else was important to him except his cigarettes. But then a book or an interview to the press would cover that very nicely, thank you. He didn't believe in money for money's sake, only for the good it could do. Sure enough, if he was a free man then he would spend it and enjoy it but he wasn't and so it could benefit others instead. Somewhat strange for an ex-gangland boss and the most wanted man in Britain.

I went to see Ron Kray in the early '90s together with a journalist who had bought the rights to an interview. The young man was in for a torrid time, with Ron kicking him under the table and telling him constantly to 'Fuck off!' But he kept most of his cool although he stuttered more and more as the meeting progressed, and finally emerged into the daylight with something that he thought his editor would be pleased with. Ron told me afterwards how much he had enjoyed the day – playing up to his image was one of the few joys he had left. He treated it all as just a crazy joke but I am sure the young journalist was having nightmares. 'I didn't like his long hair,' Ron told me, 'so I decided to have some fun.' Ron was indeed schizophrenic, good guy and bad guy all rolled into one. The problem was that this could be difficult to understand if you didn't know him reasonably well. Fortunately, being a twin myself, we had common ground and that made me acceptable – thank God!

In 1993 the Krays were again back in the headlines with an article in the *Sunday Times* about the Boothby scandal. Once more Ron Kray could see his name in the newspapers and have a little chuckle to himself. It was really all about Lord Boothby but the Krays (and Ron in particular) were featured. But he was used to all the attention and it didn't mean much any more. He was more interested in what other people were doing and listened intently to their tales. He was not a very good talker but he excelled at listening.

So when the newspapers started to talk about the loonies taking over the asylum at the end of 1993 he took it all with a pinch of salt. 'Where have they done that?' he asked.

'Here, Ron,' I told him.

'Why hasn't anyone told me?' he mocked. I am sure he was completely unaware of the newspaper articles commenting on statements from MPs and union leaders alike that the authorities had no control any more at Broadmoor. But it didn't matter – he didn't really care. As long as they all left him alone he could get on with what was left of his life. Even when further political documents were made available in 1995 under the 30-year rule Ron took it all in his stride. Boothby and Driberg were once again headline news and scandal filled the pages of the newspapers. But Ron tended his garden at Broadmoor as if nothing was happening in the outside world. He wasn't bothered about politics, corruption and headlines any more – it was only the inside of Broadmoor and his medicine that kept him going.

He continued to smoke his 100 cigarettes a day and never thought about tomorrow. He joked that they couldn't make him pay tax because he was a madman, but his health was now suffering from his smoking habit and he was taken to hospital more than once with suspected heart attacks. But the final blow came in March 1995 when he was again rushed to Heatherwood Hospital in Ascot and he was yet again headline news. This time it was for real – Ron Kray suffered a massive heart attack and died shortly afterwards.

The Sun ran the story on their front pages on 18 March 1995 and they even supplied Ron Kray's dying words: 'Oh

God, Mother, help me!' The *Star* did the same with all the usual suspects and all the well-used photographs and even the *Daily Mail* used a whole page to cover the event. The usually indignant *Mail* offered sympathetic words and even carried a quote from yours truly. But the shock didn't sink in straight away to a nation used to having the Kray twins around and in the news. One of them was dead. Was it the mad one or the other one? How long had they been in prison? Were they really that bad? The questions were endless and many prominent folk tried their best to answer them but there are still so many unanswered questions surrounding the Krays. Even the *Electronic Telegraph* ran an obituary on the Internet, where they tried to summarise the life and times of the Krays in only three pages. Impossible!

During the following days when the true meaning of his death became apparent there were more stories about Ron and his gay lovers at Broadmoor, about the heavy mob standing guard over his coffin and about the inquest that was held in secret. But the news that his brain had been removed shortly after death was kept from the media. Even now we have not had a reasonable explanation for this surgical procedure and the fact that it was so hush-hush makes me want to ask why.

Reg Kray was put on medication when he heard the news of his brother's death. He had wanted to visit Ronnie in Broadmoor some days prior to his demise but the authorities at Maidstone had refused without giving any reasons for the decision. He was furious and so too was Charlie Kray. The brothers immediately set about making plans for the funeral and part of the arrangement would be the attendance of Reg Kray at the graveyard in Chingford in Essex. The Krays once again contacted their pals in the media and laid on a funeral of funerals to mark the passing of one of the biggest and most notorious of gangsters this country has ever seen.

Reg Kray's main concern apart from the actual funeral arrangements was that he had given away his black suit to a friend only a few weeks before, so he had to get fitted up for a new one a bit sharpish. Reg was never keen on being fitted up!

Ron had one last typical request and that was to be carried to his grave in a coach pulled by six black horses decked out in plumes. It was outrageous and extravagant but he was the big showman to the end. He wanted to go out in style and Reg and Charlie made sure that they honoured this request. After all, they were honourable men.

Again the newspapers were full of stories about Ron and his burial, some of them even mentioning the hatred between Ron and one particular inmate of Broadmoor, Peter Sutcliffe – the Yorkshire Ripper. I was there once with Ron Kray, with Peter Sutcliffe sitting just behind me with a pretty woman who had come to see him on many occasions. Ron and he exchanged a few sordid words before Ron told me of his dislike for Sutcliffe, a man who had mistreated women in such a depraved and debauched way. Ron Kray always treated women with respect and expected others to do likewise. Sutcliffe shortly afterwards tried to strangle Ron, thinking that he had given information to the press regarding his pretty blonde visitor. This was of course untrue. Someone else was present that day who sought to take photographs of the visitor. It was in fact one of Ron's visitors that day who protected the woman and got her away from the press. So Sutcliffe should have thanked Ron Kray instead of trying to kill him.

On 21 March 1995 Reggie Kray hit the headlines with the news that he had been given permission to go to his brother's funeral. Star John Altman, who played Nick Cotton in *EastEnders*, and page three girl Debee Ashby were also there at the prison to lend a supporting voice or two and to add to the theatrical occasion and to ask for the release of their pal. The funeral was all set for Wednesday, 29 March 1995, with the service to be held at St Matthew's, Bethnal Green, and the burial at Chingford cemetery, alongside mum and dad and Reggie's first wife Frances, who commited suicide.

There were something like 60,000 people lining the streets from the church in Bethnal Green to the cemetery in Chingford to see the procession led by the glass-sided hearse and the black plumed horses. Among the guests were the crazy gang led by Mad Frankie Fraser and Freddie Foreman, who has only recently admitted to killing the Mad Axeman Frank Mitchell. There were tributes from far and wide, including the regulars such as Barbara Windsor and Roger Daltrey, and the US Mob sent a wreath, too, to show their respects. And the newspapers spread the news all over the following day's issues with photos of jailbird Reggie with his brother Charlie. The *Daily Mail* had a photo entitled 'The grinning gangster' while the others were again more sympathetic with tributes from show business stars and specially chosen ex-gangsters.

Reg said that Ron 'had a great humour, a vicious temper, was kind and generous. Above all he was a man.' Strange words for a twin brother to say, but they were true enough. After the funeral the 30-vehicle cortège set off on the trip to Chingford. Father Bedford led the way and the coffin was brought in by amongst others Charlie Kray, Johny Nash and Freddie Foreman while a recording of Frank Sinatra's 'My Way' issued from the loudspeakers on the church walls. Charlie joined his brother and a few well-chosen friends around the coffin and poems were read out loud. Then the congregation sang the hymns 'Morning has broken' and 'Fight the Good Fight' – typical Ron Kray. Whitney Houston's voice was heard singing 'I will always love you' as the service came to a close.

Outside the church the photographers were waiting for their best opportunity and Father Christopher Bedford explained why he had conducted the service. 'It was my duty to commend Ron's soul to God,' he told them. 'I don't make judgements. God does and thankfully he is far better at it than me.' The pall-bearers carried out the coffin and the Rolls-Royces and Daimlers were ready for the slow drive over Bow Flyover and out to the cemetery – all the way with a police escort to clear the road. The photographers got their chance and the bulbs flashed and the hands shook in greeting. Well-wishers waved to Reg as he took his place in the first of the limousines together with Charlie. Reg waved back, giving rise to the *Mail* headline about the grinning gangster.

When Ron's oak coffin complete with gold-plated handles was laid in the ground, Reg Kray was led straight back to

Maidstone Prison but not before he had had the chance of throwing a red rose into the grave. Some of their old gangland pals stayed for a while at the grave while others were left to have a drink and a chat in a nearby pub. 'To the other half of me' said Reggie's wreath left on display in the cemetery. A painting of the twins was left on the grave as a reminder to everyone of the importance of the terrible twins in the annals of British crime. Only some of the newspapers mentioned that all the time during the service and afterwards, Reg had been handcuffed to a guard from Maidstone, all part of the deal that Reg was forced to make with the authorities.

The others, including Mad Frankie Fraser, Johnny Nash, Freddie Foreman, Charlie Kray and the bodyguards, all thanked each other for being there. This was a part of their history and a day that will be remembered for a long time in the East End of London. The funeral was actually larger than Winston Churchill's, which must say something even if it is only that the Krays have many pals still who are willing to organise on their behalf. And the painting so deliberately laid on the grave by Reg Kray was just as deliberately stolen during the night by souvenir-hunters. They also took a floral boxing glove that was given by prisoners at Maidstone. Nothing is sacred.

The analysis started shortly after the funeral, with all the experts giving their opinion on the Krays and Ron Kray in particular. Even Kate, who had been divorced by Ron the previous year, was asked for her opinion. No one was left out – indeed, I myself was asked by many national newspapers to supply a remark or two for their latest editions. And this is where the problems begin since it is extremely difficult to say for certain whether or not we as a country have learned anything from the experience of the Krays. I try to give my own conclusions in chapter thirteen which I call 'The Kray Legacy'.

Was Ron really evil? Or was he misunderstood? Could his kind have come from anywhere other than the East End of London? Has nostalgia taken over, making us blind to the realities of the Kray empire? And have they been in jail long enough? These and many others were the topics of the day – Ron would have had a good laugh. He always said he did what he had to do. He didn't think about it or analyse it. And I do not think that he expected others to do so. 'It's all a waste of time,' would be his reply, as he reached for a cigarette.

What Ron did leave behind was about £10,000 that he asked to be shared among his close friends at Broadmoor and his twin brother Reg. Kate got nothing, likewise Charlie. He had given his fortune away through the years at Broadmoor. In fact he had made his millions and disposed of them as he saw fit. It was a way at sticking two fingers up at the tax man and saying get it if you can. But he couldn't. And they say that Ron was mad!

Funnily enough, £10,000 was just about the same amount of money owed to the funeral companies to settle the debts for the funeral. By August of 1995 they were still unpaid but it would have been a simple matter to settle and I am sure that it was all sorted out in an amicable way. W. English & Son, part of the world's biggest funeral services company SCI, said that they would not be using strong-arm tactics to get their money. 'We are entirely comfortable with the situation,' said a company spokesman.

As for Reg, he has been busy in recent months. An amateur football club has asked him to be their president and he has also been writing about his love of music. The piece, entitled *East End Promise*, was actually commissioned by *The Stage*, for their nostalgia pages, and he talks about the old days at La Scala in Milan, where he enjoyed opera with his wife Frances. He has also been busy remembering and honouring the name of his brother Ron. In March of 1997 he actually organised a fly-past tribute to his brother over Chingford Mount Cemetery, where a memorial service was to take place. 'Ron would be pleased that we are doing this for him. He would have done the same for me,' he told reporters, who still anxiously wait for news of the Krays.

But the latest news is not good for Reg Kray. Michael Howard, when he was boss of the Home Office, disregarded pleas for Reg Kray to be released early. It would now appear that his successor Jack Straw is also intent on Reg serving out his full 30 years in prison. So Reg could still look forward to many more years in jail. Only recently have the Home Office announced an investigation into Reg Kray and charity fraud.

Reg Kray is the most well-known lifer in the country. Those who care to remember all know what he did but in this modern day and age a 30-year sentence is hard to defend. For now Reg Kray is still there behind bars, writing his books and his letters and waiting for the time when he will be free and an instant millionaire. It may be hard for some murderers and criminals to survive in the outside world once they are released, but for Reg Kray the media of the country wait in solemn silence for the date and the time of his freedom when they can coax him to the South of France, put him up in an expensive villa and get the whole story of his imprisonment straight from the horse's mouth. Reg Kray will be rich and the rich, as we all know, are powerful. He will be the richest lifer in the country!

11. WILL CHARLES KRAY, DRUG
DEALER, PLEASE STAND

'Gotcha!' said the police officer as he arrested Charlie Kray. For Charlie it was all a case of *déja vu* or, as he put it, a case of mistaken identity. But it was he who had mistaken the identity of the man with whom he had just made a two-kilogram cocaine deal and promised to supply five kilograms every two weeks for the foreseeable future. For the man known as Jack was really an undercover officer from the Metropolitan Police masquerading as a northern businessman who wanted a new supplier of dope, his previous supplier having been killed.

The date was 31 July 1996, just another pleasant Wednesday, and a new Kray prosecution was imminent. Charlie Kray had been settling down for the evening with his girlfriend Judy Stanley to watch television at her home near Croydon, south London. He was well aware of the fact that the drugs deal was going down, because he had played a major part in setting it up, but he had covered his tracks well, or so he thought, and he was not present when the cocaine changed hands. This was an old trick and it had helped Charlie Kray out of many a hole. He was often there or thereabouts but never caught with his pants down. This time, however, he had supplied the evidence for his own downfall. For unknown to him at the time, his incriminating conversations with Jack and his friends had been recorded on tape. He was soon to be his own irrefutable witness, his own worst nightmare.

Charlie Kray was led away by jubilant police officers to Ilford Police Station, next door to the regional criminal operations unit, where he was questioned about the £80 million deal. Plain-clothes detectives involved in the arrest quizzed him about his part in the drugs syndicate and the subsequent supply of cocaine. He maintained his innocence throughout even though he was informed of the capture of his two partners in crime, Ronald Field and Robert Gould. The case against Charlie looked convincing but it all rested on police evidence; evidence that could stand up in a court of law. And Charlie had usually been able to wriggle out of trouble. The only real exception here was back in 1969 when he was found guilty of helping to get rid of the body of Jack 'The Hat' McVitie and subsequently sentenced to 12 years in prison. On that occasion, however, his luck was not with him since he had not taken part in the killing, neither before nor after when other members of the Firm got rid of the body at sea – see chapter three: 'Another One Bites the Dust'. So what did he have to fear this time around?

Judy Stanley stopped to talk to the press as she left Ilford Police Station that night after vainly attempting to see her lover. 'Charlie has done nothing wrong,' she said tearfully. 'We are utterly amazed.' As a parting gesture she asked them, 'Can you imagine a 70-year-old man who has a hatred of drugs being involved in the distribution of them?' No one answered. Later, at her Sanderstead semi-detached house she spoke again to the press. 'Someone has thrown his name into the hat because of what he is,' she said. 'He is no stranger to all this but he's 70 now and doesn't need the hassle.'

The police issued a statement saying that it was 'one of the largest and most significant drugs raids this year'. Indeed, the Metropolitan Police had been very busy that evening arresting 31 people in south-east London.

Charlie Kray had much to think about as he sat in his cell that night. What kind of case did the police really have against him? Would the others talk and implicate him in the deal? How long would he spend behind bars if found guilty? When would he be permitted to see his lawyer Ralph Haems, a close Kray family friend?

It reminded him of the days when he was behind bars in Canada. That time he was thrown out of the country, because of lack of evidence. His Mafia pals had played their cards right, unlike their English cousins, who had had a traitor in their midst – a man who almost led them to life in the Tombs, Montreal's own top-flight prison. But the Mob weren't around this time so who could he rely on? Charlie Kray began to think, to wonder why it had happened this way, to speculate on the outcome, to reflect on the events that had led to this most terrifying ordeal. The only question that concerned him was why.

It had been a long night, a night without end. But the story had only just begun to unwind. It followed a devious path: no straight and narrow for Charlie Kray. But then this had always been the case. The only way to get rich was to outsmart the other guy: why do it legally if you can do it easily and reasonably safe by using the Kray name? This same Kray name that had caused so many complications in his life. He should have known better. His brothers, Ron and Reg, had always been able to control situations, to use the Kray name to make lots of dosh. But Charlie had never really been very successful at trading on the fear and violence that the name conjures up in the minds of good guys and bad guys alike. His nice little earners often turned to dismal tales of what might have been. The get-rich-quick schemes had always worked for others but not for him. This was like 'Del-boy' out of his league, playing with the big boys, those who know all the tricks and always come out on top.

As Charlie Kray slept his mind wandered back to the first time he had met Jack and to the meeting that was to seal his fate. This lonely character, down on his luck and 70 years old, was soon to be called simply a 'foolish old man'. So what had gone wrong? And why?

'Done, mate.' That was all it took to secure the multi-million-pound drugs deal. Charlie Kray was feeling fine. It was the deal of a lifetime but he had to be careful. 'I put people together,' Charlie told Jack. 'But I won't go there when they do these things because I have too many eyes on me.' How right he was.

Jack too had to be careful. He needed the right kind of

proof of Charlie's complicity in the deal so a hidden tape recorder was always at hand. It wouldn't do to tip anyone off accidentally, because this was hard core drugs trade – intruders would be dealt with speedily and for ever. There was no room for errors of any kind.

The idea of the sting came in May when a phone tap revealed the name of Charlie Kray. The Metropolitan Police were aware of drugs deals being set up in and around London and they had arranged for numerous phone taps to try to gain useful information concerning future drugs deals. They felt sure that the known drugs barons would be involved somewhere along the line but the name of Kray must have been a real bonus. High profile, high status – a good career move in the making.

However, a recent cocaine bust involving Dave Courtney, a friend of Reg Kray's and the man in charge of security at Ron Kray's funeral, may also have played a part in calculations. He had been arrested at Heathrow Airport with £1 million of cocaine. Further back in time there was the cocaine bust involving Pete Gillet, Reg Kray's adopted son, and then there was the bust involving Joe Pyle, ex-Kray Firm member and still a close pal of the twins. There were no end to cocaine connections in the Kray family.

An introduction was made through a go-between establishing Jack (not his real name) as a northern businessman with connections in the underworld and in need of a supplier. Cocaine was his chosen vital ingredient and Jack did all he could to impress Charlie Kray with his good humour, his money and lots of champagne. They didn't call Charlie Kray 'Champagne Charlie' for no reason.

It worked well and soon Jack had been invited to attend a party, a benefit for Charlie's son Gary who had recently died of cancer. Jack and another plain-clothes man called Brian (again, not his real name) met with Charlie Kray and the discussion inevitably came around to drugs. Ronald Field, a 49-year-old builder, and Robert Gould, a 39-year-old electrician, were introduced to Jack and Brian as a good supply source of cocaine.

Later, Charlie Kray would be thankful that his son, Gary, was not alive to witness the depths of depravation that had lured his father into dealing in drugs, something that his brothers even in their heyday had never resorted to. But then drugs were not then the scourge of society that they are now. If Reg and Ron Kray were starting on a life of crime today it would be difficult indeed not to be involved in one way or another in drugs.

Soon afterwards Jack invited Charlie and his accomplice Ronald Field to visit with him in Newcastle. This was to seal the connection and to show good faith. Once again, throwing money around as though there were no tomorrow had apparently worked and Jack became just another do-gooder in the long line of Kray benefactors. The two Londoners stayed at the Linden Hall Hotel at the expense of Jack and his friend Brian, although in reality every taxpayer in the UK was footing the bill. But Jack had set things up very well. The scheming had paid off. Charlie and Ronald Field fell for the bait – they took it hook, line and sinker. Jack on behalf of the Metropolitan Police and the country and in order to trap Charlie Kray once and for good agreed to pay £31,500 per kilogram for an initial drop of two kilograms, the money to be paid in cash at a time and a place to be determined later by mutual agreement. The arrangements included future supplies of five kilograms every two weeks for at least the following two years, a deal that would net Charlie and his pals a cool £80 million. And it was all recorded for posterity on a hidden tape recorder used later in the trial of *Regina* v. *Charles Kray*.

The deal was done and all men shook hands on a prosperous business venture. And that is what it was to Charlie Kray, just another deal – another chance to make a fortune and to give Judy Stanley the good life he thought she deserved. This was to him a last chance; a chance to gain some kind of prestige and to live the rest of his petty life in some kind of grandeur.

But Charlie Kray wasn't through playing his mind games. He was well aware of the fact that he was now playing very near the line, the barrier between good and evil – some would say that he had already crossed over to the other side. If

Charlie could find a way of getting the money, and that was what this was really all about, without really going through with the deal, he would jump at the chance. After all, it had often worked on previous occasions. I do not want to bore readers with sordid details of other petty con tricks – suffice it to say that these are well documented at Scotland Yard and by other 'informed' sources. This time, however, the deal could not be termed petty. How could anyone call £80 million anything but a major scam?

There were numerous delays to the deal going through as Charlie tried to evade the question of drugs and to get on to the question of the money. He even managed to borrow a small amount (about £500) from Jack, saying that he had recently lost £1 million on a deal that had gone wrong. Now that doesn't appear to be far-fetched considering Charlie's proven track record but anyway it did the trick for the time being. Something is better than nothing has always been Charlie's motto. Again, the state footed the bill.

Eventually Jack and Brian managed to fix a meeting with Field and Gould at the Swallow Hotel in Waltham Abbey. The date was 31 May 1996. The drugs would be delivered and the money would change hands – £63,000 in cool cash. Charlie Kray had already arranged not to be present at the exchange.

As planned, the cocaine was handed over in a brown paper bag to the undercover policemen Jack and Brian in the early part of the evening at the chosen venue. The deal done, Field and Gould left the scene with their ready cash, also in brown paper bags. Jack and Brian inspected their delivery of the cocaine and phoned in to headquarters that the sting had gone off well and that Operation Crackdown was a success.

When Ronald Field and Robert Gould stopped to refuel their car at the Lakeside Service Station on the M25 London orbital motorway at Thurrock, police swooped to capture both men and cash. Further drugs were also seized. Jack was right – Operation Crackdown had been a complete success. At the same moment officers were on their way to visit Charlie Kray; his champagne days would soon be over, possibly for good.

On Friday, 2 August 1996, Charlie Kray appeared in Red-bridge Court, East London, charged with plotting to supply, and supplying drugs. The 30-minute hearing was a simple affair. Charlie smiled to Judy, Judy smiled back. Charlie even managed to blow her a kiss as he stood quite motionless in his smart navy-blue suit, waiting for a decision. He and the other accused were given a further 28 days in remand, although this was later changed to 6 days since the magistrates had made a little mistake regarding their powers in such a case. But the major details remained the same: conspiring to supply, and arranging to supply approximately £80 million of cocaine.

Judy took it well and vowed to continue her fight to save her Charlie, a man who, according to her, hated the mere mention of drugs.

The following days, weeks, months saw a routine of visits to court for all three accused. They were in deep trouble and the police were not about to release any of them so they could conveniently leave the country or intimidate witnesses or anything else for that matter. They would remain in jail until a date could be fixed for a trial.

They had a long wait. On Monday, 2 December 1996, Charlie Kray stood in court at Woolwich, South London, and was duly remanded in custody for plotting an £80 million cocaine importation and supply deal. His pals Ronald Field and Robert Gould were in court with him, accused of the same crime, and therefore all three men would await the same fate.

Judy was there again but there were no kisses this time.

The only good thing to come out of this period for Charlie Kray was that he didn't have to feed himself or to supply a roof over his own head. And his debtors couldn't get hold of him. The problems hadn't gone away since he still owed money. But they had been shelved for a while and time, as they say, is a great healer. But it hadn't worked before so why should it work this time? Sooner or later Charlie Kray would have to face up to his problems, his debts, his deals and his nightmares.

Charlie Kray was soon standing in Woolwich Crown Court

accused of offering to supply cocaine, supposedly to a value of £39 million. Why the figure had been reduced from £80 million is not quite clear. But still it was enough to put him away for a very long time indeed. It was now Wednesday, 14 May 1997, and Charlie Kray had already spent almost a year in custody.

John Kelsey-Fry for the prosecution opened with a few general remarks addressed to the jury. First of all he told them: 'Kray is an unusual name and you may have guessed that the defendant, now over 70 years old, is the brother of the Kray twins, Reggie and the late Ronnie.' He continued by telling them: 'You will appreciate that no man is his brother's keeper, and whatever his brothers may or may not have done 30 years ago cannot adversely reflect on this defendant.' In the same vein he added: 'The brothers' past actions can in no way help you determine his guilt or innocence of these charges.' Well, that was plain enough and it must surely have helped to set the record straight. The seven women and five men of the jury were, I am quite certain, put at ease by these remarks. However, to put their minds completely at rest they were told that they were being put under police surveillance throughout the expected six weeks of the trial, just as a security measure. That remark must surely have helped their concentration.

The Kray name was now established. It was time to continue. 'As the evidence unfolds it will become clear that Charlie Kray presents himself as an affable, slightly down-at-heel character, much liked for his amusing tales of the old days and the twins,' said the learned prosecutor. But he added, just for good measure, 'The Crown alleges that behind that affable and charitable image there was another side to Charlie Kray. He was a man prepared to be involved in the drugs trade.' John Kelsey-Fry had made his point and everyone in the courtroom knew it.

The prosecutor told the court that Charlie Kray took care never to be present when the drugs were handed over. He also reminded the jury of the Kray name with all the associations and implications that go with it: 'But he was the kingpin, the link in the chain without whom the deal could not be done.' Details of the cocaine itself were also outlined in the court room; it was 92 per cent pure and lethal. A five-kilogram delivery every other week would have had serious consequences. And then Kelsey-Fry delivered a telling blow by informing the jury that the other defendants in the case had admitted their involvement: Field from Raynes Park and Gould from Wimbledon had pleaded guilty prior to the trial. Charlie Kray was the last man standing.

Charlie had not helped his case by refusing to answer questions that night at Ilford Police Station when he was first taken into custody. Mr Kelsey-Fry pressed home his advantage by repeating this fact several times and added that they would be hearing tape recordings of Mr Kray setting up the deals. Also on the recordings, according to a somewhat jovial John Kelsey-Fry, they would be hearing Charlie Kray talking about his old friends Rocky Marciano and Frank Sinatra, but the main facts to listen out for were those involving the proposed cocaine deal. These first tape recordings were taken at Charlie Kray's 70th birthday party in Birmingham. It was here, according to the prosecution, that the first talk of supplying drugs took place. The jury would hear Mr Kray himself admitting to be able to supply cocaine. These were damaging remarks indeed, and the trial had only just begun.

The first witness in the case was our old friend Jack the undercover policeman and to protect his identity he was hidden behind a screen. Jack told his story of the sting and of the eventual handing over of the cocaine. He missed nothing out about Operation Crackdown and even talked about his back-up story of being a northern businessman with criminal connections. 'I told Mr Kray that my dealer had been topped,' he told the jury. He continued to relate a tale of intrigue and guile. 'Kray said he had people who were sat on a ton [of cocaine] and he could put my name on it,' he told them. 'That is a lot of puff, I told him.' Charlie Kray was then reported to have said: 'I know it is not the place – we will talk in the morning.' But no mention was made of who it was who set up the initial meeting with Charlie Kray and how his name had come up in the phone-tapping part of the investigation.

Still the prosecution had a good case against Charlie Kray

and the jury heard a lot of incriminating evidence against him during the first week of the trial. It was just something that he had to get through before he could have his own particular day in court. But a betting man wouldn't have given him very good odds during this first part of the trial.

The whole idea and presentation of the interrogation of the witness Jack had all been a little bizarre. It had been staged to impress the jury and it had been very convincing, although it would have been more at home in an American TV trial. The press had been there in force; no one wanted to miss a historic Kray trial and it was well reported throughout the media. But it didn't look as though the force was with Charlie Kray this time around. It was soon to be even more peculiar and theatrical, acrimonious even. For it was now the turn of Jonathan Goldberg QC for the defence.

On Thursday, 22 May 1997, Jonathan Goldberg QC was ready and eager to cross-examine Jack, the prosecution's main witness. Was this to be a revival of good fortunes for Charlie Kray? Or was it just a last-ditch gamble, with all the cards stacked against him? At first it looked as though he had only jokers in his hand.

'Did you tell a barmaid at a hotel in Essex that you and Brian, a colleague, were into security guarding wealthy Arabs and jewels?' he asked a surprised Jack. Was this Mr Goldberg's trump card? Jack replied that he couldn't remember.

It was now time to add a little spice to the trial of Charlie Kray. The defence QC continued to attack Jack on that point. Referring to an evening that Jack and Brian had spent with the Spice Girls at the Essex hotel where the drugs deal was supposed to be shortly concluded, he asked if Jack had said to the barmaid: 'Why don't we kidnap Victoria Adams, who is better known as "Posh Spice", then release her and put ourselves forward as bodyguards?' His intention was to imply that Jack and his colleague Brian had compromised themselves and the investigation by drinking and partying with the girls at the hotel. Four hours of such behaviour, remarked Mr Goldberg QC, was surely tantamount to misconduct. Jack denied that he had said anything of the kind to the barmaid.

Jonathan Goldberg continued to talk about the 'Spice Girl' incident; something that appeared to have happened by chance after the girls had appeared on *Top of the Pops*.

Questioned about making phone calls that evening, Jack admitted phoning Michelle Hamdouchi, a hostess he had met at Charlie Kray's 70th birthday party, to ask her over to the hotel. The undercover policeman was asked if he had said, 'Come and have some drinks with Posh Spice.'

Jack replied that it had all been a prank but that she had surprisingly arrived at the hotel. It was apparently a surprise to both Jack and to his colleague.

But Jonathan Goldberg wasn't finished with his questioning yet. 'Isn't it true that Miss Hamdouchi and your colleague Brian went for a "quickie" in the bedroom?' he asked. The idea was that both Jack and Brian wanted their own bit of spice entering their lives, at the taxpayers' expense too.

'I don't think so, sir' said Jack solemnly. The afore-mentioned sleeping together had not apparently been reported to superior officers in subsequent reports and Mr Goldberg suggested that the whole thing had been one huge cover-up to disguise their own misdemeanours as a genuine 'sting' operation in which they were 'setting up' his client. 'You got caught trying to protect him [referring to Brian] and both of you have ended up telling a tissue of lies.'

It had all been a case of 'Give me what I want, what I really, really want', suggested Jonathan Goldberg QC. Brian had managed to get what he wanted but it certainly looked as though the whole thing could have back-fired on them and blown their cover. It was a sorry and sordid episode, if a bit of a joke, and Jack had difficulty in answering the many questions put to him that day. There had been a couple of cops whoopin' it up in the Swallow Hotel Saloon but for the moment they appeared to have gotten away with it. That Thursday for Jack and Brian couldn't end quickly enough.

If these previous days had been a comedy of errors then what awaited the jury on Monday, 2 June 1997, was a character assassination. The man doing the assassin's work was none other than Jonathan Goldberg QC. And the man being crucified was his client Charlie Kray

First Mr Goldberg had a few words to say about the treatment of his client. Outside Woolwich Crown Court armed police were on patrol. People going into the court were searched, luggage was searched. His client had been kept at Belmarsh Prison, Category Triple A security (like IRA prisoners). 'The hype surrounding his case is the biggest obstacle I face in defending him,' he concluded.

Now the assassination could begin. 'Charlie Kray is no more than a skint old man trying to charm cash out of his victims.' Now that was pretty bad but worse was to come. 'He is a pathetic old has-been, cashing in on the family name and cadging drinks whenever he could.'

Charlie Kray stood in the dock motionless, head down, while his life was torn to shreds. What a sight he made. He wore a smart suit, clean shirt and polished shoes. But behind the façade stood the real Charlie Kray with fake watch, schooled smile and false reputation. In tears he told of how he couldn't even bury his own son who had died of cancer at the age of 44 the year before. His brother Reg, he told the jury, had paid all of Gary's funeral expenses. He spoke quietly and in a subdued way about living with his girlfriend Judy Stanley, a headmaster's daughter, at her semi in Sanderstead, and of how he shared the home with her three sons. It was a sad experience for everyone there.

Mr Goldberg didn't let up however. He said that police had lured a foolish old man into a carefully laid trap. 'This old fool thought he could string them along and con them.'

A pitiful Charlie Kray, his reputation in tatters, had to continue to have his life pulled apart. It must have been a terrifying ordeal for a man who had lived his life with pride. For no matter what he had done or had tried to do, Charlie Kray was indeed a man who had tried to live up to a certain code. It may not have been a recognised moral code but it was in the main the style of a man with dignity. It may appear strange to an outsider but Charlie Kray is not all bad – he has, however, difficulty in telling right from wrong and this time had gone just a little too far across that line between good and evil.

The jury were now witnessing a curious double act. First Jonathan Goldberg would say something quite detrimental about his client, then it would be Charlie Kray's turn to do himself damage and to imply a simplicity in his actions. The reason for these actions was to simply get money out of a punter. Charlie Kray didn't care who the punter was, just how much money he could con out of him.

Charlie Kray now told that jury that he had even had to borrow £50 that night when he first went out to meet Jack and his pal. He said that he had always been broke with no bank account, no credit cards, nothing. Now that is something of a little white lie since I just happen to have a copy of a cheque from Charlie Kray in my possession. Certainly he didn't have the account for very long but it did exist and it is not difficult to prove. However, the police were not interested in such sordid minor details. They had a fish to catch, and bank account or no, they wanted their man.

Jonathan Goldberg continued the act. 'Charlie Kray is nothing but he looks everything,' he told the court. He was quoting Lady Bracknell, from *The Importance of Being Earnest* where Oscar Wilde is describing Algernon. 'He might seem suave, like a million dollars, but he is just an old trouper doing his best.' It might have been his best but it wasn't working.

Something new was needed and the defendant himself had once more to step into the breach. 'It was just a load of bull,' he told them. 'I swear on the grave of my son that it's just a load of rubbish.' He was clearly trying to establish the fact, alluded to earlier, that he was trying to con money out of Jack and his pals, not trying to supply drugs.

Mr Goldberg took up the argument once again by telling the jury how Charlie Kray had 'frittered away the money from the Kray film'. Perhaps he forgot to tell them the amount involved; maybe £99,000 would have made a different kind of impression on them. He may also have forgotten to tell them of the problems Charlie Kray had with his brothers about his handling of the deal. Instead of over £1 million they only received £297,000 between them. (This included Charlie's payment as technical adviser.) Charlie, as usual, needed the money fast and took a huge discount to get cash. Ron and Reg Kray were furious with him at the time and didn't speak to him for almost a year. But that was of little interest to Mr Goldberg.

'Charlie Kray has been a victim of his surname throughout his life,' said the defence counsel. This may have been right but it was also his 'cash cow' and he had milked it for all he could get. 'He is sociable, lovable, anti-crime, a wonderful father, anti-drugs and anti-violence,' he continued. And for good measure he added: 'He is a man with a heart of gold, naïve and gullible.' Well, I may very well agree with some of that but really to call Charlie Kray anti-crime is like calling Tony Blair anti-politics. Charlie Kray has always been on the fringes of criminal activity and how any man can say such garbage about the man who laundered stolen bearer-bonds for the US Mafia is really quite beyond me.

But Jonathan Goldberg did hit the right note when he began to argue the case against the police, saying that the whole case looked like 'an elaborate and devious sting'. To clarify matters he added: 'No doubt it has been quite a feather in the cap of many officers to nick the last of the Kray brothers.' The police he said had acted as 'agents provocateurs'. There may have been some truth in this but Charlie Kray didn't have to do the business to arrange for the supply of cocaine.

It was revealed in court that Charlie Kray had been involved in various businesses. He had managed a failed pop band, gone bankrupt with a clothing company, existed as a celebrity doing talk shows and interviews and so on. Again the talk came around to famous film stars such as Judy Garland and Frank Sinatra and it reminded Charlie of the time Ron shouted at Judge Melford Stevenson at the trial back in 1969, 'I could be dining with Judy Garland instead of being here.' It wasn't the kind of thing a QC should be reminding the jury of in such circumstances.

The only other conviction that Charlie had against his

name, apart from disposing of the McVitie body, was a £5 fine for theft in 1950.

To change tack a little Mr Goldberg asked Charlie about his brothers. Ron was ill, he said, but he could be kind-hearted. Reg, he said, went crazy after Frances died, but they always treated normal people with respect. I for one would like to know what Charlie Kray calls normal people. He probably means anyone who doesn't get in their way.

The day was drawing to an end and it was time to make a point or two. To explain the way Charlie looked at people and money Mr Goldberg said: 'Charlie Kray would offer to sell Scud missiles if he thought he could get some cash out of the deal. But only as a con.' This was indeed a dangerous ploy because it showed a devious side to Charlie's character. Anything for money was not really the kind of thing to say to a jury and certainly not one trying a Kray. To balance things up the QC added that the police officers in the case had swilled champagne and encouraged Charlie to deal with them. But seeing that kind of money was too enticing – he had just explained that in open court. It was an apparent fact that Charlie Kray was a crime waiting to happen!

To Jonathan Goldberg QC, Charlie Kray was 'a pathetic old has-been, a thoroughly washed-up figure whom the hype by the police and prosecution has made to appear something he is not'. The day was over for Charlie, no time for elaborate excuses. No time for any cosy chat over a pint down the pub, only time to remember. It had been a gruelling day for everyone and now Charlie Kray had only his thoughts for company.

If anyone had imagined that this trial would continue with a whimper they were very much mistaken. Wednesday 4 June started with a bang!

'My brother found out before I did that they had removed Ronnie's brain after he was dead for experiments. Everyone was ringing up about it and was very upset about it and wondering why.' Charlie Kray was near to tears as he continued his grim tale. 'Finally they returned the brain in a casket and it was reburied,' he told the court. Exactly how anyone had recognised the brain of the deceased murderer was not made clear. It probably had a label on it saying 'Ron Kray's Brain'. The family had complained to the Home Office about it but no one had had the decency to explain the need for removing the brain or the need for keeping it such a secret. So the complaint situation had not yet been resolved.

'They didn't admit it at the time,' said Charlie. 'We thought we were burying the full body.'

In fact brain tissues were removed by Home Office pathologists and pickled in a jar. No one said whether it was strawberry or raspberry and I am sure Ron Kray wasn't bothered but the tissues did find their way to Oxford for testing. A statement was issued at the time but hidden away for only academics to find. A spokeswoman for Wexham Park said: 'Tissue is sent away to specialist centres if we don't have the right facilities.' She added: 'They can find out if there was any damage to the brain or any illness. It is not standard but it happens in about one in three cases'.

Radcliffe Infirmary in Oxford had been in possession of the tissues for almost a year – they were carrying out tests to establish whether Ron Kray had suffered any brain damage or illness prior to his death. However, officials denied that tests were linked to research into criminality. But still the brain tissue had been removed without consent or the knowledge of Kate Kray, Ron's wife, when the post-mortem examination had taken place at Wexham Park. It was confirmed by the Radcliffe that researchers had not found any abnormalities in Ron Kray's brain cells. Well, that is good to know. This was just one of many macabre interludes during the trial of Charlie Kray, but yet still more drama was to follow.

For the moment, however, Jonathan Goldberg QC was content to repeat his summing-up. He said once more that the police had lured his client because of his name and that he was a 'foolish old man' who had been trapped by devious methods. Mr Goldberg has used all his aces. The only cards left were character witnesses, who were due to appear the following week. But could convicted villains like Mad Frankie Fraser and actors such as Billy Murray from ITV's *The Bill* really get Charlie Kray out of trouble? Only time would tell.

'Charles is a lovely, lovely man who would not know how to steal a penny,' said Mad Frankie Fraser, replying to a question put to him by Jonathan Goldberg QC. 'He wouldn't say boo to a goose,' he continued as he poured praise on the man in the dock. The trial had moved on to Monday, 9 June 1997, and the former Richardson gang member (some would say executioner) was presented as a character witness in the case. It may appear puzzling that a villain such as Frankie Fraser was in court at all; especially when he was not being prosecuted himself. For during his 73 years he had been inside for 41 of them and had openly admitted to killing two people. This was the kind of man who was now acting as a character witness on behalf of Charlie Kray.

'To this day the Krays are quite rightly idolised,' he said when questioned about his relationship with the Krays. As a Richardson enforcer he had spoken with Charlie and his brothers many times, mainly to sort out minor problems that had arisen between the gangs, he told the court. He even went on to talk about the time when Ron Kray shot and killed George Cornell and when questioned further he said: 'Theory has it that he (Cornell) had called Ronnie a big fat poof.'

Asked by John Kelsey-Fry for the prosecution whether he thought Charlie Kray could deal in drugs, Mad Frankie replied, 'He could not do it, not for a single day. You are probably more into drugs than him.' This was gradually developing into the Mad Frankie Fraser show and it was not helping Charlie Kray one bit. But then Mad Frankie has always had a way of helping himself. As a final gesture to the jury he told them: 'This is the first time I have come out of court free.' He was free all right but his so-called pal Charlie Kray was beginning to pray for a miracle because that was what he needed now.

Next in line as a character witness was Billy Murray, the actor who plays Det. Sgt. Beech in *The Bill*. Charlie Kray was a gentleman he told them all; he had even been helped by the Krays early on in his career.

Then came a procession of do-gooders such as Eileen Sheridan-Price, the first-ever Miss UK; Robin McGibbon, who had written a book with Charlie Kray some years earlier;

Michelle Hamdouchi, who had been sleeping around with Jack's colleague Brian and who had been mentioned earlier in the trial.

It was all very interesting but not interesting enough. The tape recordings previously played 'live' in court where Charlie openly talked about supplying drugs had done the trick for the prosecution. From then on in it had been downhill all the way. Charlie Kray had now spent much time in the dock behind the glass screen. His only companions had been two prison officers standing by his side. His only movement was a glance or two upwards to see who was testifying. He was still the last man standing.

The five-week trial was over and the jury of four men and seven women (one man had been excused during the trial) had to bring in their verdict. Guilty or not guilty?

What would it be? Charlie Kray knew he would soon find out.

On Friday, 20 June the jury brought in their verdict. They had deliberated for three whole days. The verdict was delivered soberly and simply. Charlie Kray had been found guilty on all counts. He was guilty of offering to supply undercover police officers with a consignment of cocaine every fortnight for two years. He was guilty of supplying two kilograms of cocaine worth £63,000 the previous July. They could have added that he was also guilty of being a man named Kray.

Judy Stanley wept as she sat in Woolwich Crown Court, her hands covering her face. Other women in the packed public gallery started to cry while men just shook their heads in amazement.

But all this time Charlie Kray sat in the dock without the slightest emotion. He knew it was all over bar the shouting and when it came it was something of a relief. Judge Carroll had already earlier in the day told him that he could expect a custodial sentence. He rose from the dock to shake hands with his barrister Jonathan Goldberg QC. As he shook his hand he also found time to blow Judy a kiss, but he didn't smile on this occasion although he did manage to receive one back. He knew he faced a possible life sentence.

Outside the court Judy Stanley was too upset to speak to
the press so friends said a few words on her behalf. Diana
Buffini told them that there was evidence that the jury had not
been allowed to see. And Maureen Cox, a former *Sun* page
three girl said: 'Our biggest fear is that he will not come out
alive.' Later Judy did speak to the media but only to say: 'I am
in a state of shock.' Their only hope now was a light sentence
and everyone stressed Charlie's age, over 70 years old, and the
problems of incarceration at that time of life. For Charlie Kray
any sentence could be life.

Judge Michael Carroll began proceedings on Monday, 23
June 1997 by launching a withering attack on Charlie Kray,
whom he called a veteran villain. 'You show yourself to be
ready, willing and able to lend yourself to any criminal
enterprise,' he told him. 'But when caught you cried foul,' he
continued. 'I'm pleased to see that this jury saw through that
hollow cry.' He sentenced Charlie Kray to 12 years'
imprisonment, part of which was to be as a Triple A prisoner.
'Throughout this case you have professed your abhorrence of
drugs but the jury's verdict has shown your oft-repeated
protestations to be hypocrisy.' Charlie showed no emotion as
the sentence was passed. The game was up.

'Those who deal in class-A drugs can expect justice from the
courts but little mercy,' said Judge Carroll bitterly. Judy Stanley
waved goodbye to her ageing lover as she left the court. It was
left to Mr Goldberg QC, a man who had torn his own client to
pieces, to say that he thought Charlie Kray would have trouble
in prison and be the target for thugs. 'Every young hoodlum will
want to take a pot-shot at Charlie Kray. Public interest does not
require a sentence that means he dies in prison,' he said. Perhaps
Jonathan Goldberg had already said enough. Giving young
offenders ideas of that nature is not a good thing to do.
Personally I believe that he will survive. If nothing else, Charlie
Kray has been a survivor all his life, no matter what.

The irony of the case is that his accomplices Ronald Field
and Robert Gould received nine years and five years
respectively. And these were the men who actually did the
business. So what price justice?

Reg Kray immediately complained about the verdict and the sentence. He thought the whole case had been arranged as a set-up to lengthen his own prison term of 30 years. Then he quietly set about trying to find the man who had fingered his brother. God help him.

All the stories of stars such as Jackie Collins, Muhammad Ali, Sonny Liston, Judy Garland and Frank Sinatra hadn't helped. The stories of Posh Spice and the 'quickie' incident hadn't helped. The demeaning summing up by his own defence counsel hadn't helped. Nothing had helped.

As trials go it was an expensive and protracted series of outlandish events more at home on the cinema screen than in a Crown Court. It was a tale of iniquitous dealings and personalities, with a debilitating series of assaults on the personal character and credibility of the accused, Charlie Kray. The country had incurred all the costs and will continue to do so – in Charlie Kray's case for the next 12 years or so.

'We will appeal,' said Judy Stanley, finding her voice at last. 'Twelve years is a long time but Charlie will be fine.' She left to start proceedings for the appeal and to drown her sorrows. She began to cry again.

Further down the road, however, stood a happy and contented man. Det. Supt. Gavin Robertson, the man who led the inquiry known as Operation Crackdown, was overjoyed. He wasn't amazed at the verdict or at the sentence. 'No sad old fool has the capacity to produce that amount of cocaine,' he said solemnly. He was right.

And still Charlie Kray protests his innocence but then he has nothing else left to do. At 71 he is behind bars and facing an eternity in prison with all the low-lives he thought he was getting away from. I well remember only a few years ago when I was walking with Charlie Kray along Waterloo Road. He stopped, turned and pulled me over to the other side of the street. When I asked for a reason for this action his answer came rather unexpectedly.

'It's that Buster,' he said, referring to the Great Train Robber Buster Edwards, who ran a flower stall just outside

Waterloo Station. 'He's always trying to get me roped into things.' Charlie didn't want the aggro then but maybe he has changed just a little.

Meanwhile the old-timers have turned out to raise money for their old pal. Mad Frankie Fraser and Tony Lambrianou have organised a fund-raiser at the Ridge Golf Club in Kent, where they asked the guests for £100 just for the pleasure of being invited. Once inside they were asked for further donations to boost Charlie's resources for his appeal. The young hoods came in by the back door while the older villains were openly looking for publicity.

'Charlie has lots of friends, many of whom do not believe that he was involved with smuggling cocaine,' said Tony Lambrianou. That is quite right even though it rather distorts the truth. He wasn't pronounced guilty of smuggling cocaine – he was found guilty of selling and supplying it. Maybe Mr Lambrianou should get his facts right.

So all the gangsters turned up to pay tribute to Charlie Kray and to wine and dine the night away to the music of The Rockin' Berries. There were over 200 of them in all, just a token amount of assorted villains and rogues, all there for a reason. It was a time to talk of old times and to plan new ventures with quiet talk in dark dingy corners. Hand-shaking looked as though it had come back into fashion in a big way, or should that be in a Mr Big way?

So the team of old lags is back in business. Maybe Charlie Kray will get the help he so desperately wants or maybe the crooks will just get a little richer. In either case, I think Judy Stanley will have a long wait.

12. THE WOMEN IN THEIR LIVES

The idea of gangsters and their molls goes back to the early days of cinema and to Hollywood's impression of the reality of the early '30s in places such as Chicago and the Lower East Side of New York. The bad guy would be the stiff-upper-lip type, always ready to mow down the enemy with a machine-gun or to slap a kiss on the face of the best-looking broad in the house. Well, at least that was how Cagney and Bogart used to do it.

The Krays were different. Not least because Ronnie was a self-confessed homosexual. But their lives and the image of their times that they tried to display as being representative of those days shows something else. They followed the Cagney path true enough by trying to visibly emulate the Chicago gangsters. They even dressed like them and drove American cars. Outwardly both men tried to show themselves as good-looking, normal, everyday types, constantly in the company of attractive and beautiful women. Ron was photographed with Christine Keeler around the time of the Profumo scandal, and Reg was photographed with Judy Garland, even though he tried to hide the photo from his wife Frances. So they tried to convey an image of normality, one that they thought would do them the most good. Image, especially to Ron Kray, was an important part of being one of the most feared people in the country.

It was Ron's downfall that he could not let George Cornell get away with calling him a 'big fat poof' because it was said in public and it didn't tie in with Ron being the violent underworld boss that he so rightly was. In fact, no one is really sure if that was what Cornell said, but the intent was there sure enough.

So was the image created by Ron Kray done so as to hide the fact that he was homosexual or was it just a way to get his name in the history books? And was Reg Kray really the timid, shy lad we are told about in the books or was there another reason for his behaviour?

Women have always been fascinated by the Krays. That is a verifiable fact and they have had enough correspondence to fill the Albert Hall. It is as true today as it was back in their heyday of the '50s and '60s, so what is it that attracts? What makes women (or at least some women) wet their knickers over the Krays?

Maybe it is all just media hype. Have we all been brainwashed into imagining that Ron, Reg and Charlie Kray are just a bunch of nice East End boys who have sex appeal in abundance? I heard the opinion recently that the tabloid press helps to fill a void, a need for emotional sentimentality. In common journalistic jargon, it is expressed as the commerce of feeling or the politics of emotion – the recent death of Diana, Princess of Wales, is a good example. But is this outburst of feeling by the media representative of the country or does it just make sentimental idiots of us all?

The press try to sell newspapers and no one can blame them for that. But the trend now is for the tabloids to break one of these heart-rending stories, followed three days later or so by the broadsheet newspapers. So is there an actual void, or do the press create the void, only to fill it with this type of media sexy stuff?

Whether this kind of sexiness is contagious or not is something that I feel needs further research, but the truth of the matter is that many women do find the Krays sexy. They are attracted to these men. They want to contact them. They write to them. They fill an apparent void for these women.

So is it power that women are after or is it purely fantasy that attracts them? Surely both are contenders among the young. Possibly the older women and those from more puritan backgrounds simply want to entice the Krays onto the straight and narrow. Or maybe others just want to become natural born killers and live out their fantasies in ways that they can only dream about. Whatever it is that turns them on, it appears to work for the Krays. And the Krays love it.

To ensure the psychological background for this chapter I

have enlisted the assistance of family psychologist Audrey Sandbank, from the twins organisation TAMBA, and Tim Trimble, who lectures in psychology at King Alfred's College, Winchester.

Considering the Kray family in general and the brothers in particular, I will try to elucidate these hypotheses and to shed a little light on the reasoning behind them. Being a mere man, however, is not a good starting point and I hope the reader will forgive any apparent blunders in trying to understand the female mind. However, my academic colleagues may just come up with a surprise or two. Considering the fact that there are far more women studying psychology than there are men, some 5,800 against 1,800 at present in universities all around the country, I appreciate that my own male view may not be adequate in the eyes of female readers, but these are the risks of putting my thoughts into print.

All three Kray brothers idolised their mother Violet. She was such a strong and powerful influence in their lives that comparisons with other women would have been extremely difficult, if not impossible. Even when it came to young girls it was very difficult for the Kray brothers to form relationships because of the protective devotion of their mother. Theirs, it seems, was a male-dominated world where men made all the decisions and played out all the deeds according to their own macho rules. The only place for women was on the side-lines, urging their mate on to further great achievements at the cost of all other men – it was the call of the wild and the Krays were the king apes who dominated the landscape of the East End of London.

It was not a good environment for so-called normal relationships to develop, and remember, the boys didn't have a father figure to look up to since old man Charlie was normally on the run from the law, classified as a deserter throughout their early and most informative lives. So the dominance of their mother became an important part of their appreciation of women in general and girlfriends in particular. No one could compare with mum!

But within this mother and son relationship came the ever-growing powerful surge of egoism that was to make Ron Kray, the younger of the twins, challenge his brother's position and to assert himself as the dominant of the two. This situation did not provide for the stability and balance that Reg Kray needed when he was maturing into adulthood. It also provided many with the theory that Reg, too, was a homosexual; twins look the same, they behave the same, they have similar sexual preferences – or so it appeared to 'outsiders' at the time. But those who knew Reg portray him as a womaniser and indeed he has had his fair share of paternity suits against him, all of which he has successfully fought in court. So the question remains, did Reg have similar tendencies to his brother Ron? It is quite clear that Reg was present at parties at Cedra Court when Ron ran his orgies and invited pals such as Tom Driberg, MP and Lord Boothby. But whether or not Reg took an active part in the entertainment is still not known for sure.

To understand fully the relationship that Reg had with women it is necessary to travel back in time to 1961, when Reg was already 27 years old. It was at this time that he met the only one true love of his life, Frances Shea. Even here we have contradictions, because Reg himself has always said that his wife was 18 at this time but research has shown that she was a mere youngster of 16 and pure and innocent, even in the sexual freedom of London's roaring '60s. Frances was only 17 when Reg whisked her away to Milan and to Barcelona, much to the dissatisfaction of her father, who was employed by Reg at one of the clubs. He asked her to marry him on several occasions but she knew that her parents would not give their permission so she failed to accept the invitation. The trips continued to the South of France and to Holland, with Reg playing the courteous suitor and Frances just being her natural sweet self. She was an Irish red-head with brown eyes and long eyelashes with long hair, swept back from her cherub-like face. Reg was absolutely besotted with her and treated her with the utmost respect, so much so that he never slept with her before they were married. Some say that they never slept together even after they were married. Even now Reg doesn't like to talk seriously about sex, always having feared sexual ailments such as venereal disease and AIDS. No, sex is almost a taboo subject for the Krays.

Reg took Frances home to meet his mother on many occasions and she enjoyed the company of the Kray family at Vallance Road but she never took to Ron. She could see trouble in his eyes even though outwardly he treated her kindly. Frances couldn't understand the power Ron had over Reg and why he would almost always take the side of his brother in any disagreement. And with Ron's blatant homosexuality it was apparent that there were troublesome times ahead. She didn't understand the problems of the Kray household and Reg did little to try to understand her fears and to put her mind at rest. Everything was normal to Reg but it was a nightmare situation for Frances, torn between her love for Reg Kray and her compassion and regard for her own family, the Sheas. She was a kid out of her depth and Reg did nothing to keep her afloat.

Frances was still only 17 when Reg was sentenced to a six-month jail term and it was this that really antagonised the Sheas and turned them so vehemently against him. They didn't want their lovely daughter mixed up with a gangster who would be in and out of jail for the rest of his life. They wanted happiness and security for Frances and not the insecurity and depravity that went hand in hand with the life of a gang boss.

Not that Reg went out of his way to disappoint Frances and to complicate her life. On the contrary, he tried his best to give her everything she had ever dreamed of, but somehow his own lifestyle got in the way. Even after they were finally married, in June of 1965, the problems continued. Frances wanted a quiet wedding. Reg wanted to invite the entire East End of London. Frances wanted a family affair but Reg wanted all the razzmatazz of their club scene with Rolls-Royces in abundance and David Bailey taking the celebrity photographs. When Reg gave Frances a new car she found an instructor to teach her but Reg was jealous and she never saw the instructor again. When she said that she wanted to work again as a secretary Reg refused, saying that no wife of Reg Kray would ever be going out to work. Reg was the breadwinner and that was that. And even when they went out together they seemed to meet all of Reg's gangster friends and the talk naturally came around to crime, something that Frances hated. Reg just could not win even though he meant the best in everything he did, trying to woo and comfort his young wife who was now only 21.

The honeymoon was spent in Athens with Frances complaining about the food and Reg on the drink. In fact rumours quickly spread back to London that Reg Kray was impotent and unable to have sex with his new wife. This was not the right kind of impression for Reg to make in the East End, where he could very easily be ridiculed for such inactivity and lack of masculine prowess. This was, and still is, very much a man's world and Reg knew that his position as underworld gang boss could be in jeopardy.

But when they returned from honeymoon they couldn't move into their new apartment in the West End because the decorators weren't finished. So they moved into the Shea household for a few weeks. This was another big mistake because the Sheas could see the problems brewing between their little girl and her club-owner husband Reg Kray. Reg was out all day and night and he became an unwelcome guest at Ormsby Street, Bethnal Green. Even when they finally moved into the West End they didn't like it and quickly moved back to the East End. It was here that Ron saw his chance of upsetting their lives by getting Reg to take on a flat at Cedra Court, where Ron held his sex orgies for his boys – this was yet another big mistake to make.

It appeared that no matter what Reg tried he could not get away from his twin brother. And his twin was loving every second of it. He wanted things back like they were in the old days, pre-Frances days. He missed his twin and he would make sure that Reg was soon missing him. He was intent on coming between the newly weds and when Ron Kray made up his mind about something then he would turn heaven and hell to make it happen.

Frances became desolate and depressed – soon she was back with her parents in Bethnal Green. She had been married for only eight weeks.

The following couple of years became a routine of hospitalisation and drug abuse for Frances Kray and she even tried to get the marriage annulled. Her parents blamed it all on Reg and even said that he had supplied her with the drugs, but Reg has always denied this and I, for one, feel that he is quite sincere on this point. All during this on-off marriage her mother always maintained that her daughter was a virgin even though Reg managed to keep his reputation as a stud with various women saying that he had fathered their children. But this is a simple trick to achieve – a telephone call could pull in favours for a suitable sum and the woman would be rewarded well for her time in court. Since there was nothing to prove, naturally Reg would win the case. Simple, but it works. Whether or not Reg actually pulled this kind of stunt is not certain, but it is an interesting thought.

But the problems for Frances became a nightmare and she became more and more depressed. Her premonition that she would die young didn't help the situation and Reg continually tried to talk her around by telling her of all the exciting places that they would be seeing and the great things that they would do. Unfortunately, Reg became more involved in business at this time, when his services were needed at Esmeralda's Barn. Frances knew that he didn't really need her and she tried to commit suicide.

Ron again saw his chance of getting her out of his way for good. He hated her for coming between him and his brother and took every opportunity to demean her and to upset her. In fact he made her life intolerable. His plan was beginning to work.

Reg made one last effort to make things work by taking Frances away from everything for a holiday and Frances reluctantly agreed. On 6 June 1967 they went to a travel agent and bought the tickets but that same night Frances took an overdose and died in her sleep. At 23 her life was over.

Reg was still her legal husband because the divorce had been put on hold, so he knelt by her side all day with her listless body motionless on the bed. He drank and drank until he could drink no more. The gin didn't help, nothing helped.

And still the Sheas blamed him for it all. True, Reg Kray had made many disastrous decisions but in no way could he have known the outcome of these events. He was still in love with Frances and he just couldn't believe that she was dead.

The funeral was held at Chingford, Essex, with the Kray and Shea families split in an ever-increasing family feud. It was the first time that Reg had had to face the music alone, since his brother Ron did not attend the funeral. Mum and dad were there with brother Charlie but it just wasn't the same. He didn't have the support of his brother. He was confused and in agony. But the agony subsided long enough for him to drive to the Shea residence and collect all his letters to Frances and the jewellery that he had given her over the preceding seven years. Was this then the action of a grieving husband?

Reg turned to gin and to guns. He drank more and shot a few people just for good measure and he puts it all down to the death of Frances. But maybe it was all due to his own shortcomings as a husband and his own family relationships. I don't suppose we will ever know the truth.

In more recent years Reg Kray has had a weird way with women, one that has shone light onto his apparent inability to have relationships with the opposite sex. In 1993 Sandra Wrightson was so beguiled with Reg Kray that she was divorced from her husband Peter, naming Reg Kray as the other man in her life. She had written Reg a large number of letters and kept hidden all the replies under her bed but her husband found the letters and their pornographic content persuaded him to file for divorce, which was granted. Her sons Lee and Harvey disowned her and she lost everything that was dear to her except for the memory of Reg. He wrote to her about kinky orgies with his cell mate, suggesting three in a bed, or maybe she would like to have sex with his pal while he watched. So she started visiting him in Blundeston Prison in Suffolk and soon things just got out of hand. But not before Reg had his hands on her best assets, her breasts, and had tried to entice her into his underpants. And all of this in front of the prison guards at the visitors' room. But things went sour when Reg asked her to take care of a friend – by letting him stay at her home near Northampton – she couldn't handle it, like Frances and many others before. Reg became belligerent and threatening. It was all over and they hadn't even had sex.

Sandra is not the first to be besotted with Reg Kray and she will certainly not be the last. In May of 1995 schoolgirl Sophie Williams was pictured in *The Sun*, when she was on the way to the mailbox with a letter to Reg Kray. The 19-year-old had visited him at Maidstone Jail on a number of occasions, sitting with him in the visitors' room and drinking coffee. 'He is the most wonderful man I have ever met,' she said. 'It is so cruel to keep him locked away,' she added, as she drooled over the ex-king of gangland. In fact she had first started writing to him when she was 16 – now does that ring a bell? Guess who is living in the past? It would appear that Reg likes them young. Some may say a little naïve too.

Perhaps the strangest on-off relationship, however, is that between Reg and the actress Patsy Kensit. Reg is the godfather to her brother and an old friend of her father Jimmy Kensit, although recently Patsy has denied ever knowing Reg Kray and his twin brother Ron. But in the summer of 1988 she wrote to Reg thanking him for his kindness when her father died in 1987. Jimmy 'The Dip', as her father was known, used to run errands for the Krays and apart from asking Reg to be godfather to his son, he also asked Ron to be godfather to his daughter Patsy. As her career has gone into overdrive Patsy Kensit has sought to distance herself from the Krays, but Reg took offence in February of 1997 when he heard rumours that Patsy had denied ever having known the twins and asked *The People* to publish her letter. Patsy is now married to Liam Gallagher of Oasis, after being divorced from Dan Donovan from Big Audio Dynamite. I hope now she can reconcile herself to the fact that we all know the connection between the Kensits and the Krays, so sleep well and forgive as others forgive you. I am sure Reg Kray likewise has forgiven Patsy for denouncing him.

The whole Kray saga took a new turn on 14 July 1997 when Reg Kray married Roberta Jones, a 38-year-old university graduate, in Maidstone Prison. Ron was dead, Charlie in jail, but now the 'Double R' was back in business.

Reg and Roberta has a nice ring about it, doesn't it? I am sure that was the idea. The cynics among us will say that it is all a part of Reg's plan to get parole early in 1998 by proving that he has a home to go to and someone to look after him. Money has never been a problem for the Krays but supplying a satisfactory home life or ready-made family has always been a complex issue. Reg had tried earlier with his old cell-mate from Parkhurst, Pete Gillett, who he adopted legally and officially while in jail, but nowadays they aren't talking. Ron and Charlie have no kin to help, since Charlie's son Gary died recently of cancer. So there are only the bastards left and the Krays have disowned all of them.

So Reg Kray has married Roberta Jones – just how did that happen and what does the future hold for the lovebirds? The first mention of a new woman in the life of Reg Kray was a headline in *The People* of 6 July 1997 when Roberta Jones made the front page. 'Reg Kray is my life,' she said, adding, 'Everything I do, everything I am, is about Reg.' She had even sacrificed her home, business and her normal family life to live in a small flat near Maidstone Prison. She must have been shocked when Reg was suddenly and unceremoniously moved to Suffolk.

But the front-page news had a familiar ring to it – she was announcing the release next year of her book, telling all about Reg and of her love and devotion. Roberta, an honours graduate in English literature, moved down to London from Stockport some 20 years ago and has been involved in the marketing and media fields in recent years. It was when she was standing in for a friend who had made an appointment to see Reg Kray in Maidstone Prison that she first met the gangland boss. The idea was to talk about Ron, who had only recently died, but they ended up talking intimately about themselves. It all developed from there. She moved into a small, rented, two-bedroom terraced house near the prison just to be close to Reg, waiting for the day he would be released. Her only comforts were a few cardboard boxes for clothes and a mattress on the floor, but her thoughts of Reg kept her happy and gave her a sense of belonging.

Roberta Jones had sacrificed everything to be near her

beloved Reg Kray and where Reg goes she will surely follow. 'Regarding our love life, I have just switched myself off,' she told reporters. But then she added: 'We can touch and hold hands but we both look forward to the day we can lie beside each other.' Whether this celibate lifestyle will actually help her to come to terms with the fact that Reg Kray was, and in many people's minds still is, a gangland boss of world renown is still to stand the test of time.

The following Sunday, 13 July, *The People* had another exclusive, this time telling all about Reg and his keep-fit sessions in prison. 'The cold showers help to keep his potency,' the report stated, but it didn't say if it did him any good. And the reflexology was apparently a key element in his physical training, and Reg talked openly about the physical side of his attraction towards Roberta. 'Reg believes he has found a soul-mate in Roberta,' the newspaper continued, 'despite their 25-year age gap and their cultural and educational differences.' But the term soul-mate sounds just a little too much like cell-mate, but then that is probably what Roberta means to Reg. Having lived so many years in prison he is obviously aware of the fact that he will have many years of adjustment before him in outside life once he is released. Forensic psychotherapy can play its part in rehabilitation but without doubt the presence of Roberta in his life will play a major and dominant role in his future. With 30 years behind bars, he deserves all the good fortune he can get.

The news of 15 July 1997 in the *Daily Mail* said it all. 'The bride was late. But Reggie Kray wasn't about to go anywhere.' The white wedding was held inside Maidstone Prison in Kent with only a few close friends and officials present, under the ever-watchful eyes of the security cameras. Reg Kray was then 63 years old, the exact age of her father when he died when Roberta was only 12. So was she replacing her father with a father figure and, if so, couldn't she have chosen someone else? But they both have their own particular reasons for getting married and as long as they can live with their decisions then I cannot see any reason for doubting their mutual desire for a long and loving life together.

To mark the day Reg had planned for a laser show the night before the wedding, so the showman is obviously still alive and well and living in prison somewhere in the UK. And the following morning the bouquets of flowers began to arrive for their Church of England service in the prison chapel. Charlie Kray, who was himself in prison, couldn't attend the wedding so he too sent some flowers. The best man was there, Reg's prison pal Bradley Allardyce, and so too was Brentford FC manager Dave Webb. It was all over in 20 minutes with Reg only speaking once to say 'I do' and 'Amazing Grace' played to supply the requisite aura of majesty and bliss.

Roberta Jones had overcome the journey, made by four-wheel drive Jeep, the metal detectors, the security, the razzmatazz of a Kray wedding in an ankle-length ivory beaded dress and had come out the other side as Mrs Roberta Rachael Kray. Mark Goldstein, Reg Kray's solicitor, said after the wedding, 'Mr Kray and Miss Jones wish to thank their family and friends for their love and support and look forward to the time when Reggie is released and they can spend the rest of their lives together.' The non-alcoholic reception lasted some two hours, with other friends celebrating at the pub opposite. But in Roberta's haste to beat a retreat from the prison, the Jeep that she had arrived in actually hit one of the photographers who were waiting outside for a shot of the bride. Knowing the Krays, he is lucky he didn't get shot himself.

Her father, who taught at the Birkdale School for Hearing Impaired Children, and his wife Gladys doted on their daughter, who did well at school, eventually going on to university. But the death of her father of cancer was a blow that she never really overcame, although she would not show any outward signs of confusion. This had all changed when she met Reg Kray and all the old pain re-emerged. She could remember the agony of his death and told a journalist, 'When I lost my father, I lost my protector – the member of my family who looks after problems and sorts things out.' She has certainly chosen a suitable father figure in Reg, who surely knows all there is to know about protection. Roberta knew that people would talk about her father and she has resigned herself to the banter and back-chat.

But Roberta Jones, now Kray, has a sense of humour and how she will need that in the time to come. When Reg proposed on the telephone from Maidstone Prison she asked if he was on one knee. His cell-mate confirmed that he was and Roberta told Reg that she would think about it, but that was all she needed. She had found her surrogate father and her new husband all rolled into one in the person of Reg Kray. And who are we to say that she can't live the rest of her life in happiness and style, safe in the knowledge that her man will always take care of her?

'I live in the present,' she told reporters after the wedding. Her future is as yet undecided but most people in the country will wish her well and hope that she can help Reg Kray to survive the vigours and rigours of release and family life. Maybe the dynasty of the Krays has not been extinguished after all.

Elaine Mildener married Ron Kray in Broadmoor in 1985. Originally she had started writing to his brother Reg but swapped allegiance for some reason, probably because writing to Ron was easier than dealing with the complexities of his brother. This may seem peculiar when Ron was the homosexual of the two and the so-called violent madman. But Reg has served all his time in prison, and most of that in maximum security, so his attitude to life is urgent and somewhat forceful. Ron, on the other hand, was sedated with drugs and had convinced himself that he would never be a free man. So Ron was the casual, elegant twin and Reg became the exasperated, touchy twin. I can confirm that visiting Ron was like a Christmas dinner compared with the austerity of prisons and the impatience of his brother.

So Elaine Mildener was now Elaine Kray and *The Sun* was there to record events for posterity, even taking a photographer along with them to plaster pictures of the happy couple all over their inner pages. It was a coup and Ron greatly appreciated the photographs. And the new Mrs Kray greatly appreciated the money paid for the privilege. She returned home to her children a happy woman, ready to play the part of Mrs Kray to the full. But it didn't last; the visits became a routine and her children, Andrew and Debbie, suffered as a result.

Ron had always told her that sex was out of the question since he had his real soul-mates inside Broadmoor with him. His few close friends were all he needed for sexual pleasure but he wanted something else, something that only a woman can give: he wanted a family or the semblance of one. He felt the need to be in a family once more and to project that image of an identity within a family group. He felt safe in that environment. This made him feel at ease as though he were leading a normal life, even though he was confined in such a dismal place as Broadmoor. In a way a part of him had escaped outside those bleak walls and was living freely with his wife.

Elaine kept the visits going for as long as she could but when it began to be a burden, she decided that a divorce was inevitable. Ron agreed. After all, he may have been mad but he was no idiot. So in June 1989 they were divorced and Ron was free to set about the task of finding a new wife. He didn't have long to wait.

Only two months after the divorce, Ron Kray was married once more inside the walls of Broadmoor. This time it was to be kissogram girl Kate Howard, a divorcee from Headcorn in Kent, and again photographers were there to take their shots and record the event for public scrutiny. The story is similar to that of Elaine Mildener, in that Kate first visited Reg Kray before seeing Ron in the top-security hospital. Again the charm of Ron Kray was the clincher and she fell madly in love. The diminutive, effervescent blonde was to be gangland boss Ron Kray's second wife.

Kate Kray is now 41 and still the bubbly girl she always has been. Apart from visiting Ron on a regular basis she has also found time to write books and to do television work and I have been fortunate to meet her on several occasions. She has sex appeal in abundance and it is easy to imagine how Ron fell for her charms – indeed they always seemed to be ideally suited to each other. Laughter and giggles were the order of the day when they were together but Kate made a big mistake when she decided to go public about an arrangement that they had agreed on involving sex with other men – and it isn't Ron's sexual relations we are talking about but Kate's!

In September 1993 she was publicising a book that they had written together, called *Murder, Madness and Marriage*. She had told several journalists that she and Ron had an arrangement about sex and that he had allowed her to sleep with other men. Naturally the newspapers the following day were full of the story. Kate had broken one of Ron's strict rules about their love life: she had revealed their secret agreement to the nation and he was furious.

The papers had a heyday with column after column of spurious debate and conjecture but for Kate it was almost the end of her marriage. Ron felt that he had lost face, respect even, among his society within Broadmoor and he also had to deal with his brother Reg, who was livid with the ex-kissogram girl. Their anger is understandable when reading all of these articles; it must have shocked the criminal fraternity as well as the gay community, even the whole country.

'I told him how frustrated I was getting. So we agreed I could make love to other men until he gets out of prison,' she told reporters. She even went on to tell them of her affairs that she discussed with Ron in the visiting room of Broadmoor. But she also confirmed that Ron didn't want her to take men friends to places frequented by his pals and to keep their agreement secret, and that meant not telling his brother Reg, who he feared would not understand the pact. Ron was still keen to maintain his image and secrecy was the key.

Ron Kray had in fact taken an AIDS test before they were married and he had even told Kate of his first sexual experience with a woman when he was only sweet 16. So Ron was more AC/DC than purely gay. These revelations were, however, mentioned in the book which was, strangely, co-written by Ron and should therefore not have been any surprise to him. But the publicity did the trick and the book sold well.

But there was a darker side to Kate Kray which was apparent when she told of an incident when she nearly killed a man by running over him with her car. It was at the end of an affair while she was married to Ron and her married lover had taken her on holiday to California. But on their return he broke off the relationship and Kate took drastic action. The police even had to pull her off of the man. On another occasion Kate went on a spending spree with forged credit cards, knowingly amassing a huge debt. When Ron heard about it he told her: 'If you can't do the time then don't do the crime.' But she apologised and once again did the rounds of TV studios and sold a few more books. It really was a no-lose situation. Some may say that it was all planned.

Kate Kray was treading that fine line between intrigue and enticement, when she was lured over that line by pure fantasy. She had believed her own stories and, like Ron, thought she was invincible. It must have been a rude awakening when Ron on his sixtieth birthday filed for divorce. At the end of September he had suffered a heart attack and he felt that Kate had betrayed his trust, something that was of utmost importance to Ron. So she had to go. 'She's made me out to be flash, arrogant, rude and ignorant and I'm none of those things,' he told the press.

In March 1994 Kate went to see Ron to try to patch things up between them but it only ended with Ron being restrained from punching her. 'Ronnie suddenly raised his voice and they both started shouting at each other,' was the word on the street. 'His heart condition, obviously made worse by the heavy smoking, has made him tetchy,' said one of the nurses at Broadmoor. Ron was still adamant about the divorce on the grounds of 'unreasonable behaviour'.

Kate told me once of the many letters that Ron received from women all over the country. 'During one visit Ron asked me if I wanted to see some snaps one girl had sent him,' she told me. 'The girl was a blonde of about 22. She was posing naked on a bed in the sort of open-leg shot you see in girlie magazines,' she continued. Not, of course, that I understood what she meant, but she was not the only one to send Ron photographs in nude, or semi-nude positions; his portfolio must have been a real collector's item.

Ron Kray was a good patient at Broadmoor. With his designer suits and his well-decorated and furnished room, he was their star attraction. Kate visited him regularly and kept him in touch with things going on outside, the life he could not live. She was good for Ron Kray, even taking the place of his brother Charlie, who Ron could not forgive for his part in the Kray film where he let the scriptwriters allow his mother Violet to swear. Ron vowed never to see Charlie again. It could not have been easy for the jovial blonde from Kent to act as go-between between the three Kray brothers. Her own relationship with Ron is hard to define and the relationships between the brothers confuses the issue but now that he is dead, one day we may see a new book outlining her attraction to Ron, and giving the reasons why she felt so trapped in their marriage.

With Ron Kray no longer with us there is surely a void for all of those women who felt inextricably drawn towards his charm and reputation. And there are men who feel the same way, men who can no longer live out their fantasies in the safety of their urban and banal environment now that their 'god' has gone the way of mere mortals. Just why so many have felt this attraction is still a puzzling paradigm of modern virtues but, whatever the reasons, Ron Kray enjoyed it all and no doubt he is still enjoying it.

If Reg and Ron, the terrible twins, have a powerful sexual appeal then what of their elder brother Charlie? In recent years he has made the *Daily Telegraph* where someone suggested that he would be marrying Diana, Princess of Wales, although I am sure that no one dared approach Diana on the subject. Charlie would, I am sure, have laughed it off as a media hype and a good old East End joke. But it does display another kind of sexual fantasy as portrayed in the press, where some journalists dare to suggest such associations with an intolerable air of flippancy. Perhaps the innuendos and false assertions commonly included in tabloid newspapers actually serve to titillate the British public and are therefore just a way of selling newspapers. But this can of course be dangerous, since some people can let their fantasies get the better of them.

Charlie is the one brother who was just there for the fun and he exploited his position to the full. When it came to partying then Charlie was your man. And he loved it. He got as many girls as he could while the going was good and they almost stood in line waiting for their chance.

One such girl was Barbara Windsor, who had an affair with Charlie while he was still married to his first and only wife, Dorothy. Dolly, as he called her, had her own affairs and Charlie had a troubled time at home so he took solace in the arms, or should that be the boobs, of the lovely Barbara. Their affair was passionate and predictable since Barbara could not come to terms with his marriage because she was looking for stability and a long-term relationship. This stability she found in the unlikely arms of Ronnie Knight, club owner and crook. Ronnie Knight was brought back to this country from the South of Spain in the early '90s and is about to complete a sentence for his part in a huge robbery from Security Express. Barbara's ex-husband now has nothing to go home to since his creditors have taken it all, including his home in Spain. So Barbara was wise to get out while the going was still relatively good.

Charlie, however, returned to Dolly and his son Gary, who he dearly loved, but things didn't improve at home and Dolly divorced him while he was serving a 12-year sentence for his part in the killing of Jack The Hat McVitie. Charlie, I am sure, was innocent but his time was up and the champagne days were over, for the time being anyway. Dolly's affair with petty crook George Ince had been the talk of the East End since they didn't try to hide their feelings towards each other, and Charlie felt relieved that it was all over in 1973. His only concern throughout his life was for his son Gary, but he was to die from cancer in 1996 leaving Charlie Kray a lonely and vulnerable man.

On release from prison after serving seven years, Charlie looked up an old acquaintance, Diana Ward, who used to be a waitress in one of their clubs in Leicester. They actually lived in Upper Norwood, South London, for many years and I was a regular visitor to their flat when I wrote my last book on the Krays called *Doing the Business*, back in 1992. She was a charming person with a ready wit and good-looking, too, so I was surprised to hear that she and Charlie weren't together any more. But the one thing that had kept them together was the fact that Diana had worked abroad for long periods of time all through their long association. This had now stopped and Charlie was finding living with someone full-time a little trying. After all, he couldn't bring his girlfriends home with Diana there, so he was forced into meeting them at hotels and restaurants, something that was costing him money. And when he hadn't worked for 30 years, had refused, because of his ego, to receive benefits for all of this time and didn't even have a credit card, then he was in serious trouble. Diana knew about his misdemeanours but she wasn't prepared to pay for them. When the phone was cut off again it was the last straw and she threw him out.

Whenever I met Charlie Kray he always had a different woman on his arm and in his bed. He is an incorrigible womaniser who has lived on the legend of his brothers and on his own ability to con anyone out of money, all so he could keep up appearances. He is a charming rogue, however, and the women in his life have a way of forgiving and forgetting his transgressions. Recently, however, the dark side got the better of him and he is now serving a 12-year sentence for supplying cocaine.

Charlie's latest acquisition is Judy Stanley. This may not be exactly fair to the young divorcee but it represents the attitude of the Krays to their women. Like the gangster's moll, they are a part of the image that they have all tried to represent as being the truth. But in reality they are generally used for whatever the Krays want from them.

Judy Stanley is a mother of three who works for the company Nestlé near Croydon. She has a good administrative position and has been able to keep Charlie in the style that he has been accustomed to: good living and good loving. Although she only lives in a small end-of-terrace house, she has managed to project an air of self-confidence and righteousness; something that Charlie is now putting to good use in his appeal.

Her father, Ieuan Evans, an ex-headmaster and some 76 years old, has many concerns for his daughter. Being only three years older than his daughter's lover he has little good to say about Charlie Kray. 'I don't know why she chose to live with him,' he told a newspaper journalist recently. 'But she is a mature woman, very independent and she knows her own mind,' he added in retrospect. And at 46 years old, Judy should know her own mind. But again we have the situation of a schoolmaster's daughter and a Kray, just as in the case of Roberta Jones and Reggie Kray. It may be a case of schoolmasters everywhere lock up your daughters. But I doubt that it would be any good, and if experience has anything to say in such circumstances then the daughters would rebel just as their predecessors have done throughout history.

Charlie Kray seems to have forgotten that famous phrase of Ron's: 'If you can't do the time then don't do the crime.' He has been found guilty of supplying cocaine and is rightly being held in prison, and his chances of getting out in the near future must be bleak indeed. So once again there is a touch of tragedy surrounding the Kray women who have fought for their men but have all ended up by losing the battle.

Sometimes, indeed, it is the overwhelming maternal instinct that controls their destiny while others thrive on the edge of danger. The important father figure can also play a vital role, in reminding them of their happy childhood. They have all trodden that fine line between heaven and hell, sometimes succumbing to their fantasies, sometimes overcoming their innate desires to go beyond the tangible and to touch on the irreversible and criminal aptitude for violence. For once bitten by the bug of power that crime represents, even the most sublime and innocent of us are in danger of letting go of reality. But, whatever the needs of women and no matter how the Krays have been able to fulfil those needs, the story will continue. The names may change but the game goes on. And I am sure it will give psychologists much food for thought for many years to come.

13. THE KRAY LEGACY

Above all the Krays have taught the authorities to be more secretive and the crooks to be better and more ingenious. No one was prepared for the Krays and they were quick to seize the opportunity to create havoc in the East End and West End of London alike. But have there been any lasting lessons to be learned and will the Krays have their place in history?

It seems that the police have now realised that they are ill-equipped to combat crime, as a report showed in February of 1996 when crime researchers established that there were more than 300 street gangs nationwide with a total force of over 10,000 members. They deal in drugs and are a greater menace than the Yardies, the Mafia and the Triads combined. The family gangs, represented by the Krays and the Richardsons, are on the way out and the new gang bosses are taking over.

'These people are leaders because when push comes to shove they will walk into a pub and shoot someone,' said one top London police officer, reminding me of Ron Kray when he killed Cornell. Maybe they have learned something after all, this new breed of British gangster.

Manchester CID chief Colin Philips, who ran the research team, said: 'These gangs even have their own network, and the common currency is drugs.' Usually numbering from some 15 members up to around 20, they are well organised and are quick to take revenge and retribution. He continued to outline the modern trends by saying: 'In the '50s and '60s it was vice, prostitution and pornography. In the '80s it was car crime and then fraud – in the '90s the drug trade is worth millions.' Perhaps he should have mentioned protection, gambling, 'long firm' frauds and other racketeering, but the idea of change was brought across to the general public and to the police alike.

The conclusion of the report was that the police are ill-prepared to cope with the new crisis. It goes on to blame poor co-operation between forces and inadequate intelligence. I personally would also say that secrecy is to blame. Because of this lack of co-operation in intelligence-gathering, gangs and gang members are getting away with murder.

Recently some politically sensitive material has been made available giving more facts on the Lord Boothby case. Since it had been previously covered by the 30-year rule it had been a classified secret. But now we can see and research this case by sifting through the papers and documents released through government sources. But Scotland Yard have still refused to disclose their knowledge about the case and when I enquired about the files on Lord Boothby and the Krays held at the Yard they slapped the 75-year rule on me and told me to come back in the year 2042. How's that for secrecy!

Until we have a more open society, events will be exploited by people like the Krays. In this matter the police have not yet learned the vital lesson that it is better to let people make up their own minds by presenting the facts as they are and not hiding them away in a vault, thinking that inquisitive folk like myself will just go away. We will not!

Just who they are trying to protect is a very good and interesting question. Could it be officers high up in the hierarchy of Scotland Yard itself, who are afraid of not getting their pension? Could it be others involved in homosexuality with Ron Kray and his friend Lord Boothby? Could it be further details about the Mafia and their involvement in crime in this country, a fact that the police are keen to deny? Or is it the total lack of proper organisation at Scotland Yard itself that they want to conceal? Whatever it is, I can see no reason for withholding the truth from the British people.

In our present information age this lack of access to information surrounding the Krays fails to inspire public confidence when politicians and others in authority use such rules or Acts of Parliament to suppress the truth. It is the 'Sir Humphrey' syndrome, where we are only told enough to satisfy us, and the real reasons for their actions are hidden away from scrutiny. Not telling us what is happening, and why, is a downright disgrace. But such is the extent of secrecy in this country, this conspiracy of silence, that makes it essential that we, the general public, must urge the government to do more than just talk about a freedom of information act. They must also provide one as quickly as possible.

When the present government is talking so much about the provision of this new Act, I find it surprising that Scotland Yard are shielding themselves from investigation by imposing this 75-year rule, one that is normally only used for national security. But maybe the Krays do have something to do with national security, since Ron was often photographed with Christine Keeler, the girl in the Profumo scandal. The mind boggles.

Sir Paul Condon, Commissioner of the Metropolitan Police, recently went on television in front of a house select committee to say that in his opinion there were about 0.5 to 1 per cent of police officers in the Met who are corrupt. This then means that these corrupt officers, some of whom must by definition work at Scotland Yard, have access to information that the public are not allowed to see. Again I must ask, why? Indeed, what kind of corruption are we addressing? If it is purely criminal in content then what about the boys helping the boys? Those in high office who want their misdemeanours kept quiet so they can continue in their positions unhindered. There are too many possibilities for pure speculation – it's a minefield.

We have been informed about a new sense of awareness, change is in the air. But because the same people are still in authority, they can just choose a rule that suits them if they really want to suppress information. Sir Humphrey will always be there in Whitehall, doing what he has to do to maintain his position of power. This will be for his own benefit, however, and not in the interest of the country.

When researching this book I was denied access to files at Broadmoor, I was denied access to information held by the prison authorities, I was denied information about the Krays held at Scotland Yard, and I was denied information from the Police Federation. Even the officer in charge of the Charlie Kray case didn't want to talk to me because he thought he would get into trouble with his bosses at the Yard. This conspiracy, which finally resulted in the invoking the 75-year rule, has gone on long enough. What are they afraid of?

One of the good pieces of news that came out of my investigations is the fact that scientists have now found a way of repairing brain cells by injecting specially cultivated cells into the damaged area. This is apparently a genuine cure for, among other illnesses, Alzheimer's disease, although the method will not be available for some years to come. I can only hope that research into the brain of Ron Kray, that chronic paranoid schizophrenic, will also help in the fields of medicine and that one day his friends at Broadmoor will benefit from the findings.

One of the most curious findings of my own research has been that the Krays were never tried for anything other than murder. They were not accused of running protection rackets or doing deals with the Mafia or using 'long firm' frauds to amass a fortune or of homosexuality. The police deliberately only charged them with one murder each. They didn't even look for all the missing gang members, most of whom were presumed dead. So why? Why didn't the police press their case against the Krays when they had them under lock and key and the witnesses were ready, willing and available? Maybe that is the real reason for the long sentences, but for the time being most of the media have conveniently forgotten about the truth – instead they follow the myth. After all, it sells more newspapers and gets more viewers.

> 'I come to bury Caesar, not to praise him.
> The evil that men do lives after them;
> The good is oft interred with their bones;
> So let it be with Caesar.'

Quote from Act III, Scene II of William Shakespeare's *Julius Caesar*, written from 1599 to 1600.

These words from Mark Anthony appear to ring true for Ron Kray, some 400 years into the future. The greatest danger is to believe the hype and the myth that the Krays have tried to project and evoke. The truth is out there and history must interpret the events in an unbiased and logical way; emotion can play no part in our judgements. The truth must be told time, time and time again – lest we forget!

EPILOGUE TO THE THIRD EDITION

The files held by authorities throughout the land are still being updated at a pace that would enthuse any would-be boy racer and television or media journalist. Even Jeremy Clarkson, a specialist in superlatives of all kinds, would have a hard time keeping up. The prison service is still assimilating records on the whereabouts of both Reg and Charlie Kray; Scotland Yard are still cherishing their own files on the Krays and keeping them well hidden from view; the courts of the land are filing away appeal after appeal; universities study experiments made on Ron Kray's brain cells; and the ladies, or many of them, are still enthralled by the most famous of all home-bred gangsters. The story continues.

Even before the publication of *The Kray Files* back in June 1998, Philip Johnson in the *Telegraph* was writing about new reports of a two-year wait for Reg Kray before he could be released into the community. Reg had apparently expressed remorse during his probation assessment and the official wording included phrases such as: 'has shown no serious instance of violence over the past few years' and 'likelihood of further offences on release is probably minimal'. Naturally, the authorities have to be careful when it comes to putting anything into print and the information was as bland as expected.

Trevor Linn, Reg Kray's lawyer, who represented him at parole board hearings, said, 'Kray regrets the taking of life *per se*. He regrets the effect on those persons close to the victim but he has less feeling for the victim himself – a gangster whom he believed was out to kill him.' Reg Kray, at the very least, has been consistent in this respect, even though this definition of Jack The Hat and his sense of the occasion tend to nullify somewhat any sense of remorse expressed in his probation report. It may even be thought by some that he regreteth too much. The lawyer concluded by saying, 'Allied to a disavowal of his former way of life, this is an honest and genuine expression of remorse.'

It would appear that all lawyers have a problem with semantics, so why further complicate this issue with such statements? And to call Reg Kray an honest crook is something of a misnomer, since it took almost twenty years for him to admit his guilt in connection with the murder of Jack The Hat McVitie. Reg Kray could never become the Godfather of crime that he was back in the '50s and '60s; this is now a younger man's world, one full of violence, corruption, organisation and fear. Now where have I heard that before? Things have irrevocably changed, although crime itself is still flourishing – perhaps more than ever. The time of the Krays, though, has gone.

When questioned on the subject of parole, the prison service had a few things to say too. 'Life-serving prisoners are only ever released from an open prison,' said a spokesman. He continued, 'We would expect a prisoner to have been at an open prison for a minimum of two years before release.' And on an all too familiar note he added, 'Reggie Kray has only recently been transferred from a Category B prison to a Category C prison. An open prison would be Category D. So nothing is going to happen overnight.' This explanation is much appreciated, since I have always found the defining of prisons into homogeneous groupings as explicit as good old-fashioned social demographics, and having previously worked in market research, I have always found these so-called categories mysterious, even sometimes hilarious.

And while I am discussing hilarity, I would like to point out something that appeared in Reg Kray's psychiatric report. It was stated, quite simply and apparently truthfully, that Reg was interested in setting up a recording studio and he claimed to have been in contact with none other than Phil Collins. Other showbiz pals and pop stars were also interested and I am sure they will all enjoy their get-togethers, that is, when he is eventually released. Jokes about prison records, pop music overkill and money for nothing all readily come to mind. But maybe he will make a good 'boss', doing what good bosses do: protecting their clients, protecting their employees and protecting their investments. After all, Reg Kray is no stranger to protection.

Most of these reports tell us that Reg spends a fair amount of his time writing poems and music. Well, I suppose that is as good a way as any of killing time – oops, that one got away. But I would encourage anyone interested in his poems to take a look at one entitled 'Time', since this has appeared on the Internet recently. It may not be the best thing since sliced bread, but it does show a gentle side to Reg Kray's nature, one that doesn't always come across in his medical and psychological reports. For over thirty years he has appeased the criminal justice system of the country for the mistakes of his youth and he has remained sane. But how much longer can he endure his punishment, especially now when he is so close to being set free?

When Reg Kray heard about his brother Charlie's arrest for dealing in cocaine, he was furious. He and Charlie even held fundraisers on the same day, thus splitting their community of old pals and old 'lags' into smaller, almost worthless groupings. Reg the businessman took over and started writing to his brother. Organisation was the way to go and he needed to set the record straight, or at least the public record.

His letter was full of encouragement, reminding Charlie of the good old days and of his twin brother Ron. 'Ron and I always said you were the best-looking out of the three of us,' he told Charlie. He wrote of his hope of the two of them meeting up again outside prison and he told his brother not to lose hope. 'You must be strong and positive in your thoughts. Take each day as it comes. Be decisive in thought and action.' Humour, he told Charlie, was the key to survival. 'Keep your sense of humour, Charlie, it's good for the immune system.' Reg even sent him a copy of his latest poem, the one called 'Time', but in a way he was only pointing out what Charlie was faced with, his true dilemma: time spent in jail, with only time on his hands and bare cell walls for comfort. In closing, Reg stated simply,

'Don't mind me giving out the philosophy. It's just that I care.'

To maintain his good standing with the press, Reg Kray also released a statement regarding brother Charlie. Since this has also appeared on the Internet, I feel almost obliged to include it here, for reference's sake:

> I have been inundated recently with letters, cards and phone calls from the public and from members of the newspaper fraternity, all asking about my opinions and feelings on the arrest of my brother Charlie. These letters etc. were also in general support of Charlie and I [sic] in that we are the last of my family, once again facing adversity! The fact of Charlie's arrest I find devastating, even more so because he is now 70 years of age and he is the last of my family and next of kin. I did hope that whenever I was released Charlie would be there to meet me and I would be able to say Hello Charlie, I made it, and though Ron is not with us in body, he is with us in spirit looking down on this day of freedom!

Are these, then, the words of a gangland boss, with only revenge and hate in his mind? Or are they the words of a caring man who regrets and abhors the thought of his elder brother spending the next 12 years behind bars? It is strange that Reg has expressed the same feelings as those expressed by Charlie Kray on numerous occasions; to me it really is a case of *déja vu*, only now the words have come from Reg, and not from Charlie. I, for one, am sure that the words are sincere and that they represent true feelings. The only nagging question is the reasoning behind the statement: is it the truth, plain and simple, or is it just another cunning attempt at media manipulation, so popular with his brother Ron? Maybe we should all give him the benefit of the doubt.

The Kray Files had opened up a can of worms, in the shape of the powers that be at Scotland Yard, even before publication. When I enquired about seeing and inspecting the files held by the Yard, some of them going back some 50 years, I was told that someone had imposed the 75-year rule. This simply meant that no one, outside Scotland Yard, would be allowed to see them for 75 years.

'Just who are the police trying to protect?' was my very natural initial remark on this strange but undeniable turn of events. When I had asked for permission to see the files I was told that there should be no problem, since secretive spy stories from the '60s and '70s were now common knowledge and even some of the Boothby papers had been released. So why the intrigue and secrecy about the Krays?

I was in need of answers to some very puzzling questions when along came a cavalry charge led by Stewart Tendler, crime correspondent of *The Times*. 'There were a lot of unidentified people who went to the orgies – why should someone put an embargo on them?' I asked, hoping for a positive response. It worked!

Although I, a mere author, had been unable to get any answers from Scotland Yard, the power of the press did the trick in the case of the Krays. And when *The Times* pose a few awkward questions they generally get some kind of reply. The decision, it seems, came from the top – as I had thought. According to Stewart, a senior officer had requested that the files stay closed for up to 45 more years and kept in a secure location. This location was now the Public Record Office, a paradox if ever there was one.

'But why?' I asked. Stewart said that Scotland Yard sources were worried about the safety of witnesses and sensitivity over other people named in the files, or at least that was what they were saying publicly. He also confirmed that the original request to lock them away had been made as late as 1995. 'You were right,' he told me straight, 'they will be released on 1 January 2032.'

A spokeswoman for the Public Record Office then went on record herself by saying, 'Only a handful of staff will have access to the files to make sure they are not damaged by age.' My question, however, remains the same: whom are they trying to protect?

After scores of radio shows and a handful of television appearances, where I have discussed the Krays at length, I am still asking this same question. On 1 January 2032 I will be standing there with my zimmer frame, asking for access to the files denied me during the research for this book. Maybe I will even write a new edition of *The Kray Files* for publication sometime in 2033? But then, maybe we will have forgotten all about the Krays and their evil ways – who knows? By 2032, who will really care? But then, maybe that is the real reason for all the secrecy.

When the Queen's Speech was over, in the autumn of 1998, many inquisitive people were asking the same question: where was the Freedom of Information Act, as promised by the Labour Party in their manifesto? It wasn't there. It had got lost. It was dead.

Jack Straw has now realised that being in government isn't as easy as being in opposition and he has some major decisions to make regarding attitudes to public records: which ones to make public and debate, and which ones to hide. It would appear that the jury is still out.

Certainly there are many questions to be answered and many decisions to make. Events in 1998 such as the extradition proceedings regarding General Pinochet, the possible parole of Myra Hindley, the Irish question and the release of IRA prisoners, some of whom have committed murder – these are all problems that need attention. But I, for one, certainly hope that this law is only on the back burner, waiting to be reheated for later consumption. But unfortunately the attitude of people in authority in this country has always been the same or, as Mel Gibson told Robert Downey Junior in a recent film about the secret Vietnam War, those in command have only one outlook in life towards sharing knowledge with others: 'Treat them like mushrooms,' he told his flying pal, 'Keep them in the dark and feed them on shit!'

Charlie Kray was sentenced to 12 years' imprisonment for supplying cocaine. His defence, during the summer of 1997, was presented by Jonathan Goldberg QC, a man who tore his own client to shreds in the court in order to show a down-and-out man who was no threat to society and who could never afford to get involved in the drugs trade. His ploy lost Charlie Kray his case and cost him, for the time being at least, 12 years of his life.

Mr Goldberg has now lost two appeals, leaving Charlie Kray still in jail and with no sign of release. Losing can become a bit of a habit, so they have now changed tack and are trying to get the sentence reduced due to the unfair tactics used against Charlie Kray. The sting operation, set up by the police, was never adequately questioned during the trial. Charlie Kray had lived with only his pride intact for many, many years, living off the fame of his infamous twin brothers. Now he doesn't even have that.

Friends still offer their support: among others, Mad Frankie Fraser and Eileen Sheridan-Price, the very first Miss United Kingdom back in 1958. Frankie Fraser's help as a character witness was a one-man show, at the expense of the man in the dock. It did his own show business career a lot of good, but at what cost? Eileen, on the other hand, has always been a true friend and her feelings were conveyed to reporters after Charlie's trial at Woolwich Crown Court. 'This is the biggest miscarriage of justice this country has seen for a long time – heads will roll for this!' she told them. She was not slow to give her old pal a good ticking off too, for getting involved in the deal in the first place. She knew, as we all did, that Charlie was only in it for the money, but he didn't have to go through with it. 'Silly boy,' she told him, on her first visit to see him after the trial. 'You knew you should have turned round and walked out the moment drugs were mentioned.' Charlie knew she was right. He could only hold his head in shame.

On Thursday, 10 December 1998, Eileen, from Weybridge, Surrey, visited Charlie Kray at Long Lartin Prison in Worcestershire, where is he serving a total of 12 years' imprisonment. He was keeping himself busy trying to follow the advice given by his brother, Reg, since he had promised to be positive and optimistic in everything he did. There was one thing, however, that really bothered him. 'I am totally embarrassed to be associated with the very word drugs,' he told her solemnly. He openly admitted trying to get money from the man named Jack but felt that he was unlawfully 'entrapped' by the police and their sting operation. 'I will fight for justice for as long as it takes,' he told her bluntly, 'I'll even go to the European Courts of Justice if I have to.' His feelings were reciprocated and they both stressed their sense of injustice by agreeing that the whole set-up was a disgrace.

So what chance does Charlie Kray have of getting out of this ridiculous situation, one that he has brought upon himself almost single-handedly? Will Jonathan Goldberg QC once again lose his case? Will Charlie's old pals still support his appeal fundraisers? Will Judy Stanley stand by her man?

Charlie Kray still has a woman standing by his side all right, but Judy has now gone – for ever! She couldn't take the pressure and who can blame her for thinking first and foremost of her children and their future together. The new woman in Charlie's life is none other than his old partner of many years' standing, Diana Ward. She knows Charlie Kray probably better than anyone alive – even brother Reg. She knows of his shortcomings, of his adulterous ways, of his duplicitous deals, of his shabby schemes; and yet she is back in his life to support him through it all, no matter what it may bring. Diana knows more than anyone else why Charlie looked on this northerner, the policeman known as Jack, as an easy mark: someone who would give Charlie a chunk of ready cash. And usually Charlie would, with the help of the Kray name, get away with it. But this deal backfired in an explosive way and was the cause of Charlie's present predicament.

I have had the pleasure of meeting Diana on many occasions and I am utterly convinced that she would never have gone back to Charlie Kray if he had really been intent on selling cocaine.

Jonathan Goldberg's best move would be to tell it as it was and quite naturally still is, and not confuse the issue with all that talk of being poor, being down-and-out, being the brother of Ron and Reg Kray but living in a fantasy world where Charlie was never in contact with crooks, criminals and villains of all kinds. Of course Charlie Kray knew what his brothers were all about. Of course he knew of their schemes and their Mafia deals. Of course he had contacts in high places both here in the UK and in the USA. Of course he could have become a rich man on the back of such knowledge. The point is that he didn't. He didn't work for the Mafia. He didn't take over the family business when he was finally released from imprisonment. And he didn't make himself rich on the knowledge he had gained from his brothers. This shows the real character of the man more than anything else – and that is why Diana stands by her man.

So for the time being Charlie Kray has to serve his sentence as a Category A prisoner, equal in law to the IRA prisoners he shared his cell with at Belmarsh Prison when he was awaiting trial. Charlie has repeatedly said that he felt it totally wrong that he should be categorised along with IRA terrorists and certainly the over-the-top approach by the authorities, which included having anti-terrorist-style heavy security during the trial, was more reminiscent of the days of his brothers, Ron and Reg, who were undoubtedly the kings of crime. So was this just a show put on for the benefit of the media, or was it really warranted? For a 72-year-old man who had previously spent seven years in jail for a crime he didn't commit, it may all seem a little unjustified.

Is, then, history repeating itself with Charlie Kray back in jail? In many ways it looks like the '60s all over again. The USA had at that time, in the form of President John Fitzgerald Kennedy, a womaniser of extreme proportions. His affairs with Marilyn Monroe and numerous others have parallels with President Bill Clinton's so-called relationships with Paula Jones, Gennifer Flowers and Monica Lewinsky.

JFK was in league with the Mob in the shape of Sam Giancana, the Mafia boss of Chicago. Giancana was an old friend of Monroe's and he knew all about the clandestine meetings taking place mainly in Nevada and California. And it was Bobby Kennedy's direct action against the Mob that made them do business with the Krays in London when it came to laundering stolen bearer-bonds.

In the case of Clinton, these reported affairs, whether true or not, have been used by Republicans to impeach the President and even though the source of Clinton's campaign funds is largely unknown, there is no real proof that there is any organised crime connection – although there are naturally plenty of rumours of such.

Kennedy was Clinton's mentor – he idolised the man. So is the same old story being played out, only with different players? JFK got away with it only because he died. If the news had broken during his presidency, he would surely have been thrown out of office. It was only his untimely death that stopped these relationships from ruining his career. In fact, it was only during the '80s and '90s that the truth about Kennedy, Sinatra, Monroe, Giancana *et al.* surfaced at all.

Clinton's relationships have now been described in graphic detail – the stained dress, the DNA tests, the cigar and so on. Maybe he and Lewinsky did have sex in the Oval Office of the White House, maybe they did it a dozen times or so, but should that really matter? Is it really our business? The American people appear to be saying, 'No,' but our inquisitiveness is now getting the better of us and the age of information has left us begging for more.

The London connection, in the late '90s, is Andrew Morton, the man who made a fortune from his book *Diana: Her True Story*. He is now going to write, for an unmentionably high price, the Monica Lewinsky–Bill Clinton story. There are even stories of a film deal! Mr Morton should know all about film deals, since he has just sold the film rights to his latest Diana edition for an undisclosed figure and he has been accused by many of betraying the Princess's confidence, by including tapes made by Princess Diana in his new book. He had previously promised not to publish them but with Diana no longer alive, he has quite suddenly changed his mind. As they say, money talks!

Money also seems to be talking in the case of Linda Tripp who is trying to sell the rights to the Tripp–Lewinsky tapes, and apparently another book deal is imminent, although Monica Lewinsky herself is trying to lay claim to the tapes. There is also interest in Paula Jones and her story, Gennifer Flowers and her story, even Marcia Lewis (Lewinsky's mother) and her story. Everyone wants to get in on the act, everyone wants the fame, everyone wants the fortune! Monica has apparently been holding out for £6 million!

So the moral question rears its ugly head once again: should Monica Lewinsky receive £6 million for getting laid by the President of the United States of America? I suppose everyone should have to answer that same old question: If I had done it, then would I sell it for a few dollars, a few thousand dollars – for a few million dollars? 'You bet I would!' can be heard echoing far and wide.

When the Krays took £300,000 for their film rights and £100,000 for their book rights, nobody cared. No one said a thing about it. It was as though it didn't happen. Even when the film distorted the truth it didn't matter, since the twins didn't care either. The only thing they cared about was their mum swearing in the film – they complained bitterly to brother Charlie, who acted as co-ordinator on the picture. But it was soon forgotten. So when the Lewinsky film is ultimately made, who will really care if it resembles the truth or not? None of the above, that's for sure.

Roberta fights for Reg, whereas Diana, Eileen and their pals fight for Charlie – and for Reg too. But in fact they are all fighting for each other and for the hope they have for the future. They care because nothing else makes any sense. In this respect a Kray files update would not be complete without a look at the work carried out by Roberta Kray (née Jones) from the Norfolk countryside. She has organised a supporters club at £20 a time, including photos, car stickers and the like, and there is a promise of a quarterly newsletter. Just who will be contributing to this latest edition of Kray merchandise is anyone's guess, but already Roberta has had some interesting comments to make about the walls that separate her from her husband.

In a recent statement entitled 'JUSTICE FOR REG KRAY' she confirmed, 'Despite Reg completing the time set by the trial judge and despite psychiatric and psychological reports claiming that he is fit to be released, Jack Straw and the parole board won't release him or even send him to an open prison.' Roberta continued by saying, 'They say he drinks alcohol and is manipulative. If these were adequate reasons for depriving people of their liberty, we would have precious few politicians, lawyers or big businessmen on the streets!' And who can argue with that, although I would hope that all these good men, and women, had not been gangland bosses. It is the cumulative results of his lifestyle that have incarcerated Reg Kray and he can blame no one but himself for that; unless he wants to condemn his twin brother.

One interesting point that Roberta raised was the catch-22 situation whereby Jack Straw has to *ask* the parole board to consider release, but he can only do so on a recommendation of the board itself. As Roberta has pointed out, 'This means that Reg Kray can remain in prison forever!'

In the meantime, Roberta still produces the posters, Diana writes letters and visits Charlie to keep his optimism alive and Eileen supports them both, on television, in the press, wherever she can. When the going gets tough, it seems that only the women get going!

Reg still thinks of his lost brother, Ron. Having had a twin for all those years, this is quite natural. Any brothers would feel this way. But Reg must move on, away from the overpowering thoughts of his twin and away from the myth of their evil empire. Even in his press release on Charlie's arrest, he was writing as though Ron were still around. And in all the merchandise and paraphernalia that surrounds the Krays it is always the twins who dominate. As long as Ron and Reg Kray are still alive in the minds of the authorities then they, the twins, will continue to represent a threat to society. Right now, this is a threat to Reg himself as he awaits parole. He must let go. He must lose or dampen down the image so carefully constructed over 40 years or more by his brother, Ron. These are harsh words, but for his own sanity I am sure they are right.

The Double R is back in business, but now it is Roberta and Reg. Reg must let go of the past and look forward to the future with his new wife. Being a twin myself, I know how impossible it is to lose that twin thing, but family life is what Reg Kray should be looking forward to and a peaceful retirement far from the madding crowd.

Whatever Reg and Charlie Kray do in the future, the story of the Krays will always represent the epitome of gangsterism in this country. No matter what happens, the Kray files will always be there. Ron may be dead, but their story is still alive!

The future of Reg Kray and that of his new wife, Roberta, lies firmly in the hands of the politicians. Jack Straw, on behalf of the Home Office, now carries the mythical key to the cell door belonging to Reg Kray, once one of the most powerful gangsters in the world. Only he can unlock that door and tear down the walls that separate Reg from Roberta. It will not be easy for Reg Kray, ex-Godfather of crime, to acclimatise himself to the new and modern world that awaits him. After all, who could be normal after 30 years behind bars? But are there any good reasons for his continued imprisonment? Isn't 30 years enough for anyone? I can hear Ron Kray's voice rising from the grave as he whispers, 'If you can't do the time, then don't do the crime!'

But perhaps the closing remark should come from someone in authority, someone respected throughout the land, someone who knows the Krays and their evil ways much better than most mortals. In a recent newspaper interview, Nipper Read, the man who almost single-handedly brought the Krays to justice, had the following to say:

> He has done the length of time that the court felt was right for his crimes. I see no objection to him being released.
>
> Nipper Read, *Daily Mail*, 1998.

I agree!